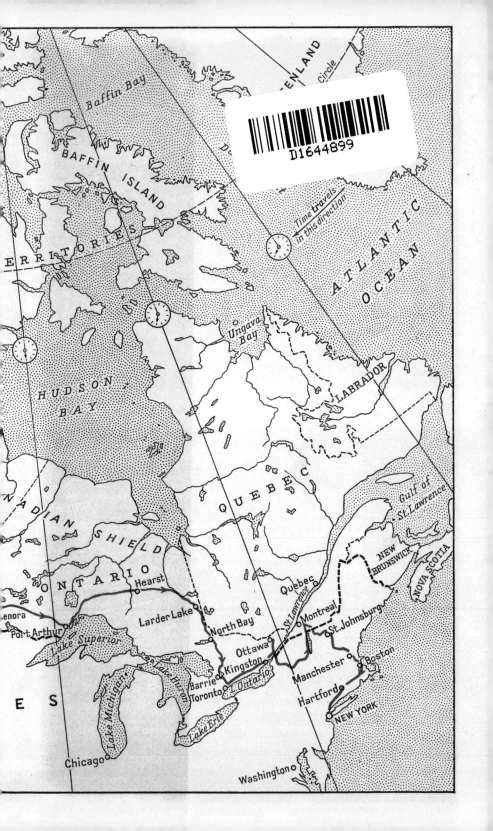

POLES APART

By the same author

*

BOLDNESS BE MY FRIEND
ARM ME AUDACITY
CAPE COLD TO CAPE HOT
FORTUNE IS MY ENEMY
SEQUEL TO BOLDNESS

Richard Pape rigged for the rigours of Antarctica, but without the dark spectacles which give protection from snow-blindness.

RICHARD PAPE

★

POLES APART

A fast-moving account of his
adventures from Alaska
to Antarctica

WITH FOREWORDS BY
LORD ROOTES
AND
REAR-ADMIRAL GEORGE DUFEK
United States Antarctic Projects Officer

ODHAMS PRESS LIMITED
LONG ACRE, LONDON

First published 1960

© Richard Pape 1960

T. 460. PQ.
MADE AND PRINTED IN GREAT BRITAIN BY
THE SIDNEY PRESS LIMITED
BEDFORD

Contents

CONTENTS

ACKNOWLEDGEMENTS

I should like to record my gratitude to Ivy and Fred Young of Auckland and to Ann and Don Meikleham of Russell, Bay of Islands, for their true friendship before and during the writing of this book in New Zealand. I wish also to express my thanks to those who helped me to obtain and to verify many of the facts quoted. Among these in particular are The Distillers Corporation-Seagrams, Ltd., for permission to use facts from *The Awakening North*, their Annual Report for 1956; The *Milepost* (official Alaska Highway guide book) and William Wallace, its Editor and Publisher; Richard Schiller, contributor on Alaska to the *Reader's Digest*; James Warner Bellol, contributor to *Holiday Magazine*, and Commander Merle McBain, United States Navy Information Officer, Operation "Deep Freeze", Antarctica.

Illustrations

Foreword

BY LORD ROOTES

A LARGE proportion of this book concerns two subjects which to me have always been of great fascination—motor cars and the great continent of North America. Both have stimulated and fulfilled my sense of adventure from my first experience of motoring in the early days with my father and my first Atlantic crossing nearly forty years ago.

The author of this book has also found the combination attractive and, like myself, has found in North America one of the most absorbing land masses in the world.

He has motored within the Arctic Circle and across Canada and encircled the original 48 States of the Union. His journeys have taken him to places where modern mechanized civilization has been brought to its highest pitch and to rich, raw and vast territories stirring under the first impact of new methods and developments.

As much as it was in the days of the wagontrains and the four-masted clippers, this is still the New World. The bold spirit which impelled Richard Pape in his race along the Alaska Highway is the same exhilarating spirit which still infects so many visitors from other continents.

The successful sales invasion of the U.S. and Canada by British cars is itself a great commercial adventure story. Among other things, this book shows how well-equipped these models are to meet the challenge of this continent.

Today the motor car has come to mean many things. It is an abundant source of commercial wealth, an indispensable tool of industry and an accepted success symbol. But to some people it is still, above all, a key to new countries, new faces and new experiences.

9

Mr. Pape has used this key effectively to open the doors of adventure—and it is worth noting that the key he used was a moderately-priced British family saloon of a type within the reach of an ever-growing number of men and women.

Those of us who are labouring to forge enduring social and trading links between Britain and North America will all hope that one day soon it will be economically possible for many more of our people to emulate Mr. Pape's motoring Odyssey.

In the meantime, I hope this graphic record will help his readers to appreciate the scale and tempo of events in these lands to which our political and economic future is so closely linked.

Foreword

BY REAR-ADMIRAL GEORGE DUFEK

THE latter part of this book is the story of men on a peace-time mission to the most remote area on earth—Antarctica. They are there to build bases in support of the International Geophysical Year. These chapters describe the adventures, dangers, the tragedies and triumphs of the men who built the bases for the scientists. It is documentary proof that our young men have not gone soft in a post-war world. They are willing voluntarily to face danger and endure hardships with little reward other than the satisfaction of accomplishment and service to their country.

It is an exciting and accurate first-hand account by that world traveller and bold adventurer, Richard Pape, who shared our adventures and meagre comforts during the conduct of these operations.

There are incidents of men falling into the icy seas, crashing with their tractors into treacherous crevasses, and lost aircraft. There are the attempts at rescue by their comrades. The stark beauty of a continent emerging from an ice age is vividly described, as well as the scanty bird and animal life.

The men who now seek adventure in the Antarctic respect as shrines the camps and equipment of those who went before them. The buildings of Scott and Shackleton erected a half century ago are still intact. They are described so well that one feels one is living with these great Antarctic explorers.

Close by are the modern bases of the United States and New Zealand. The contrasts of half a century are clearly portrayed. From dogs to tractors and aircraft. From sailing ships to icebreakers. Foods, clothing, buildings and modern equipment. Source of heat has changed from wood and coal stoves to oil stoves and electric heaters receiving energy from Diesel engines. There are plans for nuclear power plants. Men now enjoy comfortable beds with inner-spring mattresses, electric lights, hot and cold shower baths, automatic washing machines and driers, "ham" radio and moving pictures.

The improvements in comfort have been great, but there is still the isolation. This was described by one of Admiral Byrd's men in answer to his question of what he missed most in the Antarctic. The man answered in one word—"Temptation".

Rear-Admiral George Dufek, U.S.N. (Ret.),
Commander U.S. Naval Support Force
Antarctic (Operation Deep Freeze)
during the International Geophysical Year.

Preface

I ARRIVED in New York in April 1957 for a brief visit connected with the American publication of my latest book. It was a story about a journey in a British car from the North Cape to the southern tip of South Africa. At the time I had no idea that fate was directing me towards another big motoring adventure. This was to take me north of the Arctic Circle to Fairbanks in Alaska. Then Fate and "Billie", a New Zealand girl, took my destiny in hand. Together we travelled across the American Continent and encircled the United States of America. Thereafter "Billie" let me go into "Deep Freeze" beyond the Antarctic Circle, *poles apart* from my earlier journeying.

The events recorded in the book which brought me to New York had been experienced two years before. This 17,500 mile, "Cape Cold to Cape Hot" journey had been fraught with many unexpected risks. Returning to London from Africa in 1955, I had resolved to abandon further wide-scale adventuring in desolate parts of the world.

I tried to console myself that it was high time for me to relax in favour of a safety-existence. Reluctantly I became a fiction-thriller writer in the peace and sanctuary of the English countryside. But writing about actual events appealed more than penning fiction. For close on two years I accepted this "de-adventurized" state before America beckoned.

Thereafter, the spirits of Action (and Romance) winked at each other and designed to a large measure what this story is about. "Billie", now my wife, was certainly the indirect influence which again set in motion those wheels of adventure. Following the Alaska drive she became my fiancée-co-driver: together we shared thrills and tribulations on wheels on the most important continent in the world.

RICHARD PAPE

Chapter One

New York to Vancouver

I meet an old friend in the New World

THE LURE of New York influenced me to extend a week's visit into three. I found this city of 8,000,000 people far more rousing than I'd anticipated. It is the greatest melting pot in the world. Its crisp vitality possesses a dramatic brilliance and, overall, a subtle inspiration all its own. The tendency of New Yorkers towards friendship and hospitality is stimulating. Had I accepted my many invitations, despite my restricted dollar allowance I could have stayed on for months. I dared not remain, however; a gay time had to end. The tranquillity of English village life called. Before sailing for New York I had signed a contract to write an important book by a given date. If I were to keep that date I must begin to write. It would have to be a case of straight home and get down to serious work.

* * *

Four of us were sipping highballs in a restaurant high above Times Square. My publisher was dining me. Also present was a somewhat eccentric writer from British Columbia, Canada. The other guest was a vigorous publicity agent. The sun was casting a burnished glow over the upsurge of skyscrapers, the shops, hotels, movies, restaurants, streams of ant-like people and miniature-looking cars. Soon the lights would go on. Spectacular advertising signs would blaze into coloured life. The "Square" below would be transformed into the brightest spot on earth.

The Canadian author was of small stature. He wrote chiefly on historical subjects; his restless black eyes seemed magnified behind crystal-bright lenses. Frequently he removed his pince-nez and polished them. Also, he kept raising his glass as though unconsciously toasting himself. He had been described to me as an amazing personality, unpredictable and brilliant.

The publicity man addressed me.

"I've arranged radio and television appearances for you next week, now you'll have to stay."

"Sorry" was my apologetic reply, "I've booked to leave in three days, and it's definite, I'm afraid."

The publisher said, "Your book is beginning to move now, can't you stay a little longer and help push it?"

I explained carefully and politely that it was most urgent I made a start on the writing of *Sequel to Boldness*.

"Why not stay on this side of the Atlantic and write your book?" my publisher chuckled good naturedly. "You could at the same time wise-up on our blueprint of life and collect some American ideas for thrillers."

I countered. "Not possible with all the dollar restrictions, I'm afraid."

The Canadian author asked curtly: "You will concentrate on fiction in the future?"

"Unfortunately, yes," I replied, "I'm getting too old for further first person 'I' adventuring."

The Canadian perceptibly bristled.

"How old are you?" His tone demanded an answer.

"Forty," I snapped.

"Most men at forty," he snapped back, "lack ability to make quick decisions. Because they are over the half-way mark they grow fat and slow up. I hope you are not falling into that sort of self-pitying condition."

I was getting ruffled. Marc, the publicity man, nudged me to keep quiet.

"How many dollars do you possess?" the little author man asked next.

In spite of amazement at this apparently impertinent question, I answered "seven hundred".

His next words had the suggestion of a sneer about them. "Forty years ago I left Scotland for Canada with ten dollars."

Above: While living at Kelowna in British Columbia I came to know Tillicum, an Indian from Queen Charlotte Islands. He insisted I should take this photograph; it shows a house, owned by a Mrs. Tucker, on a lovely promontory in Lake Okanagan. Turn it so that the house is on your left and you will see what Tillicum declared to be my totem; he interpreted its message. See page 25.

Below: I watched the building of this bridge across Lake Okanagan. It is 4,584 feet long, the longest floating-pontoon bridge with lift span in the British Commonwealth. Princess Margaret declared it open on 19 July, 1958. It is a vital link in Highway 97, one of the strategic north-south roads linking Canada with the markets of the United States of America.

Left: Races between sledges drawn by dog teams still are popular in Canada's north, but, even among the Eskimos, the aeroplane is superseding the dog team for long-distance travel.

Below: An artist's impression of Dawson City at the height of the gold rush of 1898. Vaguely it typified for me all that I envisaged of the townships of Alaska, land of ice and snow—and gold. Just how different is today's reality I was soon to know. Alaska now is a land of contrasts. Eskimo picture writing is still in use: the scientist is opening up the vast mineral resources of the country and military considerations are responsible for the Dew Line radar early-warning network. See the pictures facing pages 65 and 80.

Right: The start from Vancouver to Fairbanks in Alaska on 22 August, 1957, was quite a show. After acrobats in vividly - coloured clothes had performed on 100-ft flexible, swaying poles, hula dancers from Honolulu gave us the 'Aloha Farewell" and some lipstick smears.

Below: I had invited David Roat to be my co-driver less than twenty-four hours before the "off". Here, relaxed and calm, he sits beside me while police on motor-cycles escort us to the city boundary and the account of our departure, broadcast by station CKWX, begins to arouse the tremendous excitement which, during the next five days, spread throughout Canada and much of America as the reports of our progress went out on the air at intervals.

Through the canyon of the Fraser River we drove for nearly 100 miles—100 miles of gravel-surfaced road that twisted, climbed and dipped, leading us at times close to the edge of mile-high cliffs that rose perpendicularly almost from the river's brink. I recalled a warning given before our start: "One false move on a loosely-gravelled curve and you'll sail out into space . . ."

"Really," I murmured, "you must have set yourself a bit of a problem."

Again the pince-nez were polished and I was studied leisurely.

"If I were you in New York tonight with 700 dollars, you know what I would do?"

"No, what would you do?"

"I would follow my destiny; head west for British Columbia. I would do my writing there. It's a land of opportunity and adventure."

I was becoming even more indignant.

The publicity man kicked my ankle.

"But why should Richard go up there?" he asked.

"Yes, why," I put in fiercely, "why pick on me?"

"Because . . ." and the piercing black eyes behind the bright lenses gleamed, "I feel he should go west. It will help him to write more decisively about life."

The little man proffered me his card, and said: "Come west, and if you do, when you're down to your last fifty dollars, contact me on Vancouver Island for a roof and a bag of porridge."

"Thank you, good night."

I turned and had taken my first step.

"Oh, and Mr. Pape," exclaimed the little man softly, "I just wish to add that I think the west will make your present and future of greater value."

At that I left, puzzled rather than annoyed.

"What a peculiarly rude type," I reflected; yet I could not think of the diminutive Canadian too uncharitably. In my room, later, I was taken aback when I observed a message on the reverse side of the visiting card in neat handwriting. It read: "The Canadian North—in this land, at once awesome and inviting, lies destiny. The awakening is as radiant as the dawn" . . .

*   *   *

Twenty-four hours before leaving New York, a package arrived from the U.K. containing mail from my home. An

Orient Line envelope with familiar handwriting caught my eye. It carried the Honolulu postal mark.

"Ah, Billie Brickman," I murmured happily.

We had first met four years before in New Zealand. Billie was a pretty, dark-haired person with sparkling eyes. During a seven weeks' sojourn I had learned to admire her a great deal. More than that. From early in our friendship I realized I secretly harboured unusually tender feelings towards this outwardly gay and versatile girl.

I read, and re-read Billie's lettter. She had no idea I was on the North American Continent. I hadn't a notion either before this latest news reached me that she had left New Zealand. She wrote:

> "Dear Richard,
>   At long last I am moving. Now en route to Vancouver and friends. I shall stay in Canada a short time before going to relations in the U.S.A. I hope eventually to make my way across the Atlantic . . ."

I sat bolt upright.

"My God," I whispered, "now isn't this just too incredible, she's in British Columbia right now."

Tripping among the words Billie had written was the image of a small man with grey hair and pince-nez. Two nights before this extraordinary author had advised me to "head west" . . . I recalled his final words in Times Square: "I think the west will make your present and future of greater value. . . ."

"Damnation," I breathed, "he must have been psychic."

I cabled the temporary address Billie had given me . . .

"TOURING NORTH AMERICA STOP COULD VISIT VANCOUVER IMMEDIATELY STOP REPLY URGENTLY."

The reply came that evening.

"WONDERFUL STOP STAYING VANCOUVER A FEW MONTHS STOP ADVISE ARRIVAL." It was signed, Billie.

I picked up the phone and asked for inquiries. A train was

leaving the next evening from Grand Central Station on the 3,000-mile run coast to coast: from Atlantic to Pacific. I booked a sleepette for the four days' journey and gave my 700 dollars its first big dent.

The great silver train wailed at intervals as it cleared New York City. It snorted on a hoarse note as it slashed through a curtain of drizzle. Faster! Faster! In four days I would be with Billie in Vancouver. Somehow, somewhere I had to write a book, too. I ordered a whisky from the dark-skinned steward. I kissed the glass in silent toast.

"To Billie's bonny bright eyes, and to you Mr. Canadian author and your beloved Northland. I'm headin' west, sir, on my 700 dollars."

I downed the drink. . . . "In for a penny, in for the Bank of England."

*   *   *

Thundering across the tremendous Canadian expanse made me feel that forever I would be spoiled for any train journey less thrilling or enchanting. My spirits rose. I did not regret my decision. I experienced a confident feeling that everything would fall into place. The silver train continued to snake westward.

It streaked past Port Arthur, Fort William, Winnipeg, Moose Jaw, Swift Current, Medicine Hat. From Calgary we climbed warily into a realm of bold, scarred precipices, the Rockies, a glorious and humbling citadel of mountains. Curving upwards and around this great range I had no idea that, before the year was out, Billie and I would race across this continent in a small British car. I would have laughed disbelievingly had I been told that Billie would be my co-driver in an attempt to beat the very train in which I now lounged.

One fact I did know; unhappily I had been aware of it for a long time. Small British cars on the North American Continent were far too few in relation to rival foreign cars. It hurt me to reflect how this post-war situation had arisen. Foreign car makers were on tip-toe, forcing a pace; had been doing so for a long time. For instance, German sales organizations in America and Canada were pumping out propaganda for Volkswagen and other products to a greater degree than Mr. Goebbels ever employed on the German public.

I mused: "The Volkswagen may be a superb little car, but it is not the best small car in the world. Why don't the British, who past and present by every test always have made the finest medium-priced cars, do something about it?"

* * *

So I came into British Columbia, a land first seen by explorers barely more than a century before. It was a sprawling giant of rock and water; of vast silent woods and the sudden pasture of valleys; of thousands of sheer hillsides reflected in great, cool, aquamarine lakes. The muscles which British Columbia flexes are youth's. Is there any land on earth more privileged to look into the future with soaring hope and sure trust than this young giant of the west?

Billie met me. Her eyes sparkled. She was just as I had remembered her four years before in New Zealand. It was a beautiful day, and a white dress enveloped her graceful figure.

"Billie, Billie," I whispered, "I can hardly believe it's really you."

Within forty-eight hours of booking in at the Georgia Hotel, Vancouver, a reporter found me. A write-up appeared which stated:

"Author here to work not to play. Mr. Pape intends to complete a novel in Canada based on the experiences of a Canadian woman in Holland during the last war."

This article was to have far-reaching effects.

Three hundred miles away to the east, a Mr. Leonard Marsh chanced to pick up the particular newspaper telling of my arrival and intentions. Len had formerly worked at the Air Ministry at Stanmore with my brother-in-law, Mr. Eric Hudson. Following my return from Africa in 1955 I had met Leonard Marsh on a couple of occasions. Being a personal friend of Eric's he had always shown interest in respect of what he termed, "Pape's good and bad peregrinations". In 1956, Marsh emigrated to Canada and that was the last I had heard of him. Now Len Marsh came back into my life as though dropped from another planet. A letter from him was forwarded via the newspaper . . .

I read of the former Londoner's life in British Columbia; about a small house he rented on the edge of the glorious Lake Okanagan. The letter concluded:

> "My wife and two children will join me in August from the U.K. If you would care to use my house over the intervening four months, you are more than welcome, Dick. It is very economical here; the scenery is breathtaking, you could write undisturbed. I have an insurance job and I'm out all day...."

That evening I awaited Billie outside her office. I had been in Vancouver over a week. She knew I was worried about getting down to writing; also about the need carefully to watch my precious dollars.

Billie read the letter from Len Marsh.

"What a small world." she said, "but this does sound a perfect place, doesn't it?"

I took her hand. Quietly I voiced my thoughts.

"A godsend, but . . ."

"But, Richard?"

"Billie darling, I hate the idea of being so far away from you."

She replied softly, "I shall miss you dear." She studied me curiously, intently. "Have you really come west to write and see me, Richard?"

I nodded.

She continued modestly. "Have you still any unconfessed yearning for adventure later on?"

I nervously plucked her sleeve and blurted out: "When the book is written would you consider engagement and marriage, Billie?" Before she could reply: "I've been an adventure-crazed nomad too long."

I was studied searchingly. "Are you sure, Richard?"

"Yes, dear, I've had my day I guess, I want to settle down."

Billie smiled affectionately, her pretty eyes twinkling.

"I would be very happy to become engaged," she said, "if you are serious about abandoning a wandering life."

It was agreed that Billie would remain at business in Vancouver whilst I went into "purdah" in Kelowna and completed a manuscript. After that, engagement, marriage and return to England: roses round the door and a perfect, peaceful Pape, evermore.

Chapter Two

Kelowna, British Columbia

Land of the Golden Twilight on the rim of the Great Unknown
Land of the painted totem; land of the graven stone;
Wrapped in its mystic folklore, yet bright with a promise new,
Land of Today and Tomorrow—fresh as the morning dew ...

KELOWNA in the Indian language means "Grizzly Bear". I fell in love with this lovely place on the edge of the seventy-mile-long turquoise Lake Okanagan. I doubt if any person could ignore the call of beauty among such outstanding grandeur.

*   *   *

Two months rapidly slipped away and writing progress was more than satisfactory. I led a quiet, uncomplicated life. Len Marsh was an utterly splendid and compatible fellow. We did all our own chores and both of us found it necessary to keep a taut drawstring on our purses. In a further eight weeks Len's family would arrive from London, I would then move on. And as time moved on I recognized, faintly at first, a gnawing desire to explore more of the vast Northland. This, in spite of my promise to Billie. The conflict grew. The ruggedly inspiring region where I now lived stirred inexorably the old adventure urge ... that spirit born in most of us. My imagination had been enlivened through a friendship I had cultivated with Dan Duffin, an old Klondiker. This durable character had recounted tales of his youth on the trail of '98. His reminiscing about all that went with a howlin', shootin' town called Dawson Creek, gateway to the goldfields, was fascinating. This veteran sourdough had once shared a cabin with Robert Service, Poet Laureate of the Yukon; he could recite his verses word perfect.

"I wanted the gold and I got it—
came out with a fortune last fall,

23

yet somehow life's not what I thought it,
and somehow the gold isn't all."

Dan Duffin had as his inseparable companion, Tillicum, an Indian of the Haida Tribe who had hailed originally from the Queen Charlotte Islands. Tillicum was widely versed in Indian art and craftsmanship, myths and mysteries, and especially was interested in totems.

Contrary to popular belief, the totem pole is not an idol, has no religious significance and is based on family and tribal history. Totem poles are deeply carved cedar logs, some standing as high as 40ft. and covered with figures of animals, birds, whales, fish and other forms of wild life. Often there are family emblems recording heroes in the family's history. The carvings are coloured with natural vegetable and mineral paints which are prepared in accordance with age-old methods. These poles in fact are beautifully decorative works of art. One of the emblems frequently carved is that of the Thunder Bird, an awesome creature of Indian mythology. Thunder came from the flapping of its wings: lightning from the flashing of its eyes.

Once the stories recorded on the poles could be interpreted by many but today this is possible only by a very few people. Tillicum is one of these and he can see more in some ancient totem poles than meets the eye: gold, in fact. He told me that in the top of the totem poles there sometimes was a hollowed-out section intended to receive the remains of some dead chieftain. Sometimes family valuables were so concealed. Tillicum was searching the Okanagan Valley for a lost treasure totem which allegedly had been smuggled into the valley at the turn of the nineteenth century. Tillicum believed that it lay hidden somewhere in a skin of protective metal. A totem pole stuffed with gold is not altogether incredible, because some Indians did make fortunes from the gold rush in British Columbia.

It was Tillicum who insisted that I take the photograph of the house which is reproduced facing page 16. Duffin backed him up; though I didn't think much of the subject I took the picture. The house is owned by Mrs. Tucker, widow of a doctor, who bought the place in 1930. It is on a promontory in Lake Okanagan.

The film came back four days later. I saw nothing extraordinary about the scene I'd taken "by request". However, I was visiting Mrs. Tucker that same afternoon; she'd probably like a print . . . so I took one along.

I was sipping my second cup of tea and Mrs. Tucker was chatting about Mexico, when I happened to glance at the opposite wall. On it was a tinted photograph about 8″ x 6″, I crossed to the wall and scrutinized it.

"Oh yes, I forgot to tell you," said my hostess, "the half-Indian who does my odd jobs found that picture in the lumber room, he brought it to me quite excited."

"Funny you noticing it," she went on, "he asked me to hang it on the wall, remarking the Englishman would like it."

I felt an odd sensation as I stared at the same picture I'd taken a few days previously, and I had the negative. The wall picture was tinted and new-looking, but it was in an old frame. I turned it about in my hands. Suddenly the reflection of the rocks in the lake formed a series of perfect images, outlines, characters. Turn the picture so that the house is on your left and see for yourself.

That evening I met Dan and the Indian. I showed them the photograph, and said: "A striking totem pole—can you explain it, Tillicum?"

"You have been good to us," he said slowly, "your reward is your own totem pole, a gift from my ancestors."

Without hesitation he translated the various features of this totem pole of nature, formed by land and water.

"First," he explained, "there is a shrunken head of some South American Indians, you will visit there in five years. Next, is the image of half-Eskimo and half-Indian, the hands are touching and his bosom is a bear's head, you will go to Alaska very soon."

"When, Tillicum?"

"Before the next snows," he answered. "Below this, is the

head of a beast, perhaps the monster of this lake, time will tell, my ancestors do not give its meaning.... Next, a fox, an English fox; to this land you will return when you leave Canada. A day will arrive when you will see a copy of this photograph; you will know how to act."

"What is the last figure on my totem?"

"That, 'Red Eagle', is a sheep, see its packing of thick wool?"

"Yes, I do see it."

"You will travel to the land of New Zealand 'Red Eagle', it is part of your totem destiny...."

And, as you will read, Tillicum was right.

*   *   *

While thinking of my Klondiker friend, Dan Duffin, I was lazing by the lakeside. The embracing mountains might have stepped back to admire still more of the sparkling waters at their feet. Nearby a massive pile-driver thudded monotonously. Indifferently I watched history in the making. The very first bridge over Lake Okanagan was under construction. When completed it would sweep out 4,583 feet with the distinction of being the largest floating pontoon bridge (with lift span) in the British Commonwealth.

This bridge would open up new horizons, forming a vital link in British Columbia's north-south Highway 97. It would connect the road systems of Canada and the United States on a direct (and the shortest) route—through British Columbia to Alaska. If a third world war occurred, this unbroken route 97 would assume big military importance. Troops and materials from all parts of the U.S.A. would travel along it to the ice-bound north. The Arctic north is a buffer between the western hemisphere and the other side of the cold war. Kelowna on the 49th parallel is a strategic starting point for Alaska, America's new 49th State.

I wandered back to my typewriter. I would have been astounded had I been told that a year hence the Okanagan bridge would be officially opened by H.R.H. Princess Margaret. Nor had I any idea that in two days time I would receive a

26

visit from Group Captain Townsend. He stayed overnight in Len Marsh's house, and when his Land Rover roared off for the Rockies the next day it also revved up sensations inside me. I, too, wanted to drive again in distant places. My secret longing was for Alaska and the northland. A roaring engine, racing the clock, the thrill of fast wheels, the glorious freedom of the open road, were calling me strongly again.

This desire increased; so one night, off the cuff, I wrote a letter to the publicity chief of a British car concern. I suggested smashing the Alaska Highway record in a small British car. I wrote:

"Alaska is top news at this time and for a long time to come. Americans have a great affection for their far Northern Empire. If a small car could set up a record and make news over the most fearsome highway on the entire continent, publicity for a British model would be enormous. For a continent committed to the automobile to a greater extent than any continent in the world, the Alaska Highway is most definitely the ultimate for testing and proving a small British car in a well-paved age."

I received by cable a metaphorical douche of cold water.

"THANKS LETTER STOP HAVE DISCUSSED YOUR IDEAS AND AFFIRM WE CANNOT VISUALIZE ANY USEFUL SALES PROMOTION OR PUBLICITY RESULTS FROM YOUR PROPOSALS STOP REGARDS"

I was hopping mad.

"There's something radically wrong," I angrily told Len Marsh, "with this so called new Elizabethan era and timid British business brains."

*   *   *

Shortly before I was due to leave, Billie visited the Okanagan Valley for five days. She stayed at the Royal Anne Hotel, Kelowna. I had not told her that Townsend's brief visit had inclined me towards another big motoring adventure.

On the second day of Billie's visit I again proposed

"You suggest engagement," she said, "yet you are thinking about another big motoring escapade. What's the truth, Richard?"

27.

I felt bowled out.

"What makes you say that?" I asked in surprise.

"Len has told me about your recent attempt to borrow a car for a race to the Arctic Circle. He has asked me to stop you; I sincerely wish to halt this new nonsense, dear."

I got hot under the collar.

"Hell, Billie darling, it's not much of a drive, really. I was only probing, there's nothing fixed or finalized, anyway."

Billie fixed me with her eye, and asked.

"Why risk your life, Richard, and pledge it to me at the same time?" I trembled slightly and she continued. "Your desire for another adventure alarms me. Speed demands sacrifices; can't you get it out of your system?"

"I want a husband for life," I was told, "not a shared life with other loves."

"What do you mean, Billie?"

"I mean your two mistresses called risk and adventure."

*   *   *

Billie returned to Vancouver after we had thrashed the matter out. I had promised to get a job when I returned there in a couple of weeks, to try very hard to become a normal work-a-day person. If I proved my salt an engagement ring would be accepted. When the writing of the book was finished I packed my bags.

"Get organized and prove your worth to Billie," Len advised, "or she'll be finished with you. Take root, chum, and dig in; she's a wonderfully kind and considerate person."

My Klondiker pal came to say goodbye. He reached into his pocket and handed me a dirty, folded paper.

"A souvenir," he said almost apologetically. "Maybe you'd like it?"

I studied the untidy scribble. It was a poem. I learned it had been written in an ice-bound cabin during the starvation Yukon winter of 1898.

The train moved off winding into the mountains. Kelowna in a flash became another memory. I began to read the poem given to me by the old Yukon goldminer. Because it impressed me, I set it out below:

> "Pray, don't find fault with the man who limps
>   Or stumbles along the road,
> Unless you have worn the shoes he wears
>   Or struggled beneath his load.
>
> There may be tacks in his shoes that hurt
>   Though hidden away from view;
> Or the burden he bears, placed on your back,
>   Might cause you to stumble, too.
>
> Don't be harsh with the man that sins
>   Or pelt him with words or stones,
> Unless you are sure, yea doubly sure
>   That you have no sins of your own.
>
> For you know, perhaps, if the tempter's voice
>   Should whisper so soft to you
> As it did to him when he went astray,
>   T'would cause you to stagger, too.
>
> Don't sneer at the man who's down today
>   Unless you have felt the blow
> That caused his fall, or felt the shame
>   That only the fallen know.
>
> You may be strong, but still the blows
>   That were his, if dealt to you
> In the self-same way at the self-same time
>   Might cause you to stagger, too."

*   *   *

So it was back to Vancouver, a mountain-flanked metropolis. This was Canada's third largest city and main Pacific portal. It offered many things to see and to do if one had dollars. I had cabled London for more funds. The reply was polite yet positive, informing me that I had received more than my full dollar allowance. It annoyed me to know that Germans could visit dollar countries and convert all they desired: no trouble, no restriction.

I was informed, however, that a passage could be booked to

Britain on my sterling funds in Britain. Two passages in fact! I didn't want to go home, I wasn't quitting or being driven out because of dollars or the lack of them. Anyway, Billie wanted to see me prove myself and get glued to a job. So I decided to hang on, if necessary to become a highly talented and ingenious beggar. I was not absolutely broke. I had 290 dollars (less than £100). My fourth-class hotel room and spartan eating lightened me by ten dollars a day. Reviewing the situation without panic (but with pain) I'd twenty-nine days in which to look forward to a bed, a roof and no dizziness from malnutrition. If I didn't strike a job, I could always pop my camera, and gold watch.

I sought employment in a lumber camp where pay was high and everything found. I would hoard my dollars and limber up among the timber. Before leaving to fell trees I would get engaged to Billie. Payment for the ring wasn't such a problem. I'd buy it on the never-never and leave my camera as a deposit. As a youth, I'd always been favourably disposed towards forests and lumber-jacks. I was now in the lumber country proper. British Columbia was the forest province.

I wrote three charming letters to the three most important forestry concerns. In my conceit I was certain I would be grabbed at not less than 150 dollars a week. I received the replies with aggrieved surprise; they came like icy blasts. "No work available". There was a mild recession in the industry and a lot of experienced lumber-men were temporarily out of jobs. I registered at the Labour Exchange. The appointments officer had read my books. Studying me oddly he asked:

"Why fell blasted trees when you can fiddle a living on a typewriter?"

The Labour Exchange found me a forestry job, the only vacancy out of ten camps. I wasn't ecstatic about it and the fascination of the forests fled. It was a position of kitchen assistant in a camp on the Fraser River. Duties: dish-washer, spud-peeler, meat-skinner, etc. Salary: thirty-five bucks a week.

I turned to other means for a livelihood and got a job as a

car salesman on a second-hand, open-air lot. It looked like a flaming fairground with its masses of bunting and fluttering flags. I couldn't go wrong. Within five days I'd flogged seven autos and made myself 300 dollars in commission. Then things did go wrong. A young immigrant from Lancashire was my undoing. He had rosy cheeks, wistful eyes and a betraying heart. He told me he hadn't much money and needed a reliable second-hand car as his living depended on it. He was all set on a 1952 Chevrolet. I allowed sympathy, idealism and British brotherly bonds to offset ruthless car-selling realism.

"For God's sake," I confided, with picturesque exaggeration, "leave that Chevvy alone. It's got a welded back-axle. the chassis is twisted, gear-box stuffed with sawdust and the speedo has been turned back 50,000 miles. . . ."

I was totally unaware that the innocent immigrant was wasting my time while he waited to woo the secretary of the man who owned the junk-heap under the bunting.

The beetle-browed employer sent for me after the immigrant had squealed.

"Why do you tell customers my cars are phoney?" he raved.

I raved too, and resigned.

That evening I met Billie.

"I'm fired." I told her the circumstances of my downfall. She chuckled, her eyes twinkled.

"Don't let an ass's braying upset you!" she exclaimed, "be grateful to that junk-car proprietor."

"That basket, why?"

"You've made a cool 300 dollars in five days," she explained. "If you can sell rubbish like hot cakes, surely you can sell new cars?"

"Tell me more, Billie, dear."

I was told to write to firms handling British models.

"Regain your self respect," I was teased, "sell shiny new cars and accumulate nice untainted dollars."

Next morning, bursting with boldness, I strode into the offices of Rootes Motors (Canada) Ltd. My previous car selling ability had fired my enthusiasm. It was money for old rope. Now I wanted money for new rope, fast and furious, too. I sought a big commission job selling Hillman products.

The receptionist, a willowy blonde, glided over to me. I surveyed her sweetly. She was haughty.

"May I see your manager, please?"

"Name," she said, "the nature of your business, please?"

"Tell him Richard Pape from London."

"Representing what, Mr. Pape?"

"Oh, just tell him," I grinned, "I'm representing punch, pep and personality for flogging Rootes Products on this 'ere continent. Here, take this little card?"

The blonde bristled, and with a wobble she passed through a doorway.

This is the East Pine Bridge on the John Hart Highway, which is the connecting link between Prince George and the start of the Alaska Highway at Dawson Creek, still 100 miles away. The road snakes across 255 miles of timbered mountains, tumbling streams, swift, clear rivers and placid lakes. In this most difficult country one mile of road cost as much as £355,000.

Left: Already we had travelled more than 800 miles non-stop in this the first leg of our journey: here was the township of Dawson Creek and Milepost Zero on the Alaska Highway. Here urgently needed tyres awaited us; we waited only long enough to change them and re-fuel.

Right: Matthew Baillie Begbie, a struggling young London barrister, who was appointed by the British Colonial Secretary to be Judge in Clinton, British Columbia, in 1858. This young country was experiencing an invasion of gold-hungry roughnecks, some of whom were quite devoid of principle. Many were Americans; unless law could be enforced these men might seek aid from the United States. Matthew Begbie enforced the law. His justice sometimes was rough and ready, but it preserved British Columbia to the dominion of the British Crown.

Chapter Three

Car Salesman to Car Racing

*The greatest pleasure in life is doing what people
say you cannot do*

IAN GARRAD rose from the desk and extended his hand.
"Richard Pape of *Cape Cold to Cape Hot* book, eh?" I nodded.
The initial impression I got of Mr. Garrad, Manager of
Rootes Motors, British Columbia, was that he was somewhat
young for the job. Intelligent eyes behind rimless spectacles,
however, were serene and confident. A little later I knew that
Garrad was a shrewd character with a fierce determination. A
chip off the old block, in fact. His father was Competitions
Manager for the entire Rootes Group; a man internationally
respected in motor-rally circles.

Discussion veered from my last big drive, to Volkswagens
heading sales lists everywhere. As we chatted, I observed that
Ian Garrad had a habit of lightly drumming his fingers on the
blotter.

"Selling small British cars over here," he confessed, "is a
high-pressure business; it's not easy."

"Who's to blame," I challenged, "for letting Volkswagens
flood the markets on every continent since the war?"

"It happened, didn't it?" was the terse reply. "My job here
is selling Hillman, and obviously my organization doesn't wish
to miss its slice of the cake."

Quietly and clearly he said. "So you want a job?"

"Yes, it's important for survival."

"What's your previous car selling experience, Mr. Pape?"

My reply was succinct: "Five days on a used-car lot. Seven
tricky sales: 300 dollars in commission, plus the sack."

A little later Garrad rose. "You're hired," he said, "all success

33

in your new job. Please report here at nine tomorrow for a briefing on selling angles."

I beamed appreciatively and thanked him.

Before leaving, he said: "We've got to attract buyers to Hillman cars at an increasing rate."

"Of course, Mr. Garrad."

"I'm always on the lookout for bright ideas. If you have any, please bring them along tomorrow morning."

*   *   *

Back in the hotel room my ambition for racing the Alaska Highway surged anew. For hours I argued with myself on the wisdom of broaching the subject next day. Inner voices conflicted. One told me to wait, sell new cars for a period and win confidence. The second voice tweaked my morale. "Don't be chicken," it said, "tell 'em, take a gamble!"

Eventually I made up my mind.

"In for a penny, in for the Bank of England," I encouraged myself.

I tried to foresee the possible reaction and the questions my Alaska-drive proposal would engender. Before I retired that night, my approach was planned. I visualized Garrad behind his rimless spectacles and in imagination heard him say gravely: "Quite a fanciful idea, Mr. Pape, but if you failed it would result in shockingly bad publicity for British cars."

A distressing contemplation to say the least. But I'd still offer the Alaska-drive, 5,000 miles in 5 days. As if to bolster morale, my mind went back to 1955—the beginning of the "Cape Cold to Cape Hot" exploit. When it was first mooted, manufacturers had turned me down right and left as a crackpot and nuisance. In the end I purchased my own car for the expedition. If I didn't break my neck I'd go broke. I did neither. Now I'd do it again somehow. If Ian Garrad issued a flat "No", too bad, so what? I'd sell his Hillman cars and hoard my earnings. Then I'd buy a British model and tackle the Alaska Highway privately. I switched off the light in a perverse mood. "I'll show British small car makers up for the craven-hearted so and so's they are," was the thought on which I went to sleep.

*   *   *

Next morning I was in a happier and more optimistic mood. "People who fly into a rage," I reprimanded myself as I caught a bus, "always make a bad landing, but spurts of personal fury achieve wonders."

The men at Rootes were waiting. I listened politely to the pros and cons of car-selling. A salesman held up a card.

"What does it say, Mr. Pape?"

I goggled at the letters, "Y.C.S.I.U.Y.T.I."

"A plain damned jumble," I retorted.

"It means," I was informed, "You can't sell it unless you tell it."

I tried to speak and failed.

Another salesman had a go . . .

"Anyone can kiss a girl, Mr. Pape, but the art is being invited again." He smacked his lips. "The same with salesmanship. It's the first impression that your prospects get of you, your products and the company that counts up to the long-run profits."

" 'Suppose so," I acknowledged and looked at Garrad who was quietly listening. His fingers were riffling a sheaf of papers. The previous day I had given a lot of thought to what I would say. Now I began mentally to take aim for pulling the verbal trigger and exploding the Alaska bombshell. I would have to be crafty, convincing, and clever, but first I would get them all annoyed.

I began with a sad little sigh.

"It all sounds pert, nice and pretty, but what draws customers into the showrooms for Hillman cars?"

A grunt of "Huh?" came from a Clark-Gable-type salesman. I followed up.

"Gentlemen, I'm joining you to chase fat commission cheques, fast. I've got to hook and book people for my dollars, but what entices these folk to the Hillman vehicles?"

I got a sharp answer.

"We have specialists," I was told, "who deal with our sales

35

promotion; press, radio and television. This aspect is not your concern. Another department hypnotizes the customers; you just concentrate on clinching the deals."

I adjusted my mental sights.

"A pity," I said, "that British firms out here are inferior at motor-car hypnotics."

"What?" . . . the senior salesman was flabbergasted.

I continued. "For instance, take the Volkswagen. The public doesn't need beguiling advertisements. Agents everywhere just scream for more and more of them. These small German cars sell themselves. Can you deny it, gentlemen?"

The voice which replied came from a flushed face. It was a chilling voice.

"We are not here to discuss the matter. Yes, it's been a battle; we're battling strenuously . . ." A pause. "Should you work for us, Mr. Pape, you've got to battle, too." He flicked his nose. "As a straight salesman and not a psychologist."

Garrad remained inscrutable and I decided to keep the Alaska bombshell a while longer.

"Personally," I went on, trying to speak with logic, "I think there's too much hot-air in salesmanship and advertising. Hundreds of thousands of dollars are let loose every week on sales promotion, honeyed words, streamlined jargon, and rosy claims by copywriters. British and rival firms in the small car field all try to create stampedes, but does all this piebald advertising start a panic?"

Garrad spoke at last.

"What's so wrong with advertising and salesmanship techniques?"

For some seconds I could think of nothing to say. When I did, I began: "In spite of super salesmanship and advertising, sales of small British cars in Canada and U.S.A. are far below Volkswagen records. I ask you, have we an overwhelming leader, say a natural best-seller like today's Volkswagen or the Austin Seven of yesteryear? Admittedly our cars are unrivalled, but they are still only medium sellers on the world's showrooms so to speak." I spoke carefully . . . "Have we a star?"

Patriotically, a salesman chipped in heatedly.

"Our cars are tops. We can't understand the public's mania for the Volkswagen curio" . . . He sniffed disdainfully. "How the hell it became a best-seller complete with fan clubs *à la Elvis*, beats me."

Garrad almost barked. "The 64,000-dollar question is *why?*" He slapped his desk. "In my opinion, it's the most over-rated car in the world, in originality, appearance, performance and workmanship."

He lit a cigarette and I knew he was riled, but I felt I was capturing his imagination and interest.

He inhaled deeply, then added. "All right, draw comparison between a best-seller car and a best-seller book complete with suggestions for our Minx to assume such a status."

They were waiting for me to fizzle out; I knew it.

"Well," I pursued after a longish pause, "take a book which leaps into the best-seller class, or a small car like the Volkswagen. The book may have had shocking criticisms, it might have been turned down a dozen times by publishers, but somehow it is published. It soars and nothing can stop it. Mystified, the publisher or manufacturer proclaims—'that unpredictable public'."

"Blame advertising!" exclaimed a salesman.

"No," I answered. "All the advertising in the world cannot make a book or a car a best-seller unless the article possesses personality or 'breast', that indefinable something which captures public imagination and sentiment. Advertising may assist at the start, but once the public has a certain impression, maybe a small section only at first, before you can say, 'kiss me Katie', there's a spontaneous world-wide attitude towards it."

Garrad stubbed his cigarette. . . . "Go on," he enjoined.

"No amount of literary polish or grammatical perfection can ever make a writer," I persevered, "if the cultivation of literary personality is neglected. 'Style is the man'—and with automobiles, 'the car is the style', irrespective of ugliness, lack of features or decorations. With books or cars it boils down to the over-all impression. What the public likes and wants, it buys." I snatched a breath. "There are no bad motor cars today, all possess reliability and personality, all make their way to the public showrooms. A few, however, can't be held back. Something about them results in a break-through, then nothing can halt public demand."

Garrad smiled, a smile of curious concentration.

"How is this warm-hearted, indefinable public affection created? Our Minx is a reliable seller over here, it should be the best-seller."

Now I pulled the trigger; away bounced the Alaska bombshell: the idea on which I pinned my hopes.

"I'll race a Minx to the top of the world, through British Columbia, the Yukon and Alaska. I'll attempt 5,000 miles in 5 days. If successful, this bold journey will bring in customers yapping, 'we want a Minx, we want a Minx'."

I heard a titter.

"Let me continue," I rasped.

"Such a drive will at once give you a live, red-hot advertising gimmick if your Minx achieves something spectacular on this North American Continent. Stir the hearts of the people, show the flag. Let a British Minx put up a show unsurpassed on terrain loved by English-speaking Canadians and Americans. Let the Minx roar out a living adventure story to win affection and loyalty in one fell swoop."

"How?" Garrad demanded.

"By affecting mass mentality," I replied. "If you dramatize a true-to-life, action story...."

I was looked at as if I were nuts.

The Clark-Gable-type salesman groaned.

"A thousand miles a day, come off it buddy. You've no idea what it's like up in that wilderness. My God, it's enough to make a tough Land Rover burst into tears."

"If you failed," Garrad murmured contemplatively, "it would be frightfully bad publicity for British cars."

He rose, addressing the others ... "We'll conclude now, I would like to speak to Mr. Pape alone. . . ."

Garrad closed the door. He started taking long strides about the room, paused suddenly and said:

"Congratulations, I'd like to come as co-driver, but there'll be too much organizing to do at this end."

A friendly satisfaction had eased into his voice. For seconds I could think of nothing to say.

"You are with me, aren't you?" he asked.

"You mean," I said disbelievingly, "you've agreed on the Alaska drive?"

He laughed. "Of course, I'll loan you a Minx for this 5,000 miles in 5 days marathon."

I wanted to whoop but merely said: "In that case, begin calling me Richard."

"When can you start?" came the swift inquiry.

My mind was not responding at its fastest. The Alaska proposition had magically materialized out of the limbo of ridicule and speculation; like a wraith taking shape. Reality seemed unreal.

"When can you start?" Garrad repeated.

"I leave as soon as details are completed for success."

Garrad's eyes showed excitement.

"Today's the 19th and August is dying out fast," he said. "Okay for take-off in about four days?"

"Suits me, Ian."

Garrad spoke again: "You know, every year we get dozens of opportunists who are crazy to do spectacular drives for us. I don't rate you in that category because I believe what you have put up to me has been well reasoned out beforehand. The fact that I'm backing your idea shows that. But I want a straight answer to one question: have you considered the risks and personal dangers involved?"

"Yes, I have."

"Look here," I told him, "there won't be any blasted regrets. I like the thrill of challenge, win or lose. It's life and a wife to me. Everything is an adventure in the far north. The Alaska Highway was made for conquest."

"Yes, indeed," agreed Garrad, "but will you answer me one other question truthfully?"

"Yes."

"If you couldn't have got a British car, would you have driven a foreign model in certain circumstances?"

I laughed scornfully.

"Would have written my own death sentence first."

Garrad eyed his desk thoughtfully and confessed to me.

"I'm in this Alaska business with you to the eyeballs; I've got everything to lose, too."

"How?"

"I've O.K.'d this gamble without first contacting London for permission. Simply this, if you fail I'm fired."

"The man who is fired with enthusiasm for his firm," I retorted, "is seldom fired by his boss."

Ian half closed his eyes: "On the face of it," he murmured, "a thousand miles a day non-stop for nearly a week doesn't seem mechanically or humanly possible in that God-forsaken territory. Our four-cylinder engine will have to work at maximum efficiency for 120 hours. Every square inch of the Minx will be hammered to hell."

I waited and wondered . . . Would he change his mind?

Then: "It's on," he exploded, "we spend all today and tonight checking the route, everything. Grab your briefcase, we're in action from now, Richard."

I seemed to change gear inside.

* * *

Within two hours of entering Rootes Motors Ltd., Vancouver, the situation had changed dramatically for me. I was elated. Instead of pacing a polished floor awaiting customers, I was poring over maps planning my big run.

A demonstration Minx with 6,000 miles to its credit was

loaned to me. It was in the workshop before noon. A bucket seat would be fitted, plus safety straps and extra powerful spotlights for night running on the tortuous mountain roads. The bed would comprise a two-foot-wide sheet of plywood. It would extend from dashboard to rear alongside the driver's seat. The engine would be tuned to its highest standard by a specialist. Armour plating would be fitted to protect the sump and differential against rocks. A reserve tank would go into the boot. "Alaska-Minxy" as the car would be named, would carry twenty gallons of gas; enough for approximately 600 miles range.

Garrad worked fast and secretly. The British Columbia radio station (CKWX) saw at once the immense news value in this drive. This station allied itself wholeheartedly with us. I planned with CKWX executives for radio communication to reach the car as it devoured space in the Yukon and beyond. The Minx would be equipped with a powerful trans-oceanic receiver. At frequent intervals messages would be radioed to me.

CKWX chief agreed on the wisdom of top secrecy until a few hours before the actual start. Frequent announcements would then go over the air to all British Columbia. Excitement would be stirred throughout Canada and beyond. It was agreed to call the adventure, "World-record Power Drive". There were reasons for maintaining secrecy. I recalled the "Cape Cold to Cape Hot" drive in '55. At the eleventh hour following world-wide publicity, rival drivers with foreign cars decided to race me to Capetown from Lapland; they had wanted to steal my thunder.

*   *   *

I had to have a co-driver. I interviewed three willing men. I led them to believe that a reliability run was being planned southwards to California on tarmacadam; not to the northland on rock and gravel surfaces. The first fellows didn't impress me greatly. I felt they would not stand-up to five solid days and nights of round-the-clock driving. The third type with some experience of rallies was very enthusiastic. He had a devil-may-care personality, but oh! was he garrulous! I was not fully happy, but time was short. I would have to take a chance.

It was mid-morning, 21 August, 1957, and thirty hours before I was due to make my start. Zero-hour would be 8 p.m. the next night at the Pacific National Exhibition grounds, Vancouver. The drive would be officially checked and timed. I found Ian Garrad pacing the floor inside his office like a very exuberant schoolboy.

"What's new?" I asked.

"Boy, oh boy, think of it! A bevy of imported Honolulu dancing girls to serenade you on your way."

He flopped in his chair, snatched a quick breath, said "phew", and continued: "I've arranged a motor-cycle police escort to the outskirts. The CKWX radio will keep it up non-stop when the run begins. We figure thousands will gather to see you off. The Mayor of Vancouver will hand you a salutatory letter for the Mayor of Fairbanks, Alaska. You know what, Richard?"

"No, what?"

"There'll be acrobats in the Exhibition grounds on 200-foot poles to draw the crowds." He slapped his forehead unbelievingly. "There'll be press photographers, the lot. Boy, oh boy, I can't believe it."

"Believe what, exactly?" I asked.

"Colossal publicity for our little Alaska-Minxy, and all free. Boy, it'll be worth a goldmine."

I strove to keep calm and easy but secretly I was experiencing "pre-take-off twitters". In R.A.F. language we used to call it the "time-twitch". It was an awful sensation of suspense which lightly flicked at the bare edges of one's nerves and brain. Usually it disappeared when one got into action, but I'd all of thirty hours to live with this particular "twitch". The knowledge that I'd still got to break the news to Billie didn't make things easier.

*   *   *

We got down to the question of final briefing for the garrulous co-driver at 9 p.m. that night. I was still uncertain about him. Somehow I imagined he'd develop into a gramophone after three days of keep-awake dope. I visualized his bleary eyes and repetitive wailing. It was too late, however, to pick and choose elsewhere.

I reached for the phone. Garrad had met Billie once and briefly previously. They liked each other. I had not seen Billie for a day; she believed it was due to my training as a super car salesman. As I dialled her office I felt a nasty throb of compunction. It was going to be damned awful, especially when she was throwing a small cocktail party for me that evening. It was in my honour for taking a nice, steady job at long last. Ian had been invited, too.

"Billie," I announced breezily, "a million regrets, dear. Ian and I just can't come to the cocktail party this evening, er, urgent car business. I have tremendous news for you though," and I arranged to call at Billie's apartment at 4.30 p.m.

After a day of intense preparations I took a taxi to Billie's place.

She looked charming in a black dress. Two white earrings, however, seemed to stare at me like eyes, probing my guilty conscience. Her own eyes were laughing.

"Tell me your tremendous news, dear." She kissed me. "I know you are going to be a wonderful salesman."

I poured myself a stiff drink, I needed it. Thrice I opened my mouth and couldn't say anything. I sipped the brandy and heard Billie saying sweet remarks about my becoming a normal person instead of a demented roamer-writer.

Instinctively, she knew something was wrong. It had to be told. Quickly, desperately, I got everything off my chest. Followed a constrained silence, she seemed frozen and was very pale. I was probably miserably statuesque, too, clutching my glass at the end of the settee.

Then the tears spilled. I hate tears. A crying woman gets me dithering; like a bird with a damaged wing. I did everything to reassure Billie that I would keep on living. It was hopeless!

"You, you, hopeless adventurer," she sobbed, "you reckless . . ." There was a fresh flood of tears. "I can't stand this kind of life. You'll kill yourself in that frozen north, can't you see you'll kill yourself. Please, don't go Richard!"

I answered stupidly: "Nothing to it, it's the Arctic summer, y'know. They even grow tomatoes up there."

I put my arm around her slender shoulders and she cried on. "Richard, will you please go and leave me now."

"Billie darling," I said softly, "I'm doing the drive. Have some confidence. Meet me in five nights from tomorrow."

I wiped the perspiration from my face and left. I remember banging my pipe on the outside wall; it splintered.

My lady luck was waiting right outside the front gate: or rather, a motor car from which two men were climbing. The first guests had arrived. One was Barry, the other a fellow called David Roat whom I had never met.

Barry asked: "What the devil's wrong, Dick?"

"It's Billie in hysterics. I'm leaving for Alaska tomorrow, that's what!"

"But, but," he stammered, "you're a car salesman, aren't you?"

"Oh, hell, Barry, go to Billie. Try and calm her and tell her I'll be all right." To David Roat I said: "Can you run me back to town?"

Roat popped into Billie's apartment and told them he was driving me to my hotel.

I was compelled to notice the easy way he handled the big American Ford. The way he glanced easily from the road to me, then back to the road.

I blurted out details of the coming drive. Outside the Castle Hotel, I suddenly got a hunch.

"Have a drink with me, I'd like to talk to you, David." I laughed. "A strange coincidence meeting you tonight."

"What's strange about it?"

Ten minutes later I fired the question.

"I want you to join me as co-driver and come to Alaska tomorrow night."

"Me?"

Roat's face was a study in incredulity.

* * *

David Roat hailed from Ashford in Kent. He was 25 and had emigrated to Canada two years before. Here was a calm, clean-cut man of medium height. His speech was soft and measured. He possessed, I knew it, a dogged self-assertion with nothing aggressive in it. He was the soundly-educated and nicely-brought-up type of Englishman which appealed to the R.A.F. for aircrew. To a shrewd observer here was a type who would hang on and shine in danger and difficulties.

I was greatly struck by David Roat.

Over years of unusual motoring I'd recruited quite a number of co-drivers one way and another. They varied like the wind. One I'd left in hospital. Another had walked out on me because he said I was heartless in making him drive a dozen hours on four Coca-Colas and half a tin of bully-beef. One had developed a nervous breakdown. Another had joined the Navy saying he never again wanted to see the inside of a motor car. Still another had deserted military duties in favour of driving with me across the Sahara, a grand type. Some had been magnificent, others a dead loss.

I worked on Roat for three-quarters of an hour. He listened absorbed; his face betraying no enthusiasm.

"Well, why choose me?" he asked quizzically. "What's wrong with the chap you've already primed?"

I answered honestly, more a statement than a reply.

"I got a hunch soon after meeting you," I told him. "I want you as my co-driver. Don't ask me how or why. Say you'll join me, and the other goof's fired."

He grinned in a friendly way.

"But I'm a typewriter salesman for Remington Rand. How the hell can I just walk out on them for five days?"

I jumped to my feet.

"Another coincidence," I said. "Do you know that a pal of

mine, Joe Bandy, happens to be the Public Relations Officer for Remington Rand in London?"

Roat smiled vaguely.

"Okay," he said. "Cable him now at Commonwealth House to cable back so I won't get fired."

The cable was sent.

An hour later we were at Ian Garrad's home. The garrulous one was fired on the turn.

* * *

I went to bed early. I had to chuckle to myself: "Cocktail party guest to co-driver in three hours. A woman's tears can achieve wonders." I thought of Billie and murmured, "Thanks dear."

It seemed like fiction. At the same time the next night David and I would be snaking through the mountains, roaring north, north, north.

* * *

Radio CKWX began its campaign at noon the next day, 22 August; it pumped out news of the Power Drive on a wide coverage. Half hourly, the announcer put it over. Immediately the public was agog, amused, interested and speculative. Reaction was rapid and considerable. Ian Garrad was inundated with calls from rival but friendly concerns. He was repeatedly asked if he was out of his mind.

"A thousand miles a day for five days and nights over the toughest of this continent's terrain," said one motor executive. "If Pape peters out, it can do no good for British cars."

Motoring opinion grew like a Chinese artificial water flower. "Impossible", it pronounced and the project was mocked. "The Alaska Highway," many said, "will rip that baby-car to ribbons." Others openly doubted if the Minx would reach even the start of the Alaska Highway 800 miles away. "If speed is attempted," forecast another authority, "the Minx is a gon'er, the drivers, too."

Experienced motorists quoted facts and figures laid down in the official Alaska Highway handbook. It stated:

The trip to Fairbanks in Alaska, covering approximately 2,500 miles from the border, requires a minimum of at least eight days for *one way*, under normal and most favourable conditions, employing a heavy and high-powered vehicle.

Special equipment and precautions were laid down as "musts" . . .

*   *   *

David and I drove into the Pacific National Exhibition grounds at 7.30 p.m., that night. Prediction was correct. Thousands had collected to see us off. Excitement ran high. Dozens of youthful Vancouverites had gathered in their hot-rods. They openly jeered the small, light-blue British car.

As I mounted the platform to speak into the microphone, a gawky youth rudely exclaimed: "Power-Drive, my Aunt Fanny! Where's the power, buster?" he added.

"Under the bonnet, you blasted goofs," I hit back.

The Mayor's letter of greetings and goodwill was given to us for the Mayor of Fairbanks. The Hawaiian dancing beauties did their stuff and gave David and me the "Aloha Farewell"; lots of kisses and lipstick smears, too. The police escort opened up with hooters and led us to the city limits.

We said goodbye to Ian Garrad. We were off! I opened up the little British motor, 60, 70, 80 m.p.h. It was growing dark as we wound through sombre forests and into the mountains leading towards the mighty Fraser River Canyon. Our search-lights probed ahead. The compass showed north. It was the way to the Arctic Circle.

"At last", I yelled at Roat, "this is it. Switch on the pilot light and begin entering up the diary. One day I may write a book."

I began dictating.

Chapter Four

Through British Columbia to Dawson Creek

Keep driving. It is only from the valley that the mountains seem high

THE ENGINE hummed rhythmically. Pine-scented air flowed into the car. I gulped it deeply. It was wonderful to be in action again. The run to the start of the Alaska Highway at Dawson Creek was almost 800 miles. Then followed 1,530 miles of Alaska Highway to Fairbanks. The first hundred miles were quickly covered. Roat drove for a time to get the feel of Alaska-Minxy; he handled her smoothly at 70 and 80 m.p.h.

From the town of Hope, the challenge would really begin. We would roar into the awe-inspiring cleft of the famous Fraser River Canyon, and this we would follow for nearly a hundred miles. The gravel road would climb and twist, leading us close to the crest of mile-high cliffs rising perpendicularly from the river. Garrad had brought in a man from the Yukon to brief me on the route north. His words came to my mind vividly: "One false move on a loosely-gravelled curve and you'll sail out into space."

In imagination a picture flashed before me. I saw our headlights curving down, down, through blackness, like a falling meteorite, until the rushing waters of the Fraser engulfed us. I steeled myself: "Cut it out," I told myself, "remember two words: care, speed! Care, speed! Don't speculate!"

I had been told: "The way to the Arctic Circle is ruggedly beautiful. It is also dangerous at speed." The authority from the Yukon had said:

"At frequent intervals the side of the rock and gravel road

48

drops dizzily away. It is a highway literally on a razor-edge. There are no white lines, no people or lights. If you overshoot, nobody will see it happen; you'll never be found."

We had to average about 40 m.p.h. for almost 5,000 miles. It was obvious that the best of every minute and mile counted. I'd done a lot of boasting that this drive was possible, now I had to pull it off. On my last big drive across two-thirds of the world's surface, I had come to learn that the greatest mistake I could make was continually to fear making one. In wartime flying, in prisoner-of-war camps, during years in Africa, I'd met a lot of men who had worried too much about getting the "chop". Quite a lot of them had literally thought themselves into it.

*   *   *

The lights of Hope vanished. Gravel soon began to lash at the underside of the car. Tyres squealed as we pulled around harsh bends. In a few hours we would reach the romantic and historic Cariboo Trail. This pioneer road was carved a hundred years previously through a wilderness. It was the old-time trail of gold-seekers, fur-traders and settlers, whose oxen teams, freight wagons and pack trains were the vanguard of the builders of Canada's great empire west of the Rockies.

Our headlights slashed the velvety black of the Black Canyon Gorge, and I tugged at the wheel, left, right, right, left. Parallel with the highway swirled the Fraser River, ever tumbling and restless. The dark of the night was packed around us like layers of black wadding.

I mused on the town of Hope we had left behind. Formerly it was the Fort Hope of the Hudson Bay Company, a famous encampment of the Fur Brigades. Later gold-seekers abandoned their boats and rafts here before journeying overland to the Cariboo Trail, now an historic landmark. It was brave hope in the hearts of men which once brought them to Fort Hope.

In the ancient mountains which surrounded Roat and me, the tough pioneers of the past had ridden into this country and stayed to make history. Husbands left their wives and young ones. Beardless boys ran away from school. Soldiers deserted their posts and sailors fled their ships. All were in search of gold. Many grew suddenly rich and many of these became penniless soon afterwards. "Easy come, easy go" often applied in the days of gold stampedes.

The gold fever which started in British Columbia in the spring of 1858 became a madness. (This was forty years before the next great gold rush in the Yukon.) Hard bitten miners, imbued with dog-eat-dog philosophy, poured into the terrain through which we now drove and set a pace of lawlessness. In consequence of this gold rush, the mainland Crown Colony of British Columbia was inaugurated in 1858.

*   *   *

"Shall I drive now?" asked David.

"No, we'll change over at Williams Lake. I'll try and do 350 miles to get my wrists flexed. Thanks, David."

We were on a high place when the moon made its debut with spectacular suddenness. It appeared to shoot from dark clouds as if jabbed earthward on the end of an invisible rod. A celestial switch might have been pressed. A limitless and spectacular world spread about us, washed in a greenish, gossamer sheen. It was wild, breathtaking and almost frightening. We were in a realm of dense forests and phosphorescent-looking mountains: a timeless world of unspoiled magnificence. We stopped for a few minutes.

Whispered David: "What a lovely, glorious sight." I didn't answer but thought a lot. I'd seen many strange parts of the world bathed in moonlight. The Arctic Circle on the other side of the globe in Lapland, the Sahara, the Congo, the Mountains of the Moon, but never before had I seen anything like this.

"C'mmon, David."

We got back into the car to tackle a series of hairpin bends. I screeched round one corner too wide. There was a violent swing before the car levelled out. I shot a glance at my co-driver, his lips were compressed but he never uttered a word. His nerve was good. We pressed on at speed through the Kamloops-Cariboo country, a wilderness renowned for wild life. This was a paradise for the hunter and the fisherman. The area is bounded by the Rockies on the east and heavily forested coastal mountains to the west. It is a region in which moose, caribou, deer and bear flourish; over which fly migrating ducks and geese and it is the home of a variety of upland game birds. About us were lovely lakes silvered by the moonlight. Here sportsmen from the world over matched wits with the famous Kamloops trout. Below us, its course showing like a thread of glistening twine, lay the Fraser River, far wider in fact than it appeared from our rapidly moving viewpoint.

We flashed through the small township of Supzzum where Indians had once attacked miners, killing many during days of battle. We raced on toward Jackass Mountain, so named because so many mules fell from the narrow-shelved trail over the cliffs before the construction of the road. In those days it was described as half-a-mile of perpendicular ascents and dangerous descents where it was necessary to crawl along the edge on a path sometimes no more than a few inches wide. We climbed, bounced and descended towards Lytton. The modern road over the Cariboo Trail even yet means tough travelling.

A malignant wind gulped and sucked at the speeding Minx. The air became markedly chilly and the car's heater was switched on. David was rigid, shadowy and silent by my side. For this I was grateful. I thanked my lucky star he'd come into my driving life at the eleventh hour. We thudded over a rough stretch, the suspension taking a hammering.

I laughed aloud.

"What's wrong?" asked David.

"Just wondering," I said, "what the old pioneers would have thought had they been able to look into the future and observe this little bundle of roaring metal streaking over the route they traversed on foot."

"Yes," said my companion, "on Shanks's Pony and weighted down with a heavy pack."

It was indeed thrilling to race between places which old timers had taken weeks and months to reach. In those early days none could gamble on a safe return. This Cariboo Trail, however, had proved the pivot upon which the fortunes of British Columbia turned. I reflected on the miners who had punched out the trails which had opened up the country. It was the gold they had found which brought in settlers and paid for the Cariboo Trail we now followed. This road was the finest piece of work ever undertaken in Canada. It is referred to as the "Appian Way" of British Columbia. When the gold petered out, this river country yielded another wealth. This time a bonanza in lumber, cattle and farming. The real winners were not the high-booted, hard-talking grizzled sourdoughs, but the generations which followed.

I rounded more bends and half expected to bear down upon slow-plodding camels or gangs of pig-tailed Chinamen. In 1862 the "ship of the desert" was tried out on the Cariboo Trail. Twenty-one camels were brought from Africa in the belief that their ability to carry 1,000 lb. compared with 200 lb. by other pack animals, would help enormously to solve the difficulties of transport for the gold seekers. It wasn't the climate, but the terrain which defeated those camels. Their feet were unsuited to the rocky ground. Moreover there was trouble with the owners of other pack animals which were thrown into panic by the strong odours of the camels. So they were sent away, some to the coast and some to the area of the Thompson River where the last of the camels died about 1905.

In 1883, 6,500 Chinese labourers and 2,500 whites toiled in the heat of summer and through the freezing winter cutting a route along steep canyon walls and burrowing tunnels through mountains. Man, the architect of civilization, scored a dramatic victory in cutting the Cariboo Trail. Each mile we covered as we headed to the gorges of the Northern Rockies—the Alaska Highway—onward to the land of the midnight sun, represented a heavy outlay of toil and sweat, and even of blood.

*   *   *

North of Lytton, 170 miles from Vancouver, we emerged from the Canyon to link up with another magnificent river, the Thompson. The mountainous road became extremely dangerous. It was narrow and winding; my wrists ached and my eyes throbbed. Perspiration dripped from my face. I dared not speculate on what our condition would be when we should return over this same route on the way back from Fairbanks.

David checked on the map.

"We're approaching the tiny junction of Cache Creek", he said.

Here, Indians used to back-pack over the trail; in winter dog teams were used. At elevated places, watery moonlight silhouetted shapeless forests. They suggested sprawling black scabs in a universe of mystery. A purplish haze surrounded their outlines.

I swung round a sharp corner and two things happened.

Ahead, in the light beams, two grizzly bears playfully pawed each other. As I braked and hooted, the strident alarm clock went off. David jumped.

"Switch off that blasted clatter," I shouted.

After a mesmerized pause in the glare of the headlamps, the bears, their eyes glinting like fire, scurried off like mammoth rabbits.

The clock with the vociferous alarm served an important purpose. We set it to warn us to tune-in to Radio CKWX, Vancouver, for special broadcasts. David switched on our powerful trans-oceanic receiver in the rear. In spite of steep, surrounding mountains, the announcer's voice came to us clearly: "We have just time for an Elvis Presley recording called 'Teddy Bear' before the midnight news." David laughed.

I cut the engine. We waited expectantly listening into the void. I prickled with impatience. The wind soughed. To have the motor noiseless was disturbing amid the vast mountains, black and silent about us. It was different when it was throbbing and growling. Then it spelt life and gave a sensation of reality and promise of success.

"Two more minutes," reminded David.

I turned down the rock 'n roll melody. It sounded ridiculous. part of a giggling, insipid, artificial world which was far away. I climbed from Alaska-Minxy and stretched my legs. The silence was heavy and oppressive. A shrill, quavering cry from a moose floated from the forests. The news was read out and mention was made of our departure from Vancouver. There was a pause, then the announcer said:

"Calling Power-Drivers, Dick and David!"

I felt a blaze of excitement, and increased the volume of sound. David looked at me blankly, and I, too, felt an acute sense of unreality as the voice in Vancouver reached out to talk to us personally. Standing among the moonbeams I seemed momentarily to grasp an understanding of the utter immensity of space. The infinity of the Sahara had once promoted similar reaction, but not with such vivid intensity.

"We hope you are making good time," continued the voice from the radio set. "Hand in a progress report at Williams Lake for broadcast to your anxiously waiting public. Please tune in to Radio CKWX at seven in the morning for weather report."

A slight pause.

"Don't forget you will traverse three time zones to the Arctic Circle. At each, set your watches back one hour. Good-night and good-luck Power-Drivers, Dick and David."

The radio was switched off, the engine switched on. Its roar was stimulating. David marked the map for time zones. An impression exists that the Alaska Highway and the road we were now on which leads to it, follows a meridian course from south to north. In truth, we would travel as far west as we did north. Fairbanks below the "Circle" was almost as far westward as the Hawaiian Islands. As a consequence, our route times were (1) Pacific Standard Time (British Columbia), entering (2) Yukon Standard Time (Yukon Territory) and lastly (3) Alaska Standard Time (Alaska). A difference of one hour existed between each zone.

We roared along the winding road, the moon riding high above. We entered the small town of Clinton, which was asleep and dreaming. I allowed my thoughts to dwell on its past, particularly on a certain man associated with it. A photograph I had seen of Judge Begbie had impressed me enormously. We passed little houses with the ghostly moonlight reflected from the window-panes, and the spectral image of Judge Begbie grew before my mind. In the headlights of "Alaska-Minxy" I imagined his silhouette stalking down that main street. He was a fearsome figure in his great black cape and hat. Matthew Baillie Begbie had been a law unto himself, enforcing rough and ready justice for Britain on this far northern frontier.

I braked before a big, spreading tree and quickly checked oil level and tyre pressures.

"Wonder if that's the tree," I must have spoken my thoughts aloud.

"What tree?" asked David.

I answered: "Hangman's tree," and in the same breath, "get some sleep, will you?"

Roat gave a derisive laugh. His face was tight-set and white in the moonlight.

"Impossible," he shouted, "why not ask me to sleep on a roller-coaster or a bucking bronco?"

"You will, you'll sleep like a dead man when accumulated weariness starts its wear and tear." I smiled to myself about the truth of this statement.

Through experience I had a good idea of what would happen. It had been the same with other co-drivers on the "Cape to Cape" run. I figured on another thousand miles before he would be smitten with fatigue. About that time I'd give him some keep-awake drugs, and, if acute tenseness gave the feeling that dark spirits were eager to push us to disaster, the drugs would clear it away. About the third day a challenging weariness would induce an hypnosis of intolerable routine, but a strange power of determination and discipline would come into play. When this happened, the bed in the bucketting metal shell would become more welcome than a feather mattress floating on air. The roaring engine would become a lullaby and car-obatics, a soothing cot-like motion. After a further thousand miles of non-stop driving my co-driver should become possessed by an automatic urgency. A feeling of being pursued by a single desperate terror ... *time*! He would experience an intolerable anxiety to squeeze the utmost in distance from every minute.

*   *   *

Came the dawn. It was a vague arc of light stretching over the world and dipping into the infinite. I was giving Alaska-Minxy everything. The terrain was tortuous. The engine was straining furiously and my arms and wrists felt like lead. Unexpectedly, David said: "I can't get it off my mind what you said about that big tree in Clinton, Richard."

"You mean Hangman's Tree?"

"Yes, what made you say it?"

I glanced at the man by my side. His calmness was exceptional. I was beginning to feel the strain and it was a release to talk, even if we had to shout most of the time.

I told Roat what I knew about Begbie.

For many years Clinton was the meeting point of the stage coaches. In the early days assizes were held there but until Begbie came, the law depended mainly on a man's own strength of character. Some of the 30,000 gold-hungry trail-pounders who swaggered into the land were devoid of all scruple. Get gold, that was their only purpose! Get it by gambling, claim jumping, swindling—or even over the sights of a smoking gun.

There was always the possibility that if the law-abiding majority organized themselves against banditry they would seek aid of the United States authorities, for most of them had come from the south. If a precedent were set by the intrusion of U.S. troops or marshals, who could say whether England would maintain its hold on the Pacific Coast?

The British Colonial Secretary knew that when the Crown Colony of British Columbia was born it must have a strong watchdog. He decided that the man who would be judge, must

56

be able, if necessary, to "truss up a murderer and hang him from the nearest tree". In 1858 he appointed to that position a struggling young London barrister, Matthew Baillie Begbie, a heavy six-footer with black hair tinged early with white at the temples. His trim Van Dyke beard also was shot with grey despite his 39 years. His black moustache was waxed at the ends. His eyes were described as "luminous". Begbie's rough and ready justice soon gained fame. See picture facing p. 64.

On one occasion he was smoking in a saloon when a drunken giant challenged him. Begbie flattened him with one blow. He shrugged off threats on his life. Another Begbie legend concerns a plot he overhead while seated on a hotel verandah. Some roughs below were scheming to shoot him. He went to his room, returned with a bucket of slops, and emptied it over their heads to show his contempt of them. He was fearless, just and merciful.

Often he was enraged with the incompetence of his juries, who were frequently as guilty of lawbreaking as the accused. On one occasion a jury brought in a verdict of manslaughter when evidence showed that the prisoner, a gunman named Gilchrist, was clearly guilty of murder. Begbie's remarks were as follows:

> "Prisoner, it is far from a pleasant duty for me to have to sentence you only to imprisonment for life. Your crime was unmitigated, diabolical murder. You deserve to be hanged. Had the jury performed their duty, I might now have the painful satisfaction of sentencing you to death. And you gentlemen of the jury, are a pack of Dallas horse thieves, and permit me to say, it would give me a great satisfaction to see you hanged, each and everyone of you, for declaring a murderer guilty of manslaughter."

Often the judge would add a flogging to the sentence. "My idea is that if a man insists on behaving like a brute, after fair warning, and won't quit the colony, treat him like a brute and flog him."

Subsequently Matthew Begbie became, in 1870, Chief Justice

of British Columbia; he was knighted in 1875 and continued in office until 1894.

We rolled into what was mapped as the Chasm; breathtaking views of a great gorge were revealed. To the west, mountains etched splendid scallops in the ashy sky.

I thought to myself. "To millions everywhere, mountains are a challenge, a fascination, a solace. Wherever mountains are, people exist to whom mountains are life."

I stopped for a quick leg stretch. There was a cry of sudden alarm from Roat.

"Christ, a big blob!"

I swung round to see David kneeling by the nearside front wheel. I cursed and breathed thankfulness at the same time. The wall of the tyre showed a blister the size of half a big orange. As if to assure myself that it was real I pressed my pipe stem into it before walking to the edge of the road, and peering downwards into a murky depth. It was uninhabited country and I felt an involuntary rush of terror.

There, but for the grace of God . . .

"A miss is as good as a mile," Roat seemed quite unemotional.

I found his coolness in the circumstances irritating until I had recovered my composure.

"We're lucky," I said. "Death would have been a certainty had that tyre popped."

I studied the mountains which enclosed us and in my mind's eye I saw Billie. Her voice echoed faintly.

"You'll kill yourself!"

For seconds waves of sheer panic engulfed me. To break the tension and change my mood, I joined Roat in changing the front wheels and inspecting the rear ones.

Alaska-Minxy carried three spare tubeless tyres. The four tyres on the car had been brand new. Our inspection showed that rubber was ripped and the walls bruised and lacerated with cuts. These tyres were unsafe. It was apparent that about a thousand miles at speed over such pitiless terrain was the maximum lifetime of a tubeless tyre if one wanted to keep on living. We hadn't got to the torturing Alaska Highway yet and I had bitter misgivings about the tyres. Roat seemed to interpret my thoughts.

"We should have put tubes in the tubeless."

I reached for the American Automobile Association guidebook and read aloud from the section, "Car equipment and service."

> "The car should be fitted with heavy duty tyres at the start of the trip. Because of the rough sections of the highway, cars equipped with tubeless tyres should carry spare inner tubes in case of air leakage or damage to the rims. Two mounted spares, preferably six-ply or nylon should be carried with tubes."

At once I wrote out a message to be telegraphed or phoned back to Vancouver. I wanted four spare tyres to await our arrival at Dawson Creek and another set for immediate use. Also yet another set and spares to await our return there from Alaska.

After 8½ hours we came to Williams Lake. It was 360 miles from our starting point, so we'd averaged over 40 m.p.h. Our next leg was 426 miles to Dawson Creek where we joined the Alaska Highway. This savage stretch would test every inch of the British car as few small cars are ever likely to be tested. We faced hundreds of gravelled miles beset with hairpin bends, through gorges and ravines. Beyond Prince George the road would go up and down like a switchback. In the mountains it would frequently cling to the sides of cliffs many hundreds of feet high.

I checked maps and times. Our first 80 miles followed the Fraser River to Quesnel.

"We've got to make it faster, David."

The reply was icy—

"How . . . in this country?"

To achieve victory, Alaska-Minxy would have to average over 40 m.p.h. for 120 hours, inclusive of all re-fuelling and other unforeseen delays. I was suffering from an attack of pessimism and I knew it. David had similar reaction.

"Hope we haven't bitten off more than we can chew," was his comment.

* * *

We refuelled at Williams Lake. Friends brought hot coffee and cold water. The latter for external refreshment. We handed over a CKWX progress report. Our urgent communication to Ian Garrad for more tyres was to receive top priority.

"I'll get these instructions off immediately," promised Ross, a tall, fair-haired Canadian and a Rootes man.

Cables would be sent over the North-west Communications System, whose vast interlacing lines tied together the far-flung people and settlements of massive British Columbia. Where smoke signals of Indians once wreathed, the voice of the telephone and radio had taken their place.

When we left Williams Lake Roat put his foot down and drove admirably. The coffee, food and head dousing had made us brighter and inclined to chat. I felt I had known David for two years instead of a couple of days. He was a grand type and a splendid driver. The relentless urge to make speedier time was circulating in his bloodstream. I indulged in chit-chat, it was good for morale and camaraderie. I knew it wouldn't last long. As the monotony of miles and weariness again set in, so would follow silent resignation over seemingly endless hours.

The night was dying, the day's new born light aided speed. I tittered as I marked the map.

"What's funny, Dick?"

"In ten miles," I answered, "we come to Whisky Creek, and fifteen miles beyond that is a place called Soda Creek."

Roat shot out his tongue, and moistened his lips.

"In five days," I said, "we'll be sitting back comfy and cosy, sipping our whiskies and soda, eh?"

* * *

We continued to chat cheerfully as we skirted the Fraser River, matchless and magnificent. It was a realm of ponderous mountains and far-reaching valleys.

"You and Billie," David inquired, "will you get wed?"

"Yes, we will. And then there'll be an heir, I hope!"

"Will you keep on writing?" was the next question.

"Not much," I replied, "I hate writing really. I've been told I might develop a style; this is the beginning of the end for any writer."

I grinned at my companion.

"What about you," I chivvied. "Are you tied-up with a dainty piece of femininity?"

Roat swung the Minx around the edge of a sheer cliff face at 50 miles an hour.

"I'm going out with a very nice girl called . . ."

In a flash loomed disaster.

"Christ, look out," I screamed.

We were almost on top of it. I experienced a stab of anguishing emotions. An overturned vehicle straddled the road, its wheels upward, like a dead animal with elliptical, drawn-up legs. The rear end of the car was near the edge of the ravine, it looked a gap of about a yard . . . I ducked. David braked and heaved the wheel. Alaska-Minxy was thrown into one hell of a shrieking dry-gravel skid. He de-clutched, spun, accelerated and braked again. We rolled crazily, but he'd judged it magically. We did not finish up a pile of wreckage; we didn't hurtle through space. Our car whipped around more than half a circle. It squealed to a standstill with its rear bumper denting the capsized Plymouth Sedan. See picture facing p. 33.

I gripped David's shoulder.

"Bloody magnificent," I yelled.

First instinct was to rush to the dead or injured. My feet had barely touched the ground when I heard shrill laughter. It came from a woman wearing only a white chemise, she lurched about the rear of the overturned Plymouth and dangerously near the edge of the ravine. Her chalk-white face matched the colour of her undergarment.

I bellowed fearfully: "Don't walk, stand still."

Three people had experienced miraculous escapes. They

were shaken, bruised, but unbroken. A quick surge of disgust alienated sympathy; all were the worse for drink. The woman, about 35, had a hard, angry face. She was using filthy language. A man crouched on the far side of the vehicle gibbering like a lunatic about a double-crossing dame. The second man was reeling slightly. When I addressed him, the pupils of his eyes seemed to melt into the whites and his lips twitched continuously. He was unshaven, a heavy brute wearing ornamental cowboy boots and shirt.

"Skidded, a goddamned skid," he panted heavily. "Got a drink for a buddy, buddy?"

I ignored the words.

"Any of you people needing first-aid?" I asked.

It was maddening. The big American car blocking most of the road would seriously hold us up. The slatternly woman, to cap the climax, told me to "----- off, and mind my own bloody business". The big man suddenly put a convulsive grip on my arm.

"Youse police?"

"No," I barked, "get that hand off me."

"We don't want police!" he went on in a rasping voice. I didn't like his menacing attitude. I moved away, urgently whispering to David.

"Offer no consolation, ask no questions. Get over to the car, grab a heavy spanner. Quickly!"

For no apparent reason, the woman continued to swear luridly. Her face was tough enough to chop wood on. David returned. Unnoticed, he pressed the spanner into my side.

"Keep it," I ordered, "cover me, I'm taking a picture. Brain that big bastard, if necessary."

The burst of my flash bulb astounded the big hulk in the cowboy boots. He lurched towards me and my gorge rose.

"Get back," I cried, "or I'll drill a hole through your brain." I pointed my pipe like a pistol. "Don't be damned fools," I went on quickly, a new twist in my thoughts. "I was signalling friends in the valley, we want to help you."

I lied, saying we were schoolmasters, that we were camping with our boys and they would help to put the car back on its wheels. This pacified the scruff. He spoke in a smirking way.

"Buddy, I'll give you 500 bucks if you get my auto sittin' right."

"I ain't no bum, mister," I answered in his own jargon, "you'd help me in the same way, wouldn't you?"

"Sure would."

We measured the space between the end of the Plymouth and the edge of the ravine. The Minx could be squeezed through, but the nearside wheels would be just five inches clear of a drop of hundreds of feet.

I spoke to the tough in the Tom Mix boots.

"We're going to bring our boys back to give you help."

David put in cleverly: "And a bottle of brandy for you and your friends."

The woman in the chemise was nursing a bruised shoulder. The other member of the trio was still crouching near the Plymouth, involving himself in a drunken one-man hate conversation.

I manoeuvred Alaska-Minxy until its nose was in the narrow gap.

"Will the earth hold?" asked my companion in a nervous tone.

I moved forward a little at a time, sweating freely. I glanced to the left across the wide valley. The drop was so sheer that I might have been looking out of the cabin of a plane. I dared not take another look but turned my eyes to the Plymouth. Slowly I grazed alongside. Half way through I stopped until I once more became aware that I had breath and feet.

David's voice came to me, its tone brittle and urgent: "Keep it moving, don't collapse the earth."

I sucked a deep breath, fear gave me a prod. The earth was supporting the weight and I let in the clutch and pressed the accelerator. "Get it over . . ." Alaska-Minxy shot forward and I grazed its right hand side against a part of the Plymouth. I was through. For a few seconds I thought my brain was upside down. Then I stopped the car and got out.

Roat followed me.

"Go back and get the number of their car," I urged. "Hurry!"

Then the awful woman came over and put her head into the window at my side. She was whimpering now.

"Honey, Honey, run me back to Beaver Lake, I'll pay you fellas."

Mr. Cowboy boots roughly wrapped an arm around her. The language she let rip outstripped anything I'd ever heard used by prisoners against the Gestapo.

David jumped in and slammed the door, repeating to himself the number of the Plymouth. I moved off, stopping a safe twenty yards distant with the engine running.

"You filthy, low-livered bunch of . . ."

I finished my little round off, pulled my head through the window and drove away. Transition from anger, to enthusiasm for the job in hand seemed to take scarcely any time at all.

Later, upon our arrival at Prince George, the occurrence was reported. The registration number of the Plymouth was handed over. A polite version of the accident was broadcast by CKWX. I hoped the Mounties grabbed that trio. I hope that the chemise-clad bitch received a strong disinfectant mouth-wash, and Mr. Cowboy Boots got gaoled.

*   *   *

We drove on and on, fast and furious. The sun came through the clouds like a blessing. The dusty, winding road seemed to shoot out like a telescope, section after section. Dust was now a damned nuisance. We spat it from our mouths and it made our eyes smart.

Quesnel was behind us. One of the strangest stories connected with this place is that of the turnip rush. To avoid scurvy from rough trail diets in 1860, miners flocked to the farm of a Norwegian farmer called Charles Danielson. He had grown a large patch of turnips. This vegetable patch was more productive than many of the gold claims. Miners paid between 25

Above: This photograph of the Alaska Highway was taken on mile 456 east, but not by me. You can see that even on this comparatively good surface any tyres running fast are bound to throw up a constant barrage of stones; though armour protected the differential I had neglected the petrol tank under the boot ...

Right: The occupants of this Plymouth sedan were drunk. They had skidded and turned upside down without incurring more than bruises. Behind the Plymouth is Alaska-Minxy.

Fairbanks, Alaska, terminus of the Alaska Highway and our destination. I was staggered both by the size of this city of the Northland and by the mildness of the climate—though the Arctic Circle was only 100 miles away, the air had the caressing warmth of a British summer day. In winter, however, temperatures drop to minus 50° F. Fairbanks is a polite, up-to-the-minute city and, beside developing a skyline of skyscrapers, had parking meters for cars long before they had been introduced to London.

cents and one dollar for each turnip. The dumbfounded farmer cleared 3,000 dollars.

We drove into Prince George, 520 miles from Vancouver, at 9 a.m. on the morning of 23 August. Swiftly, steadily, the new day had approached. This booming hub-city lay at the confluence of the Nechako and Fraser Rivers. It was founded in 1808 as a post of the North-west Company. Today it serves the northern interior (the greatest-fur producing area in British Columbia). Huge forests which support a large lumber production extend north and east of the city. Vast natural gas and oil reserves are being explored in this region.

After re-fuelling we raced from Prince George for the John Hart Highway. This stupendous creation, part of the ceaseless development of the northland, was officially opened to public travel on 1 July, 1952. It is the vital connecting link between the Alaska Highway at Dawson Creek and Prince George. It snakes across 255 miles of rugged land, timbered mountains, tumbling streams, swift, clear rivers and placid lakes. In the forests roam moose, bear and mule-deer in their thousands. In this most difficult country, one mile of road, I had been told, cost as much as £355,000. Engineers encountered frightening obstacles, and the completion of the Hart Highway represented a great triumph. The wealth that is Alaska, the Yukon, and northern British Columbia, demanded quick access to the lower mainland. After the early miners had carved out the Cariboo Trail, the probing Highway stopped just north of Prince George for a decade or so. During this time, men knew that sooner or later the short route followed "down north" by the long boats would be paralleled by a roadway. This is the John Hart Highway.

Now we climbed the forested foothills of the Murray Range, part of the northern Rocky Mountain chain. The higher peaks ranged between 5,000 and 7,500 feet. Our motor growled determinedly. We settled down to fast relay driving.

Grim, unshaven, tense, David climbed Alaska-Minxy towards the 2,800 foot summit of Pine Pass, overlooking the beautiful

65

Azouzetta mountain lake. I relaxed and dwelt on the "Awakening Canadian North". It is well to give readers some idea of this wilderness, as unchanged and challenging as when first penetrated, but with a difference. Today its surface has been scratched, it is being brought into active production and significance.

New vistas are unfolding, the opening-up of the Canadian north is a thrilling and exciting story, not only in contemporary Canadian history, but in world annals. Over recent years, more than ever before, the eyes of Canadians have been focused on the north. Because of the north, the eyes of the world have been focused on Canada. The great natural resources which lie hidden in these forbidding areas spell an increase also to the wealth of the world. In the north is mineral wealth, oil and water-power.

To the outsider, Canada is the north, and he thinks of her people in terms of northern symbols; the Mountie, the fur-trader, the bush-pilot, and the prospector. The native Canadian sees himself and his northland in more practical and less romantic terms. He knows the north is a barrier between the western hemisphere and the opposite side in a possible future war. Beyond the Arctic mists, enormous aircraft are continually landing on strips of ice in a vast scheme of defences against surprise attack.

Where does this northland really begin? Generally speaking it is what lies north of the fifty-fifth parallel; a land mass twice the size of India and far more varied. It is a land of extremes and contrasts. In winter, the thermometer can drop to 83°F. below zero; and in summer it can soar to 103° above. In parts of the north the delphiniums reach a height of six feet in August; in other parts a birch tree takes a hundred years to grow a foot. There are mountains four miles high, fissures a mile deep, fiords a hundred miles long. There are sinuous green lakes so lovely that they seem painted on the landscape, and others so foreboding that they well could be part of purgatory itself.

There are two fresh water seas, each as big as Holland, an

island larger than Sweden, a river twenty-six hundred miles long, and more lakes than in the rest of the world put together.

Canada's biggest source of silver is at Keno in the Yukon. Her fourth largest goldmine is at Yellowknife in the north-west territories. Three-quarters of Canada's iron production and half her uranium production come out of the northland. The world's biggest fur-trading post, where as many as three hundred thousand muskrat pelts are collected every year, lies far north at Aklavik on the MacKenzie River delta. What may turn out to be the world's largest untapped body of lead and zinc (120 million tons at the most cautious estimate) lies in the far north on Great Slave Lake.

What may be the world's greatest untapped source of iron ore (perhaps sixty billion tons of it) lies in the Canadian north near Ungava Bay. What is certainly the world's greatest untapped source of oil lies in the north, mingled with the tar sands of Athabasca. There is enough to supply global needs for a century, but it is still unexploited because no practical process has yet been found to separate liquid from sand. In the cracks and fissures of some of the oldest rocks on earth, geologists and prospectors are finding unrealized mineral treasure, nickel, copper, cobalt, all within reach of man's probing hands.

Spectacular developments are certain in the foreseeable future in this sub-arctic region. There are many challenges to be met, great problems to be conquered. The "Awakening North" is still a frontier-land, and as far as man can see ahead, it is likely to remain so.

*　　　*　　　*

A generally untrue idea exists that Alaska and the Yukon are permanently frozen and frigid lands. It will come as a surprise when I state that inland summer temperatures have risen to over 95°F., and on the third day of our record breaking run, the temperature was well over 60°. David Roat and I drove all day and night in open-necked shirts. We were plagued at one stretch by mosquitoes; Alaska has billions of pestilential mosquitoes in summertime, they are as bad as in Central

Africa. Even a wintertime temperature of 70° below zero doesn't kill them off.

In summertime, these northern latitudes have long hours of daylight (16 to 20 hours), and above the Arctic Circle weeks pass with no night-time at all. Here it is as much a land of the midnight sun as is northern Norway. In wintertime, it is different. At the Arctic Circle on the shortest day of the year, the sun touches the southern horizon at noon, then disappears from sight again. At four degrees north of the Circle, the sun is not seen from late November until late January. At Fairbanks, 2.5° below the Circle, on 21 December, the sun rises at 9.5 a.m. and sets at 1.40 p.m. It is then a sombre, shaded world.

Roat and I were racing towards Fairbanks in early autumn, with the length of the days the reverse of winter. Darkness would be very short and the strange splendour of the Northern Lights would illuminate the polar skies during the brief hours of darkness.

Chapter Five

Alaska Highway

Success covers a multitude of blunders ...

IT WAS 2.30 p.m. when we came to Dawson Creek, or mile-post zero of the Alaska Highway. This was no settlement of log-cabins, but a boom-town of Canada's north-west. It had rocketed into prominence following the war. The Alaska High-way and the Hart Highway, were responsible for the town's growth of population from 500 to 10,000. Here the urgently needed tyres were awaiting. We changed Alaska-Minxy's wheels and refuelled, but we didn't stop for long. Once on our way again forty miles were quickly dashed over, and we approached the 2,130 ft. Peace River suspension bridge.

"Aha!" uttered David breaking a long silence; the way he said it spoke volumes.

"Aha!" I acknowledged.

Legend said: "Drink once of the waters of the mighty Peace River, and forever you will want to drink again." This river had been a boundary of truce between the warlike tribes of the Cree and Beaver Indians, hence the name of Peace.

Our journey now became rugged and jarring. Stones drummed on the metal below our feet, a continuous and hellish clatter. Roat bawled in exasperation: "Why the hell didn't we think of earplugs?"

The strident alarm clock let loose and we turned on the radio. We were climbing into the Pink Mountains, the gateway of the real virgin wilderness.

"C'mmon Minxy", I coaxed, "open up, give me just a little bit more."

The broadcast from CKWX was rousing. Our report left at Dawson Creek was read over the air. The announcer then said:

"The Power-Drivers are on the Alaska Highway, here is a message for them. Calling Dick and David . . . all British Columbia and Northland wish you well, listen carefully to these instructions. Try and send a report for the midnight news. You will locate a North-west Communications Repeater Station at Trutch Lodge, also at Fort Nelson 300 miles from milepost zero. Is your tripmeter correct? Was it re-set in Dawson Creek? All North-west posts into Alaska have been alerted to track your progress. Re-set your watches at the new time zone at Watson Lake, milepost 635. A weather report will be given you at midnight. Good luck Dick and David."

I hurried off 195 miles in a domain of desolate loveliness. To the west was a panoramic view of the northern Rockies. At intervals spectator bear and moose stared mystified at our approach and passing. At milepost 200, we stopped and tumbled from the hot and dusty car.

"Heck," said the Trutch Lodge operator, "you've gotten here mighty fast."

Without delay the progress report was handed over and we were off towards the second highest point (4,134 feet) on the highway. Came Fort Nelson at milepost 300. There are many strange tales of the country hereabouts, which can be called "Land of the Vanishing Men" because many of those who have been tempted to journey into the region to investigate have simply disappeared.

Fingers and forearms were feeling numb so I handed over to David. We were hungry and I opened a tin of meat. Slapping the meat between hunks of bread we washed it down with orange juice. This was our staple diet.

We wound through the most northerly extension of the Rocky Mountain Range, up and down the steep gradients to milepost 392, at a height of 4,156 feet. The compass needle was veering westerly; it should do so for another 200 miles. I began to think of unpleasant things that might happen. This was caused by "mountain mania". I had had a similar experience in northern Norway. Such speculation was unhealthy, and I grabbed our highway bible to tune my mind to other thoughts.

This "Milepost-guide to the land of the midnight sun" is a must for all who travel in British Columbia, the Yukon and Alaska. The maps are magnificent, the information often invaluable. It said of the area we now traversed:

> "Many of the curves in this section seem without reason, appearing to follow the aimless wanderings of a moose."

Panoramic beauty was coming at us so fast it proved an aggravating distraction; eyes had to be forced back to the road. I began getting funny ideas that this region was familiar. My eyes were prickling and I felt as limp as a rag doll. The time had come to take pep-up, keep-awake dope. I swallowed a capsule to alert my senses for twelve hours; I handed one to David.

"What's it do?" he asked.

"A mind reviver, take it," I instructed.

"Do they affect the heart?"

"No, take it," I ordered.

He still hesitated.

"Take it, or I take the wheel," I said firmly.

I met further protests with sharp command. I was scared that he would become drowsy while driving. I wasn't going to sleep with the fear I might end up at the bottom of a ravine. I didn't like the idea of my ghost soaring out of it. These tablets were medically prescribed, I had taken them on previous drives. They didn't damage one's health, but helped to dispel the lassitude that can induce error—and at high speed error can be killing.

*   *   *

We'd been on the road exactly twenty-four hours, recorded mileage was 1036; average speed, 43 miles an hour. David wiped dust from a weary face. "Is it humanly possible," he growled hoarsely, "to keep this up another four days?"

We started hitting pot-holes; I cringed. The highway was badly pockmarked over this section. Every time we banged down, our coil springs seemed to compress solid. I clenched my teeth; I couldn't do anything else.

Tugging at the wheel, Roat's face glistened, perspiration ran down dusty cheeks leaving white furrows: "Car suspensions weren't designed for this sort of hammering," he said bitterly.

His nerves were getting prickly, but I knew they'd get worse. In two days they would be raw, and in three days they'd be utterly ragged. It was a result of the stress and strain that a drive of this kind imposed on the human element as well as on the vehicle. This was a crucial stage for us. Strain was beginning to show. The human mind suddenly hated cruelty towards mechanism, because though he wouldn't admit it, each of us was beginning to hate the physical strain to which we were subjecting ourselves. I reacted unmercifully and taunted: "Perhaps you're worried about yourself snapping, and not the bloody suspension?"

Crouching low over the wheel, Roat bit his lip.

"Tell me more," he said sourly.

"I will! Flog this car still faster, I want you to burn out its guts and smash up the suspension by keeping straight on with fast driving. Bust it up. Try it, David?"

I was thrown a fierce look, which pleased me. Roat was getting combative. This was important for success.

"You asked for it," he bellowed, and the needle swung higher.

Approaching a sharp bend, I yelped: "Oi, take it easy!"

"You asked for it, Pape, now stop belly-aching."

"Sorry, David . . . bash away, chum."

Tyres rebelled. There was a mad, mixed noise of squealing rubber and pinging gravel. The suspension took sledge-hammer crunches repeatedly. I thanked heaven for the armour-plating. Had it not been attached, the sump and axle would have been the anvil. Alaska-Minxy was performing magnificently. Hot and eager, the car, too, might have taken a revivifying capsule. Driving demoniacally, David was seized by a whim to give me a dig at every dangerous bend.

Safely around, he would ask: "Better than Bleddy Pape?"

I couldn't have driven better and I kept silent. The reference to "Bleddy Pape" caused me unvoiced amusement. It emanated from my *Cape Cold to Cape Hot* book. It contained reference to a Norwegian, Johan Brun, who also had spat out "Bleddy Pape" when weary, ireful and the going was tough.

It was policy to leave David to think and drive, so I studied the guide-book under the hooded pilot lamp. I read a poem by an unknown American soldier of the famed Corps of Army Engineers who had constructed the road to Alaska, known then as the Alcan project (coined from the words, Alaska-Canada). In 1944, however, the word Alcan was dropped. The official name of the famous road is now Alaska Highway.

SONG OF THE ALCAN PIONEERS

They gave us a job and we did it;
They said it couldn't be done.
They figured that time would forbid it.
They licked us before we'd begun.

But there she is—eagles above her
The Road—See, she steams in the snow.
She's ours, and Oh God, how we love her,
But now—marching orders—we go.

We started with nothing and won her.
We diced for her honour with death.
We starved, froze and died upon her
And damned her with agonized breath.
Blood-red ran the snow where we lay—
Blood-red rose the sun at her setting,
Cold white are the graves we're forgetting—
Cold white are our ashes today.

We levelled the mountains to find her,
We climbed from the pit to the sky.
We conquered the forests to bind her,
We burrowed where mastodons lie.
Smooth, straight, and true we have fashioned,
Clean she is, living, aglow.
The Road—feel her, vibrant, impassioned—
And now—marching orders—we go.

Go from the stardust of June night,
Go from the beauty we won.
Little lost lakes in the moonlight,
Snow-steepled spires in the sun.
We lend you the Road—we who made it,
And bright may your victories burn,
We lend you The Road, we who laid it,
Until the day we return. . . .

I think readers should have a brief history of the Alaska Highway and Dawson Creek.

It was 15° below zero on a bleak 20 November, 1942, when 250 shivering soldiers, civilians and Royal Canadian Mounted Police on a windswept hill, opposite milestone 1061, Kluane Lake, watched officials from Alaska and Canada cut the ribbon stretched across the frozen road at "Soldier's Summit". This opening ceremony marked the end of an epic of road building, the task had been begun only eight months before. The actual breaking through and first connecting of the road took place at milestone 588, where a tiny bridge crosses Contact Creek, and where a small sign bears this legend:

CONTACT CREEK

This marks the point where U.S. Army Engineers working with caterpillar bulldozers from the north were met by engineers from the south. This marked the breaking through of the Alcan Military Highway, 23 September, 1942.

First built by Army engineers as an overland lifeline to relieve Alaska from wartime supply problems caused by shortage of shipping, the pioneer road was turned over to contractors for widening, gravelling, and the replacement of primitive log bridges by structures of steel. The road had also to be re-routed at many points.

Since that day in March, 1942, the Alaska Highway has become a legend in the annals of road building. For years only a dream of far-sighted engineers of the north country, the present-day reality of the Alaska Highway is rapidly becoming an important artery of commerce and travel—a link between the industrial regions of America, and the fabulous natural resources of the State of Alaska, a great trade route penetrating the incredible riches of north-western Canada's wilderness, and a permanent monument to the friendship between two great nations.

The completion of the Alaska Highway against what seemed like insuperable difficulties has been compared by many with the building of the Panama Canal: some experts think even surpassing it. One of the most formidable obstacles was muskeg, a slimy mass of decaying vegetable matter into which trucks and tractors alike sank and became helpless. However, once America had entered the Second World War as a belligerent, the building of the highway became a matter of military importance. America threw everything into it, men and money counted for nothing. As bulldozers broke under the strain they were buried to form solid road foundation. Many men died, but the Alaska Highway wound its way to the Arctic Circle over 2,000 formidable miles. Today, Alaska is a vitally important military base. Across a great void of mountains and glaciers extends, and is being perfected, what is termed the Dew Line. This invisible line has been built at a cost of thousands of millions of dollars and employs armies of men. It is the distant early warning radar chain. Its military importance is emphasized by the fact that American-owned Little Diomedes Island is only 2.4 miles from Russian-owned Big Diomedes Island across the Bering Strait.

*   *   *

It was close to midnight, the eerie flare of Aurora Borealis was present in the sky. I dreamed with open eyes as we rolled on over the Alaska Highway. It winds over five mountain ranges, and skirts the shores of innumerable lonely lakes. There are no stop lights, and few motorists. It is the loneliest highway in the world, yet it sponsors a great sense of friendliness. It is an ancient law of the Yukon never to withhold help from anyone needing it. Once a visitor did drive past a ditched car.

The number of the disregarding one was given to the Mounties. It was flashed ahead. Thereafter, no room was available to the callous one anywhere over the route. He had to sleep in his car for the whole of his trip.

Mileposts along the highway have become street addresses. A letter sent to Bill Smith at milepost 1,050 will reach him. People hundreds of miles apart discuss each other as familiarly as suburban neighbours. Gossip races along the magical "moccasin telegraph" with lightning speed. The entire country through which the road threads is frozen over from mid-October to mid-May. In 1947, near milepost 1,180, the temperature dropped to 83° below. In winter a sickly ghost of a sun is visible for a few brief hours daily, then the Northern Lights provide brilliant firework displays in the heavens. In summer, yellow dust kicks up giant plumes behind every car. On windless days it hovers like thick fog and even by day headlights may have to be used if one is driving close behind another car.

Engineers perform a heartbreaking job. Where the road is built on permanently frozen ground, it buckles and heaves. Where it crosses jelly-like muskeg, continually it is sinking. Bridges spanning rivers are swept away in sudden floods. Every spring, when the frozen waters melt, miles of the roadway get washed out. On mountain sides one can tell the age of the road by counting the remains of previous roads that have slipped down the slope.

Knife-sharp gravel is hell on soft tyres. A bad driver can easily rip up a dozen tyres on the trip; their carcases drape mileposts from British Columbia to Alaska. This is a land as lonely as the valleys of the moon, and sometimes as strange. Great stretches of white poplar stand like weird forests of toothpicks. In the spring and summer, however, the road runs amid a carpet of flowers. The Forget-me-not is Alaska's floral emblem.

*   *   *

The moon rode high, dense forests grew tight against the highway; a thread which showed ahead like a ribbon of burnished brass. Often though, as we changed direction, it became as dark as Hades, an alternation of garish moonlight and funeral black. The alarm clock pealed noisily, it was again CKWX-time. David was asleep, this time insensitive to noise and the car's rock and roll. I didn't disturb him but switched on the set. Atmospheric disturbance was annoying. The unseen voice read our previous despatch. Then he continued:

"This is the Power-Drive of the century and officially timed. It has aroused sensational public interest and CKWX will now broadcast bulletins every half hour."

Bad news followed.

"Calling Dick and David. Severe storms are forecast during the next six hours between Muncho Lake and Whitehorse. Extreme care is required in low-lying areas, you may encounter washouts. It is vital we track you, and Army Signal Corps have been alerted, and North-west Communication posts. You will find radio repeater stations at Watson Lake, milepost 635, at Teslin, milepost 804.5 and Canyon Creek, milepost 996. These posts will put you through to us immediately. We are anxious to make a tape recording of your voices at earliest opportunity. Gasoline supplies await you at Watson Lake whatever the hour."

As if the weather gods wished to testify to the accuracy of the meteorological forecast a brilliant flash of forked lightning split the heavens. Half-an-hour later a vicious cross-wind whipped up swirling dust. I oozed sweat, spat grit and cursed. The weather rapidly became worse. The howling wind set our nerves on edge. Hurricane gusts seemed to be trying to force Alaska-Minxy off the road. I clutched at my morale and tried to ridicule fears that the record would be washed-out.

When the full force of the storm struck us we were zigzagging warily towards the Toad River. Reverberating thunder followed intense lightning, wind gusts and torrential rain mixed together; the sting in the tail of it all was a terrifying hailstone bombardment. Frozen ice marbles lashed at the car like grapeshot. I imagined I'd been steeled to the worst of freak storms in Equatorial Africa, but this Yukon outburst really took the lolly. We had to stop. Several times I experienced a sickening stomach-gripping sensation when the car was rocked and moved by wind gusts of hurricane velocity. I thought Alaska-Minxy might be flung into the Toad River—and not in toad-like hops. David rigid by my side seemed mesmerized.

When the avalanche of water changed to balls of ice, we were in a white-out and a most infernal noise. I was too panicky to smoke. These ice balls battered at the car's metal skin with a noise that was satanical. It was so intense that I imagined our windscreen would shatter; I was half convinced that a headlamp glass had gone.

"God," moaned David, "is it the end of the world or something?"

Then it stopped. It might have been halted by the closing of a celestial switch; a sudden peace ensued. The weather demons must have temporarily prostrated themselves. It was quite impossible to move, however. The downhill highway was amorphous, just an abominable torrent carrying away billions of ice-balls. Sudden temperature change created wraiths of luminous mist, in the headlamp beams it floated in eerie patches.

"Rocky Mountain spooks," I muttered in a tedious attempt at cheerfulness.

During the lull, groups of frightened deer plunged and splashed over the canal-like roadway into yielding undergrowth. They emitted a concord of shrill squealing, sounding like a damaged gramophone record with a stuck needle.

Fifteen minutes later the Yukon storm curtain rose again on the second act. Apparently the weather demons had recovered and were anxious to give us another prod. This time a dam might have burst above us. Roat was dumbfounded, he'd never seen the like of it before. In the first round we'd almost been blown away, now it looked as if we might be washed away. I was tormented with the idea that if such violent storms persisted, the record was humanly impossible. I was also fearful about swollen rivers ahead. Would bridges have gone? I had been warned about the Arctic weather. After what we had experienced I was now prepared to believe anything. I felt that driving over the Alaska Highway would be like playing Russian roulette, waiting for something to happen, realizing that with the weather, sooner or later one was bound to "cop it".

The storm endured for two hours, but we were immobile on that waterlogged highway in all for three-and-a-half hours. I popped another sleep-killing capsule in my mouth. We had met with a serious setback and somehow we had to make up lost time. When the waterway became a discernible roadway again, we crept forward. The engine growled reassuringly, it might have been trying to articulate, "rely on me". Fortunately, we were soon on higher, firmer ground, and within fifteen miles it was hard to believe there had been any deluge at all. I was furious and stubbornly refused to accept any possibility of defeat. Savagely I kicked Alaska-Minxy: "faster damn you, faster blast you," I yelled. It was uncalled for, the little motor was doing its utmost, straining itself to abnormal degree over rugged terrain. It was a case of 60, 40, 50 miles per hour, 70 60, 80, braking, speeding, slithering, bouncing.

We again settled down to stoic, stolid driving, nothing un-looked-for happened. We passed milepost 455, and for nine miles curved along the perimeter of Munco Lake, reputed as one of the most beautiful in the world. The deep, cool waters reflect heavenly colours from turquoise to aquamarine, the lake's oversize Mackinaw trout are renowned for their fighting qualities. We speeded over the 1,143-foot suspension bridge and the Liard River, on past Mount Prudence, named after Prudence Smith, an adventurous girl who belied her name by shooting the dangerous rapids with her father.

*   *   *

The inside of my thighs burned, the skin seemed scalded and it gave me an irritated feeling. Being seated for long hours in a bucket seat promoted undue perspiration on tender parts. I stopped and put on a clean pair of cotton pants, first plastering the inside with Vaseline. I handed the wheel over to Roat and sprawled on the bed. We were now in a zone showing evidence of the glacial age. We streaked at 84 m.p.h., across the Coal River so named because on the sandbars are found lumps of coal which have been washed down by the current. We screamed over the Hyland River and at milepost 627, the road at long last crossed the boundary into the 208,000 square miles of the Yukon Territory.

We drove at a speed for which we seemed scarcely geared and eventually pulled into Watson Lake settlement for refuelling. A rising rim of red sun showed on the skyline. We visited the North-west Communications Repeater Station and learned that anxious inquiries had come from Vancouver.

"They're worried about you," declared the radio man. "I guess that storm was one of the God Almightiest cloud explosions in years."

I gave him a cynical laugh.

"Explosion is right," I admitted.

Contact with Radio CKWX 1,420 miles away was made with remarkable speed. A sound recording was taken of our voices and our reports of the storm delay were promptly broadcast.

We got off our mark to devour the remaining 280 miles to Whitehorse, capital of the Yukon. The vast frontier country we now slashed through was starkly beautiful and forbidding, and river tributaries seemed innumerable. The principal highways of Northland are her rivers. In summer they are liquid roads for the kayaks of the Eskimos and the canoes of the forest Indians, also for river steamers. In winter, after the freeze-up, they are transformed into broad, smooth ice highways on which dog teams and tractors travel with equal ease and safety. We crossed the Upper Liard and Little Rancheria rivers, the Young, Swift and Morley rivers and went on to the 85-miles-long Teslin Lake. "Teslin" means in Indian dialect, "long waters". We shot the 2,300-foot Nisutlin Bridge, the longest water span on the highway. In the Indian tongue this means, "Quiet Waters". Next we came to the McClintock River, then to milepost 914 and a side road leading to the notorious Whitehorse Rapids. Here the mighty Yukon River foams and dashes through a tortuous rock-strewn channel.

We passed a sign saying "Welcome to Whitehorse"; a few

Above: Each of these parabolic antennae is 60 feet in diameter and is made of aluminium. They form a part of the Dew Line radar early-warning network which rings the Northland and is one of the factors which have helped to open up Canada's Far North. Scientific exploitation of mineral resources is beginning.

Below: By contrast with the wonderful scientific apparatus above, but equally as much a feature of the Northland today, is the relatively primitive writing of the Eskimo. Here the Eskimo historian of an Arctic Circle community is recording in picture writing the events of the year.

Upright on its wheels at the bottom of a 50-foot ravine was a cream-coloured Dodge. It had left the Alaska Highway and sailed through space. Had not one of the badly injured occupants managed to climb back on to the Highway, to be revealed to us staggering about only half conscious, the crashed vehicle might not have been found for months. We feared the woman had a broken back. While Roat ministered to her I took this photograph (on which the number plate of the car has been painted over to save the owners any possible embarrassment). Later American Army men took over the work of rescue.

This photograph was taken when Roat and I, both very tired, were back in Vancouver at Radio Station CKWX. We'd done what we set out to do: Fairbanks and back, 5,000 miles in five days, thus beating by a full 24 hours the previous American-set record of six days. Later I found that the top of my trousers had sandpapered away four square inches of skin on the right side of my waist, which necessitated a visit to Vancouver's General Hospital.

This stretch of road beneath the frowning mass of Mount Eisenhower lies between Banff and Lake Louise. It is wide and well-surfaced. Some of the other roads in the Rockies were far otherwise: once, while snow was falling, the track was so bad that I was tempted to go back, but Billie disagreed and tackled a nasty stretch in masterly style and at a fast pace.

minutes later we were in the capital of the Yukon. I inquired the way to the garage for refuelling; thirty yards from the facade, David stiffened. He gave a low laugh in which concern had almost driven out the chuckle.

"Hell, look, Royal Canadian Mounted Police, and one's beckoning us over."

Three RCMPs in their cavalry, yellow-banded blue caps awaited us. The sergeant was easily 6 ft. 4 in. tall. In exchange for a stern smile I greeted him.

"Nice to be here, Hello."

Roat surveyed the trio of picturesque police with a look of fascinated dread.

"Hello, Power-Drivers," greeted the big man, "you're sure creating a lot of commotion."

The sergeant's eyes travelled up and down us, the other two Mounties began strolling around Alaska-Minxy.

I was asked: "Which is Dick of the foolhardy pair?"

Nervously I jerked my finger towards my neck.

The sharp eyes wrinkled: "What am I to do with you two?" he asked.

"What have we done?"

He glanced at his watch and remarked: "It is now 7 p.m. and Vancouver happens to be 1,700 miles from here."

"That's right," I admitted, trying to turn over in my mind what was wrong, what depredations we might have committed.

The tall sergeant pushed his head into the car, studied the mileage indicator, tickled his nose reflectively and continued: "It was zero and sealed when you left, eh?"

I nodded.

"Then you've travelled 1,738 miles?"

"S'right," sniffled David.

Calculations were made in a notebook.

"We've followed the broadcasts," we were told at length. "If you left Vancouver 48 hours ago, you've averaged 37 miles an hour."

"S'right," confirmed David incautiously.

Another Mountie intervened. "That's excluding stops and delays?"

I assented meekly.

"Meaning," he went on, "you've been pushing the needle off the clock?"

"Right," I acknowledged, "but technically we're still under the 50 m.p.h. speed limit, aren't we?"

The sergeant proceeded with his homily.

"Are you both capable of full control? It's dangerous to drive if you're not physically and mentally O.K."

I gulped: "I affirm confidently and emphatically Sergeant, we're both driving fit." After a pause . . . "you can't judge sausages by their skins."

The shortest of the trio jerked out:

"It's 610 miles to Fairbanks, you'll have to do it in under fifteen hours to maintain the 40 m.p.h. average."

"It's justifiable," I added. "We're not exhausted, mortified or morally shaken and time is precious."

The big sergeant winked. "A British car for a British record with British boys, eh? On your way, good luck, we'll take your reflexes as read."

The three RCMPs strolled to their patrol car. The big fellow turned and exclaimed cheerfully:

"Should your average speed exceed 50 m.p.h., you'll both go to gaol."

We ignored the chaffing nature of the remark and just grinned. I obeyed the dictum that it's fatal to argue or be funny too long with coppers, right or wrong, irrespective of species! We hurriedly took on petrol and oil for the car and coffee for ourselves. Then we got moving from Whitehorse. This was the territorial headquarters of the world-famous Royal Canadian Mounted Police, responsible for the administration of law and order in the Yukon since 1898.

Today, aeroplanes and automobiles have supplanted the more romantic horse and dog-team as the modes of transport for these colourful officers of the law. Comparatively small as the force was (as of 1 January, 1958, 5,098 uniformed strength, 350 special constables, and 564 civilian employees), it is hardly possible anywhere in Canada for one to pass twenty-four hours without evidence of the existence of the Royal Canadian Mounted Police.

There is a subtle uniformity of manner and approach about Mounties. The eyes of all the men of one of the greatest police forces on earth are much alike. Eliminate the effect of uniform, the manner and the stance, and you are left with the eyes. There is a quiet pleasantness in them, for it is a tenet of RCMP training that its members are infinitely courteous and co-operative people. Though a smile crinkles readily, there is also a look of vast, cold distance in the eyes. In casual conversation, the eyes of the Mounties seldom leave yours. If you have anything to conceal, that look in the eyes of the watching policeman can with reason be alarming; those eyes miss little.

*　　　*　　　*

We kept going fast towards the International Canada-Alaska Boundary and its customs post. "The Lights" (Aurora-Borealis) waved in milky curtains of pale green and violet from the vault of heaven to the vast reaches of tundra on the earth beneath. This aurora light was pinned to the dome of the universe by diamond bright stars.

Not far to the north-west was Dawson, the Klondike city once famous for gold. We were now probing the true country of the Yukon gold stampeders and around us were the old-trodden paths of the "Trail of 98". In this area, occasional rotting, sunken remains of log buildings still stand as monuments to the fever and fury, the colour and agony of the gold rush days at the turn of the century.

David instinctively felt the strange, inexpressible excitement of the region too. Turning to me with bloodshot eyes, he said:

"It's not easy to believe Dawson City is over there. Weird to know that such a place really existed."

"Real enough," I said. "I'm returning this way after the drive to collect notes. Join me?"

"It'll be close to winter."

"It won't be a long stay," I promised.

Roat didn't say yes, but there was a strange perplexity in his face.

"You know Dick," he remarked, "I'm not sentimental or melodramatic, but already I feel this drive has put ten years of maturity into me."

"How?"—but already I knew what he meant.

"A trip like this makes you discover something," he continued, "it's hard to conceive what it is, maybe danger, physical endurance, the magnificence of all this nature . . ." He laughed, "I just feel wiser and more tempered, anyhow."

"Good," I joked, "it's subtracted ten years from my cynical, older self, too."

He studied me intently, then asked: "Will you ever stop wandering?"

I thought it best to quote from a verse by Robert Service, once the poet laureate of the Yukon:

> *Ye who know the Lone Trail fain would follow it,*
> *Though it lead to glory or the darkness of the pit.*
> *Ye who take the Lone Trail, bid your love goodbye;*
> *The Lone Trail, the Lone Trail follow till you die.*
>
> *Bid goodbye to sweetheart, bid goodbye to friend;*
> *The Lone Trail, the Lone Trail follow to the end.*
> *Tarry not, and fear not, chosen of the true;*
> *Lover of the Lone Trail, the Lone Trail waits for you.*

*   *   *

It was difficult to believe that in a few months this wild landscape would be blanketed under feet of snow. Then, the millions of trees which now boasted foliage of red and gold would flaunt mantles of lacy white with icy needles of hoarfrost. The temperature would skid below 50°, colder no doubt than temperatures at certain places in Antarctica. In 1955, a radio announcer had reported that a south polar base was enjoying day-round sunshine with a temperature of 39° above, while at Fairbanks on the Arctic Circle it was 53° below: 92° colder than Antarctica.

*   *   *

I pressed the accelerator to get a little more speed. Vainly I tried not to keep looking to the right where the ghost-town of the once fabulous Dawson City lay. During its hey-day, it is reputed that 50,000 hard bitten, boisterous miners flooded the place. When they washed gold from the creeks, invariably they trekked into Dawson City for a wild orgy of booze, women and song. They would come from the lonely creeks of the Yukon River where for months they had survived on bacon fat and "Alaska strawberries", namely beans. Few struck it rich, 99 out of 100 dug in vain in that muted region. I urged Alaska-Minxy forward. As I did so I thought of the optimists who had been led to believe that gold could be swept up literally with brooms. Thousands had frozen to death, many more were driven to suicide, others went stark raving mad with the cold, isolation and disappointment. Those who found gold for the most part dissipated it in the saloons.

> The lonely sunsets flame and die,
> The giant valleys gulp the night,
> The monster mountains scrape the sky,
> Where eager stars are diamond bright.

*   *   *

We thundered over the Takhini River bridge on our way towards the snow-capped ramparts of the St. Elias Range, which includes Mount Logan, 19,850 feet, Canada's highest peak. Down the valley of the Aishihik River our route was shadowed for a dozen miles by snow-capped pinnacles. We made excellent time towards Haines Junction and milepost 1016. Here I made a grave mistake. The Haines Highway forked off for 160 miles to the port of Chilkoot in the Gulf of Alaska. I swung left instead of right. David was not party to this mistake, he was asleep on the bed. We had followed the Alaska Highway for over 1,000 miles without a major turn and it just didn't seem possible that any other highway existed. I boobed!

When at length I turned a weary eye to the compass I was driving in the wrong direction. I'd travelled forty miles. I stopped and checked with an old, gap-toothed Indian. In response to the words "Fairbanks" and "Alaska Highway", he jerked his thumb in the direction I had come. Angrily I reversed. I was amazed at my mistake. It had cost us ninety minutes or most of a hundred miles. To the average motorist, it may sound ridiculous that large signposts somehow can become invisible, but anything can happen in the way of mental tricks when the effects of weariness begin to show.

Once on the right road again I urged the hot little car to the highest point between Whitehorse and Fairbanks (elevation of 3,280 feet). Moonlight bathed a scene of breathtaking beauty. We ran beside the fifty-mile long Kluane (Kloo-ah-nee) Lake for most of its length until we came to Slim's River, 38 miles later to Duke River; 35 miles beyond that was the 1,617-foot eight-span bridge over the multi-channelled Donjek River. Then we rushed at 70 m.p.h. to the White River. It is so named because of quantities of volcanic ash and glacial silt which descend from the headwaters in Alaska's Wrangell Range. Now we neared the border.

*   *   *

We braked. This was the Canadian Customs on the Alaska-Yukon frontier. There was no sympathetic reception, no life or hot coffee, only a dark dawn with angry cloud masses skudding overhead. A cold wind stung our faces, making our eyes water. We flashed a torch and glared in blank misery. A notice stated that traffic must stop for clearance or face a penalty. Hours were from 7.30 a.m. to 10 p.m.

"Closed," muttered David, "now what?"

I was stunned. Fairbanks, our turning point was 300 miles away. A long hold-up would be fatal to our plans.

I blew the hooter long and noisily hoping that the frontier officer might be asleep inside his post.

In my last message to Radio CKWX I had particularly stressed the importance of contacting the Yukon frontier officials to prevent delay and facilitate our fast passage into Alaska. What added to my puzzlement was that CKWX had reported that an officer would remain at the frontier until we had passed through.

"It's really closed," muttered David gloomily; his face showed strain and tiredness.

A few minutes later I yelled: "Look!"

A couple of hundred yards diagonally behind us in the smudgy growth of dawn was a flash of lights.

We found a thin man in the doorway of Beaver Lodge. He asked stonily: "Why the devil are you kicking up such a noise?"

Quickly, briefly, I attempted to explain our situation, our desperate need to get over the frontier into Alaska.

"You're wasting your time," said the thin man in a bored and perfunctory manner. "It opens at 7.30 a.m., you can have a bed here."

"We've got to get through tonight," I told him with exasperation.

David interrupted and gave him an idea about the "5,000 miles in 5 days!" The man issued a sardonic snort, studying us suspiciously and disbelievingly. We were scruffy, unshaven, weary, and I am sure the man at Beaver Lodge thought we were crooks, gaol-breakers, murderers on the run, or something of that kind. He kept squinting at us sideways, and instinctively I felt he would call the Mounties when he got a chance. We learned that official vigilance at the frontier was strict. I was warned that gate-crashing was a serious offence, that we would be caught and gaoled.

I was throbbing with impatience. This was a contingency out of ordinary circumstances; I resolved in the name of expediency for the honour of the British drive to act first and argue later. In 1955 I had "jumped" a frontier in Africa when I was in a car and in a hurry. I was still having diplomatic dealings with the Ambassade de Belgique, 103 Eaton Square, London, for departing from the Belgian Congo for Northern Rhodesia via an unauthorized bush trail.

I took hold of David's arm.

"History will have to repeat itself," I told him sombrely.

"What do you mean, Dick?"

"C'mmon, my friend," I directed, "back to the frontier, if there are any poles we saw them down, if it's wood and wire we use the crowbar. . . ."

Fifteen minutes later were were soaring along at 70 m.p.h., this was Alaska.

"Cripes," said Roat in a somewhat nervous key, "we may have overplayed our hand!"

"Don't get panicky!" I soothed him, "we'll be in Fairbanks soon with a letter for the Mayor."

Nevertheless, I was tremendously anxious to get through to CKWX, Vancouver. I would explain why we had been compelled to crash the frontier. If officialdom got rough it could be slated by a powerful radio network, and I was sure that public sympathy would be on our side. I felt sure the issue would be dropped. I drove with odd exhilaration, I breathed again, I think I swore against the restraining practices of civilization.

*   *   *

The highway from the frontier was heaven after hell. It was mostly macadam, which enabled us to pick up speed and to maintain it. We raced through the broad valley of the Tanana River and passed some of the greatest nesting grounds in the world for wildfowl. Here was the home of many varieties of ducks, geese, even the rare snow goose, sandhill cranes and whistling swans. During April and May, the long echelons of migratory wildfowl converging on Alaska's immense breeding grounds, provided breathtaking spectacles. Equally impressive were the long wavering "Vs" of these birds, greatly increased by summer broods, winging southward in September and October.

We climbed, and a tremendous view opened up from the south. We saw three great peaks of the Alaska range in all their awe-inspiring glory, Mount Hayes, 13,940 feet, Mount Hess in the centre and 12,030 feet, and to the west Mount Deborah, 12,540 feet. Their bases were lost in amber mists.

Alaska-Minxy was running well. Thirteen miles before Fairbanks we rushed through a village called North Pole. It is unique, insofar as one can buy here "One Square Inch of Alaskan North Pole" real estate. Can any place beat this for something different in souvenirs?

*   *   *

We arrived at Fairbanks, terminus of the Alaska Highway, our destination and turning point, at 8 a.m. on Sunday, 25 August, 1957. This was the magic moment we had dreamed about across 2,500 miles. Of a sudden I felt tremendously alert, our most urgent job was to find the main police station for the official check-in.

I was staggered, not only at the sight of this far northern city of 10,000 population, but at the extreme mildness of the climate. The air had the caressing warmth of a British summer day. It didn't make sense that the Arctic Circle was only a hundred miles away. For ten minutes we cruised slowly around on a quick reconnaissance; it was luxury. Fairbanks was a secure-looking city. After sixty hours of dreaming about it, now at last it was real. It seemed ridiculous that just beyond the environs stretched tens of thousands of square miles of harsh, empty wilderness, as forbidding as anything God has created. Contrary to general belief, this Arctic Circle city was no rough, tough, god-forsaken mining township. Admittedly almost half of Alaska's present-day gold production comes from the Fairbanks region, but the city is a polite, up-to-the-minute well-planned centre. It is typical of the nicest type of mid-western community. I stopped before a cinema. Posters advertised a current Danny Kaye film which I had seen in New York. It gave a pleasant, "safe-at-home" feeling; it took me a few minutes to get the size of reality, we'd twenty-five hundred miles to motor before we got home for a picture show again.

"They are even rearing baby skyscrapers," remarked Roat.

It was true, Fairbanks was creating a skyline. Ahead was an eight-story building, also an eleven-story structure with two probing TV masts. We cruised along the short main street called Second Avenue, flanked by two- and three-storey plate-glass-fronted shops. There was plenty of evidence of snappy neon-signs, too. It was all very pleasant, and David in elated mood sang jauntily: "We're here because we're here, trah la, ain't it grand to be bloomin' well alive."

I retaliated in song: "This is the hour, it's time to say fare-well, Vancouver in fifty hours chum, or we'll finish up in hell."

Roat pointed to the parking meters.

"They've got 'em up here already, and London has just decided to install."

Fairbanks also had electric hitching posts to keep motor engines warm. A driver tied-up to a headbolt heater and current flowed into a heating coil in the engine's water jacket, warming radiator fluid and allowing easy starting. A radiator with a 17-quart capacity requires some 12 quarts of permanent anti-freeze for central Alaskan winters.

A party of Eskimos passed us and this confirmed what I had been told. In spite of its mid-western appearance, Fairbanks still bears the marks of a frontier town if one searches around. Log-cabins rub shoulders with clapboard homes; on the streets Eskimos and Indians mingle freely with prospectors and trappers.

The sergeant of the central police station was a grand fellow called Raymond Hill. We experienced friendly assistance and hospitality and the letter of greetings from Vancouver's Mayor was passed over for the Mayor of Fairbanks. The Alaskan Mayor was out of town hunting, I was glad about this as I desperately wanted to get moving with the minimum delay. Raymond Hill was a dynamic character—within fifteen minutes he had cleared a line to Vancouver. Roat and I spoke to CKWX and a recording was made of our voices for broadcast. We learned that the "Power Drive" had aroused tremendous excitement. CKWX headquarters was being flooded with day and night inquiries in spite of frequent progress reports. Ian Garrad spoke, too. One showroom had sold a dozen Hillman Minx in half an hour. I

City of Fairbanks

STANLEY J. ZAVERL
Chief of Police

REPLY AIR MAIL
Police Department
City Hall Annex
321 Twelfth Ave.

Alaska

8.15 a.m.,

25 August 1957

TO WHOM IT MAY CONCERN,

On this date I had the pleasure to meet Mr. Richard Pape and his co-driver Mr. David Roat when they completed their trip from Vancouver B.C.

The Mayor of the City of Fairbanks, Mr. Douglas Preston, is out of town for the weekend and unable to be contacted. The letter from the Mayor of Vancouver to the Mayor of Fairbanks will be transmitted to him upon his return.

We all join in wishing Messrs. Pape and Roat the very best of luck and success on their return to Vancouver and the best of everything to Radio Station CKWX Vancouver, B.C.

Respectfully,

Raymond H. Hill
Sergeant of Police

The Golden Heart of Alaska

thought of my words at the salesman interview ... "A bold journey will bring in customers yapping, 'we want a Minx, we want a Minx'."

A young policeman brought us a tray of hot food.

"With the Sergeant's compliments," he said, "it'll brighten your wait while he writes out an official document.'

It was 9 a.m. when we shook hands with Raymond Hill of the Alaska Police Force. I've met lots of "coppers" in my time all over the world. Most I've accepted with resignation, some I've loathed worse than the Gestapo, some I've acknowledged as good as anything the world produces in damned fine men, and Raymond Hill belongs to the last category. I hope he finishes up Chief of Police.

We cleared Fairbanks and I zoomed Alaska-Minxy up to 80 m.p.h. We had two-and-a-half thousand miles to do in 2½ days and I realized anything could happen. We'd just keep our fingers crossed and press on regardless. We'd had plenty of practice at keeping awake and driving at speed. The small car had been hammered in every part, yet the great test for car and drivers still lay ahead. Could the relentless grind be maintained mechanically and physically for another sixty hours?

Chapter Six

The Long Way Home

Nothing will make a man put his best foot forward like getting the other one in hot water

TYRES screamed their treads off. To the right loomed a barricade of snow-capped mountains; to weary eyesight they seemed to be marching alongside. To the south, but unseen, lay Mount McKinley, the highest peak on the North American Continent, permanently snow-covered for two-thirds of its way down. It strains towards heaven to attain a height of 20,300 feet above sea level. The Indians call it "Denali", meaning "the home of the sun". As we drove on, contorted valleys opened up. Here was lifeless matter. I felt a trembly disquiet; of being in this world yet walled off from it.

Four massive B.29 aircraft enlarged from the like of sparrows into eagles; they roared overhead on their way back to the Eilson Field outside Fairbanks. David said: "We must look like a tiny slug in some far-off kingdom."

I noticed his strained eyes had white rings round them giving him the look of an Adélie penguin. He broke gaze with the disappearing planes and suddenly remarked: "So this was Seward's Folly, eh?"

I thought awhile on Alaska's history before replying.

"Thank God Russia was crazy enough to sell for a song," was my eventual answer.

I let my mind run on the second largest real-estate deal in history. Alaska was purchased for a mere 7,200,000 dollars (less than two cents an acre) from the Russians in 1867. A century ago neither the Russian Czars nor anybody else for that matter had the slightest notion of the potential mineral resources, natural wealth or vastness of the land. It was a sale Russia will never easily forget or forgive. "Seward's Folly" and "Seward's Icebox", were the derisive terms that once rang in the ears of William Henry Seward, an American Secretary of State. He was ridiculed at the time, as most Americans could not see any sense in buying a frozen, god-forsaken wilderness. Czar number 11, who was luxuriating in St. Petersburg, 12,000 miles away, had no idea of the great Empire he was slinging away, for literally a handful of roubles. Today, world strategists salute the keen far-sightedness of W. H. Seward, who by his acquisition of what was then termed Russian-America (Alaska), eliminated a tremendous Russian beach-head from the North American Continent.

Today, American naval bases and airfields guard against an invader considerably more dangerous and insidious than the Russia of the Czars.

Neither David nor I realized, as we streaked across the "Bigland", that within twelve months it would be voted Statehood and become America's 49th State. This new American frontier is one of complex modern society where educators, business men, scientists, military personnel and planners constitute a new breed of frontiersmen. In steam-heated huts the scientific expeditionary parties are a few minutes away by phone from Seattle, Washington or New York. Tremendous steps are being made to link-up all Alaska. Even the remotest villages are serviced by aeroplane the year round; it is the cheapest and best means of travelling. With only one short railway of consequence and few roads, a traveller must choose between dog team and aeroplane. An Eskimo owning his own dog team, and to whom time has small value, still finds it more economical to buy an aeroplane ticket. Alaskans probably fly more per capita than any other people in the world.

*   *   *

Alaska-Minxy was devouring ground about two hundred miles from Fairbanks. We were fast separating ourselves from the Arctic Circle zone, in fact already the words sounded no more important to me than the name of a pub. David was stretched on the bed, and the growl of the motor was like an anæsthetic. For two hours we had not seen a living soul; the jagged mountains had dissolved, now the landscape was wild and desolate. My eyes stared glassily across the ribbon of road, I drove in that state of relaxed nonchalance which car drivers experience after many hours continuously at the wheel. A comfortable condition when a lazy little voice floats around a skull whispering: "But nothing, simply nothing can happen."

Yet something did. About 300 yards ahead a shape suddenly loomed in the road. I was struck by its tottering appearance. I punched Roat. He sat up with a groan.

"For Christ's sake, what's wrong?" he spluttered.

I pointed ahead and started slowing down.

"He's drunk," snapped my companion.

"Another delay," I murmured, watching the figure of a tall man wildly clutching at air, lurching about as though blind. I felt no panic, an apparently drunken man didn't exactly spell disaster.

But, as we soon found out, the poor devil was not drunk. He was middle-aged and the front of his windjammer might have been dipped in blood. Blood came from his mouth, too, like crimson foam on a milkshake. It trickled from his ears. The forehead showed an awful wound and white bone. I slipped an arm about the stranger's waist; the thin body trembled violently.

"Look at the back of his head," wailed David.

I looked and saw a large piece of flesh dangling from the neck.

"What happened?" I cried.

The man gazed heavenwards as if trying to call to witness what had tried to make away with him. His nostrils were dilated and he kept opening his mouth, gasping and mumbling something.

"Get the brandy, David."

Five minutes later the injured one flung out an arm and shook his head in a strong effort. He had come out of his darkness and muttered clearly: "Go to her, she's dying, she's over the side."

Roat bounded to the road edge. Then he pointed downward for seconds as though struck dumb.

"What is it?" I called.

"A car down there," he cried out, "I'm going down."

With that, he started to clamber down.

I took one of our foam-rubber pillows and stretched the man out.

"Don't move," I ordered.

Upright on its wheels at the bottom of a fifty-foot ravine was a cream-coloured Dodge. It must have left the Alaska Highway and sailed through space. David stooped over something and I heard a dog's furious yapping. His voice came up to me urgently.

"A man and woman down here, badly injured, bring the first-aid box, brandy, blankets."

I slithered to the bottom with the items, also my camera. I found the woman on her back. Roat had already supported her head with something from the Dodge. A black terrier dog writhed against her side, snarling and snapping. An unconscious man sagged half out of the vehicle. I dragged him clear His leg was grotesquely twisted and I assumed it was broken in more than one place. From appearance he was nearly out of this world and in the next, so I hastened to the woman. The sobbing labour of her breath was pitiful and the terrier was whining and licking her hand. Its rear legs were broken and it was crazed with pain. It tried to attack me so I grabbed it by the tail and pulled it clear. This was no time for doggie ministrations.

"Where are you hurt?" I asked the little woman, "we have to raise you to my car."

Her face quivered, but she answered bravely enough.

"My back, it's my back," she groaned, "and my legs seem useless."

Gently, we examined the small lady with the large, dark eyes. It was my unhappy conviction that she had broken her back, the legs, however, were visibly undamaged.

"Paralysis from the spinal cord," I whispered to Roat.

Thoughts of continuing the record run vanished, this was as issue of life and death. These injured people had to be lifted to Alaska-Minxy, and rushed back to Fairbanks.

The dog, unobserved, had crawled back to the woman's side. It bit me. At once I opened the teeth punctures with my knife, bled the hand and poured in iodine. The beast was in pitiful distress and I realized a merciful duty would have to be performed before we left.

We gave attention for three-quarters of an hour; at first the little woman passionately sobbed and cried: "Is Fred all right, dear God we mustn't be robbed of our happiness."

After a time she fainted.

David returned from our car with ropes and tackle. We were fashioning a stretcher when he jerked upright, perspiration dripping off his chin. He listened, sniffing the cool, quiet air. All my senses were alert, too, as I strained my ears and stared at the wall of rock and scrub rising to the road.

We classified the sound; a more welcome noise it was impossible to imagine. The hum of an approaching engine came steadily nearer. Roat sprang at the bank like a jack-in-a-box, clawing himself upward like a mad thing. He was on the road before I was half-way to the top. We intercepted an American staff car, trailed by a jeep. In the vehicles were eight men.

I rubbed sweat and dirt from my face. I found it all strangely thrilling and repulsive, stimulating and sickening at the same time. The men went into action while Roat and I gave the officer details and exchanged names and addresses.

"You fellahs the Power Drivers?" he exclaimed with some surprise. "Bad luck this delay, but we'll sure handle everything from now."

He kept his word to contact Sergeant Hill at the Police Station in Fairbanks so that a message could be flashed to CKWX, Vancouver. Later, a broadcast informed the public what had occurred.

*　　　*　　　*

97

We maintained silence as we sped towards the Yukon frontier; that recent episode had been unnerving. My thoughts were jerky; I speculated on what would have happened if we'd not found the staggering man on the roadway. The Dodge and its occupants might not have been found in months. For the crashed car was invisible to vehicles passing on the road.

I glanced at young Roat sitting deep in thought, eyes wrinkled, mouth tight-set. He hadn't batted an eyelid, but I was concerned about his possible reaction. R.A.F. methods were still a part of me and I decided to push Roat into the driving seat to keep his nerves tied-up. During flying days, after a prang, or if aircrew witnessed another kite dive-in, invariably the Commanding Officer sent the boys straight back into the air to ease off twitters and safeguard nerves.

I braked.

"O.K. David, take over and drive flat-out for the next three hours, please."

"But," and he spoke in a low voice, "you've still got forty minutes to drive before it's my turn."

"C'mmon, drive this bastard from now as you've never driven it before."

Roat looked at me searchingly.

"Keep your hair on," he said, "I'll hammer it just the same as before."

I stretched on the bed and tightened the safety straps. I'd ignored these straps before, but the recollection of that accident nagged . . . "Nerves," I told myself. Vainly I attempted to push from my mind the picture of the sobbing little woman with the broken back. It was futile, so I unfastened the straps and sat upright with a curse.

"What's wrong, Dick?"

"Thirsty," I answered.

"You're not," announced Roat stifly, then unexpectedly, "Every day, everywhere, human beings are getting smashed-up in motor cars, so why worry about that ugly accident? It's luck, if it's with us we'll get home unscathed."

Roat forced a laugh, and I pinned a grin on my face.

"O.K. David, for our own safety we'll forget that accident."

"Fine," he answered, "don't worry about me and I won't worry about you."

I flopped back on the bed.

"Damned amusing," I thought, "the pupil teaching the schoolmaster," and fell asleep.

*   *   *

A sign warned us that we were approaching the Alaska Yukon customs and frontier post. The 300 miles from Fairbanks had been covered in six hours (not counting the accident delay).

"Now we crackle on the hotplate," said Roat uneasily.

"When I spoke to CKWX from Fairbanks, they promised to put things right," I replied optimistically.

"Officialdom will be waiting for sure," said my companion, "they are not going to wax enthusiastic over what we did."

Officialdom was waiting for us all right. What a to do! The number-one Administration Officer had quick eyes, a big nose and restless black eyebrows. He looked us up and down, down and up. Like an incredulous parrot he repeated, "Power Drivers and law violators."

It was evident that the CKWX intervention hadn't done much good. I was in a hurry and dog-tired; delay for me was akin to a red rag to a bull. I tried to put over a reasonable viewpoint. so had CKWX. I explained that I could see no rational grounds for the commotion. Came a titanic dressing down and threats of gaol poured more red on the rag. I never liked gaols. I confess I used some of the strongest epithets in the English language in support of British cars and freedom. Bellowing patriotism, I asked Mr. Black Eyebrows if he wanted to have British cars ousted from the continent because of piddling rules. Mr. Black Eyebrows wasn't a man easily subdued.

"Desperadoes," he stormed, "you've committed a most serious offence."

He must have had military training too; some of his language was hardly of angelic origin. Valiantly I tried to snatch aces

99

from the air. I demanded an immediate call to radio station CKWX in Vancouver.

"They'll contact Ottawa and the Prime Minister," I threatened.

David joined the fray: "You'll cop it, all British Columbia is following our progress; are you fifth column? You're sabotaging a possible world record and honour for a British car. Think you're ruddy Hitler?" he jabbed. "We're not smugglers, crooks or escapers."

I took over: "We've come back, haven't we? Search the car if you think we are smuggling Polar Bear Perfume or Arctic Circle Pearls."

I had regained the initiative; painstakingly I obliterated the Yukon/Alaska frontier bulge. The official began to reel . . .

"But you violated the law, you violated the law," he kept clucking uncertainly.

In the end, Mr. Black Eyebrows cried in a quivering voice: "Go, go, but I warn you, this is not the end of the matter."

Our documents and passports were checked and all numbers noted. We moved to Alaska-Minxy and I smiled at Black Eyebrows.

"I'll have Mr. Diefenbaker investigate your delinquency," I snapped as a parting shot.

"Me, me, me?" The official must have damaged his finger by the way his chest was stabbed by it. His big nose was all of a twitch, it reminded me of a caricature of "Punch".

"C'mmon," hissed David, "leave the basket."

Roat subsided into the bucket seat and we sprang away.

Another obstacle had been overcome.

* * *

A time had now been reached in our journey when senses were dulled to extravaganza of scenery, when nothing made much difference except "Vancouver on time" . . . in one piece. In a larger sense, paradoxically, we had ceased to think of fear or to fear personal disaster. Our faces were against mighty odds; in peace or war, in the name of victory, men must have small thought for themselves. Unconsciously, what we perhaps feared most was mechanical let-down. To attain our goal every minute of each hour counted. Not only had we to battle with the considerable difficulties of this highway, but our own reaction rates were becoming impaired. It was not possible to take more than three hours at the wheel at one time. Keep-awake drugs appeared less effective than the pouring of lemonade over our heads to counter bleariness, or the slapping of our faces with a crêpe-rubber sole. Eyesight was subjected to severe strain in the peculiar northern light. Since our previous passing, stones seemed to have grown larger and harder. The road surface seemed much worse. Perhaps it was our nerves.

The continuous din we had come to know so well while going north, at times on the homeward run seemed to echo like thunder. We met with patches of bad weather; this did not improve surfaces. Repeatedly we slammed in and out of water-filled potholes; it seemed a minor miracle that Alaska-Minxy could endure such a beating. It was pointless to try to dodge the potholes for this cut down speed. We kept straight on. If any hole was deep enough to break an axle that would be just too bad!

The windscreen by now was chipped and pockmarked. A headlamp glass had shattered. The Alaska Highway, too, was very dusty. Overtaking another vehicle was difficult and dangerous. Clouds of blinding, suffocating muck rose and swirled, making what lay beyond rolling wheels a matter for speculation . . .

Since our turning point we had slashed 680 miles off the 1,530 to Dawson Creek. The worst part of the Yukon Territory had been put behind us. We had clocked fast time, everything seemed to be going our way. Darkness was settling in a great valley as we wound around the shoulders of rocky hills. The slopes covered with birch, spruce and pine fell away to the shores of a great lake. Far away a solitary twinkling light might have been an earthbound star. The alarm clock shrilled: it was again time to change over. David was prodded into wakefulness,

I could scarcely hold my head up. Over the last hour, from time to time, objects had heaved and danced. We stretched our legs for a couple of minutes and gulped fresh mountain air. A lighter patch in the sky revealed sharp-fanged peaks like cut-outs on a Christmas card. David asked: "What's the approximate position?"

"The last settlement was Johnson's Crossing Lodge, I reckon Teslin village is about 100 miles away."

As we re-entered the car I glanced at the petrol gauge and goggled in amazement. It showed less than quarter full! Something was radically wrong! At our last stop only 200 miles back we had filled the standard tank underneath the car and also the large reserve tank in the boot: twenty gallons in all, enough for a minimum of 600 miles at our customary 30 miles to the gallon.

We were in a desolate, hushed world. A night wind soughed through the pine trees. Roat slithered below the vehicle and let out a sharp cry: "Tank's burst, petrol's gushing out like hell!"

My heart sank.

The tank had been mercilessly battered and dented by stones, it might just as well have been pounded with a sledge-hammer. Petrol was gushing from an inch-long gash on a ridge of creased metal. We saved what we could of the escaping fluid and so added perhaps a gallon and a half to the contents of a jerry can. We set about fixing the leak.

A wedge of hard wood was shaped and wrapped in a piece of waterproof cloth; this was driven hard and fast into the ripped metal. Chewing gum was moulded around it, calico followed and next a layer of plastic sealing compound. A sheet of tinfoil covered everything and was held in position by liquid solder, adhesive tape and sticking plaster. Finally, a doormat was lashed over the battered tank to cushion the impacts which it yet must endure.

We were nervous, silent, and expectant. As gravel rattled on the car's underside I ground my teeth. Whenever a big bump was felt I held my breath in suspense. At intervals we tested for leakage. Our luck held : our workmanship was satisfactory.

We came to Teslin with perhaps half a gallon to spare and the gauge showing zero. The kindly proprietor gave us six containers to provide some insurance against further contingencies.

The fact that we were now juggling with luck brought with it a change in our outlook. It woke us up to a sharpened determination to try to drive the 800 miles to Dawson Creek in one hell-for-leather burst, win or lose. If the wooden plug remained fixed over the next long leg, well and good, if it didn't—well we'd done our best.

David went to the North-west Telegraph and Telephone hut whilst I stowed away the emergency containers of petrol. He left a despatch to go off to CKWX reporting the damage to the petrol-tank. Our time margin now was narrow, so we lost little before engaging the gears in what I was determined should be a non-stop run to Dawson Creek. Alaska-Minxy rolled and shuddered; we settled again to relay driving, a rhythm which seemed unending. Two hours later, high in the mountains, we turned on the radio. Full volume was necessary to overcome the shrieking of the wind. David's last message was given out. The announcer then said dispassionately :

"Following the recent accident-delay south of Fairbanks, this latest misfortune, is indeed, very bad luck. We trust this tank trouble does not hold promise of further unpleasant setback. Success is still possible and we all wish Dick and David trouble-free driving over the 800 severe miles to the end of the Alaska Highway." The judicial voice in Vancouver continued... "Over to drivers Dick and David. A team will await you at Dawson Creek to offer all assistance. Remember to hand in reports at . . ."

Roughly I switched off the radio.

Roat looked at me questioningly.

"We don't send or listen to any more reports," I told him shortly, "until we roll into Dawson Creek. Feeding the public tit-bits takes time."

I thought of all those who had sneered that Alaska-Minxy

would not outlive the first 1,000 miles. Instead she had survived nearly 3,000 of them at speed. It would be tragic if she quit now.

David was feeling as I felt. We sometimes reached a state of cold frenzy in efforts to sweep forward faster. It was now a case of two hours on and two hours off. Hours became remote, the reality of a place in the world called Dawson Creek, otherwise referred to as milepost zero, almost became a tantalizing hallucination. Yet in fact it grew steadily nearer. The distance declined from 200 to 150 to 100 miles. At last the town appeared to sprout out of the horizon; fantasy and fatigue stopped their slow rotation. Jaded jubilation grew into enormous relief, real and reviving. David slapped me on the shoulders and yelled: "We've made it!"

All doubts on the subject were hastily removed when we drew up before the Rootes Garage. It didn't seem true, but it was an accomplished fact, we had driven the entire length of the Alaska Highway, inclusive of all delays in 34 hours.

From the turning point near the Arctic Circle we had clocked 1,541 miles, and averaged over 45 miles an hour.

*　　　*　　　*

The engine was checked over, oil changed, new tyres fitted. Roat and I plunged our heads into icy water, but this did not relieve our eyeballs. They smarted as if they'd been fried in grit. A Rootes man hopped off and procured a soothing eye-lotion from a chemist. The ecstatic realization that only one more leg of 783 miles remained offset personal discomforts. We had twenty-three hours in hand, but were acutely aware of the rugged terrain we had to traverse in British Columbia.

Alaska-Minxy was put on a ramp and I inspected the weak link, the tank. It was not leaking, but the door mat which we had tied on to protect it had disappeared. A mechanic was working to take the tank off.

"We'll have it off," he said, "welded and on again in less than three quarters of an hour."

"You won't," I replied, "we're racing the clock. Stick rubber over the tank and strap plenty of old carpeting around the lot. Hurry!"

"No, no," expostulated an official, "you dare not overstrain your luck at this stage."

"Get us moving," I heatedly interjected, "or I'll begin raving."

I didn't have to blow my top. The official said no more but hurriedly handed us two cold chickens and flasks of coffee. Blurting thanks, I pressed the accelerator and Alaska-Minxy fled headlong into the night. Our next stop was to be Prince George, 265 miles to the south. A brief pause there, to refuel and hand over a CKWX report, then a non-stop dash for Vancouver, finish and bed.

A purple dawn filtered over a landscape of savage beauty. It was viewed with mingled feelings by Roat and myself: we prayed the weather would hold up on this, our fifth and last day. During the night there had been heavy rain for over an hour. Yet we had cut the distance to be covered to 550 miles.

This was British Columbia, a wilderness with innumerable waterways, lakes, mountains, forests and plains. It was a realm to be described only by superlatives. It seemed a long time ago since we had roared along this Highway 97 on the outward run: it seemed rather three years than three days. Soon we would cross again the mighty Thompson and Fraser rivers. After Prince George would come the town of Quesnel. Then once more we would take the historic Cariboo Trail.

After leaving Dawson Creek, I had become aware, when my body was slumped in the bucket seat, of an acute burning pain on the right side of my waist. I believed it was due to chafing, a tenderness through sweating. At intervals I loosed my belt and poured lemonade into my shirt to ease off whatever the trouble was. "It'll soon wear off when we get to Vancouver," I told myself.

*   *   *

We were scudding along at a fine lick and approaching Prince George, when death decided to look us straight in the eyes, smirk and slink off. This region comprised the foothills of the Murray Range, part of the Northern Rocky Mountain Chain. The road was narrow and rough, it revealed deep lacerations caused by heavy road construction machinery. The drama began when I swung round a tight corner at speed; ahead, throwing up a frightful dust screen, loomed a big military transport. Four times I closed in to overtake, but four times blinding, yellow dust compelled me to fall back. It was aggravating in our mad whirlwind of haste to be slowed up like this. Then, suddenly, an opportunity to sneak through on a downhill gradient presented itself. It would be a tight squeeze, but I knew it could be done, snappily, cleanly.

As I crept up to the truck's tail, everything of course, was partially obscured by the swirling dust. I pulled Alaska-Minxy to the left, calculated carefully, changed gear, stabbed the accelerator and moved into the gap. Something vastly different from what I expected, happened. The big truck began to converge on me. I had a blurred recollection of a wall of rock inches to my left, and a swaying truck's side pressing in on the right.

"Brake," screamed David.

I dropped back just in time, but this tension immediately threw me into a further dangerous situation. The damned truck slipped past, but in poor visibility I wrenched the wheel too sharply. I gravely miscalculated my speed and the narrowness of the road; what occurred was almost an irreparable error. The roadside fell sheer away into a gorge, and for one terrible moment I thought we'd "bought it". The front off-side wheel went over the edge, and my heart sank in a surge of terror. The explanation I offer for our being alive today is that unconsciously I whipped the steering to the left and instinctively rammed the accelerator. I recall a roar in the ears like a tempest, obviously panic, and distantly heard David's piercing scream.

"Jesus Christ!"

The right rear wheel went limp as it tore at soft, crumbling earth, the car sagged. It was a lucky turn of fate all right that we possessed just that extra thrust and fraction of traction to shoot us back to the hard surface.

This was not the last straw. Unnerved and enveloped in murky dust, I again shot across the highway and ploughed over a layer of road construction stones. There was a terrible noise of crashing and grinding, I felt twinges as though I had been touched on an open wound.

From start to finish it had all happened in a matter of seconds. I fell from the car in a trembling dither, words of disaster boomed in my brain: "You've stripped off everything below . . ."

I expected a storm of words from a pale-faced David, instead of the storm he put his hand on my arm and whispered: "We scraped through a good one there."

It was simply incredible. The damned car seemed indestructible. Lying underneath checking it over, I almost felt it was laughing at me for making such a fool of myself. The front suspension was not wrecked, the transmission and differential were visibly intact; I offered fervent prayer of thanks for the armour plating which had saved the sump. The armour protecting the differential, however, had been ripped clean away. The matting which the Dawson Creek mechanics had wrapped about the tank had been shorn away too. The metal revealed dents in it as big as small pineapples. Sickeningly, petrol spurted from three punctures, yet surprisingly the old repair job itself had not re-opened.

In a terrible hurry and state of worry I drove Alaska-Minxy furiously up and down the road. Her responses to the tests I gave her seemed like miracles; the long-suffering car was fully operative and roadworthy. With aching hearts, Roat and I worked frantically to stem the swift drain of petrol with more wooden plugs and calico. Our efforts were only partially successful.

"So near, yet so far," I bitterly reflected, and the stench of escaping petrol was depressing. In despair I cursed the designer at Rootes Motors who had placed a petrol tank under, instead of above and behind, the boot. Then I turned on myself for not safeguarding this vulnerable unit with armour-plate. I should have known better.

The tank was doomed, we'd never see Vancouver with such a piece of busted, leaking metal. An idea came to me. Reserve fuel in the loose containers plus the little in the tank amounted to approximately ten gallons.

I hailed David: "Hurry! Drive like hell for Prince George. We might make the fifteen miles before we lose the lot."

Two miles from Prince George, the engine spluttered, we'd poured everything we had into the tank, but we were among homes and people. I put a phone call through to Mr. Geister of West End Motors, Hillman agents in Prince George.

The manager was at first flabbergasted, but quickly recovered.

"Lucky thing getting so near," he said, "we have a reception party waiting here for you."

"To hell with the reception party," I snapped, "get your breakdown wagon to us, fast!"

"It will look awful towing in Alaska-Minxy," the voice bemoaned, "especially as reporters are awaiting you."

"O.K.," I said, "send out some petrol and I'll drive the car, wetting the road behind it, straight into your arms."

Before replacing the receiver Mr Geister had his breakdown truck racing to our rescue.

"Take it easy," he consoled, "I'll have a new tank lined-up for you. We'll get you on your way in an hour. Stand by for our truck and the gas."

It was heartening the way the boys in Prince George got down to changing the smashed tank. They shared in the Power Drive and the car's prestige. After only the promised hour's delay we departed from Prince George for home, 520 miles to the south with less than twelve hours in hand. We'd have to average 45 miles per hour. We were coming to know that the margin of human endurance was growing small and we were only too well aware of the strain that high speeds were imposing on our small-horse-power engine. But Alaska-Minxy roared monstrously as if to express her private fury at the frustrations of the day and probably also at our doubts about her.

Soon, we were winding our way once more over the historic route of the fur brigade and the gold-seeker. We flashed past the mile-houses still marking old stage posts, on past the turn-off leading to the ghost town of Barkerville, which in the days of the romantic gold rush, was the second largest town west of Chicago.

In his book, *The Cariboo Story*, F. W. Lindsay, noted authority on British Columbia, advises:

> Don't speed on the Cariboo Highway; go slowly and savour the romance that the Road holds for those who know its stirring past. Built of a crying need, by heroes long gone, it has beckoned the covetous, lured, with its siren call of gold, adventurers from every corner of the earth. . . .
>
> Don't sell the Cariboo Highway short. No matter who you are or where you come from, whether Italian or Swede, Chinese or Greek, Jew or Gentile, the Cariboo Highway has someone of your blood gathered to its bosom. The Road has felt the heartbreak of the disappointed, the joy of the lucky miner who has 'struck 'er rich.' The Road has been reviled by travellers who yet return again and again to drink the magic of its beauty. In the Cariboo Highway is the warp and woof of a nation. It is truly an International road, a road of many nations, a road of history, and now a highway of destiny—drive slowly and listen to the tales it tells . . .

The advice is sound, but it was not for us this time.

*　　　*　　　*

Two hundred miles from Vancouver, radio messages came through to us that a team of people would await our arrival outside the town of Hope. This was a hundred miles from the finishing post. We kept moving fast and, with no cross traffic to hold us up, arrived punctually. My exhausted co-driver was taken in another car with Ian Garrad. His place in Alaska-Minxy was taken by a radio announcer who made notes as we shot away to CKWX headquarters. This last little stretch was on safe, tarred road, a straightforward dash. It was a "piece of cake". I was doing 85 m.p.h. when a speed cop on a Harley Davidson motor-bike snarled alongside. He waved encouragingly and fell into line astern.

A big crowd, including Billie, awaited our arrival. As we tumbled from Alaska-Minxy the news went out over the air to all British Columbia.

> The Power Drive is over. It has been successfully completed in four days and twenty-two hours. 5,000 miles in under five days in a small four-cylinder British car. 1,000 miles a day over the roughest and most spectacular terrain in the North American Hemisphere. Through British Columbia—the Yukon territory and Alaska without a single mechanical failure. Average speed is well over 40 miles an hour.

I was handed the microphone and concluded a brief speech with the words : "I hope this trip will help to make this North American Continent conscious that British cars are invincible; can take it and take it tough."

The manager of Rootes Motors undressed me in a suite in the Vancouver Hotel. Off came my trousers for the first time in five days for a hot bath and a comfortable bed. Now we spotted the trouble on the right side of my waist. An area of four square inches was like raw beef, the top of my trousers had literally sandpapered away the skin. A doctor was called to clean the pussy wound and give penicillin injections.

"I didn't notice the burning sensation," I told him, "until the Dawson Creek vicinity on the return run."

The wound started to go the wrong way. Three days later, Billie and Ian Garrad took me to the Vancouver General Hospital at midnight. The diseased flesh was scraped and treated. Today I boast a four-inch pure-white patch. I have nicknamed it my "Alaska-Scar". Billie, now my wife, laughs about it and remarks : "Snow white to match Alaska, but what is a scar anyway. The spirit is always stronger than the flesh."

Chapter Seven

Interlude

Coming together is a beginning;
  Keeping together is progress;
Working together is success.

IAN GARRAD was not sacked for the part he had played in
the Alaska drive. Instead, the sack he received was crammed
with letters of congratulation. Later, Press cuttings flowed
in from far and wide. Had he not allowed his imagination to
be fired in the first place there would have been no drive. He
had taken a chance, events had taken their course, the result was
success. When the drive ended, valuable publicity blazed for
Garrad's firm in particular and United Kingdom car prestige in
general. British and Continental journals splashed the story,
Commonwealth and American papers, too. Even Japan gave the
record-run publicity. Thank heaven men with spirit of determination and faith still exist in this atomic-space era of
strangled, uneasy, frightened progress. People of the world
still hanker after the interesting and dramatic on earth, because
the genuine soul of man is essentially adventure-loving. The
vital substance of any living nation is the spirit of adventure.

*   *   *

Within a week of the drive ending, Billie said "Yes" and we
became engaged. She reviewed my vagabondage roots with
clearer understanding; the unpredictableness of my nature with
a new trust. I received a cable of congratulations. It read:
"Cupid, one who when he hits the mark usually Mrs. It."
Betrothal gave my heart wires a wrench, sternly I talked
to myself. I realized it was obligatory that I took life more
seriously; to learn to adore the insufferable monotony of a
damned job, a safe, steady anchorage synonymous of the love

of a constant woman. A few days later Lady Luck beamed on me. A Vancouver man leaving for a long European holiday accepted my sterling cheque, swopping it for dollars. I bought a supply of coloured film and cancelled the car-salesman job offered to me. I decided to return along part of the route which David Roat and I had raced, shoot a documentary movie and take notes for a book.

Delicately I explained to my fiancée that the glorious stay-at-home and wash-the-dishes state of existence we had to face in the future, could be successfully achieved only by feminine tolerance, during a natural masculine breaking-in process. There was no storm, no arguing nor entreating expostulation. So we left Vancouver having agreed to share the driving, also resolved to heed the advice of the writer who proclaimed: "Don't sell the Cariboo Highway short, drive slowly and listen to the tales it tells." However, unknown to me or Billie, the fates were busy setting the stage for more driving adventures at an early date.

Before our departure I knew that Billie had driven for many years in New Zealand without any offence, but I'd never considered her any better or worse than the average woman driver. The average female driver, for that matter, had always given me pain when contemplating hell-for-leather action at the wheel. After sharing the driving with my fiancée, I discovered to my surprise and delight that she could drive, and fast; she more than passed muster. Her handling of the car over rough, dangerous and desolate terrain revealed precision and a cool matter-of-factness.

Our first motoring partnership rather softened my views about women drivers. Most male drivers are too glib in denouncing the fairy fingers of the fair sex about steering wheels; dainty toes on the foot pedals. Disallowing credit to the ladies under circumstances of city driving, traffic-jammed conditions, isn't fair! One of the reasons they go to pieces in congestion is largely because of the monstrously evil and disdainful looks they receive from the dominant sex; almost a natural aspect on the road today. But try them on tough open highways, mix

We got to Toronto ahead of the schedule of the trans-Canada express train. Dick Williams, Rootes' Sales Manager in that city, made us welcome in his office. For the benefit of television cameras we drove Alaska-Minxy through a huge paper-covered frame on which were the words "Trans-Canada Record— First 1958 Model Across". This picture shows it happening. We were yet bleary-eyed when we left Toronto on the way to Ottawa, Canada's capital city, at the behest of British-car publicity.

We reached Ottawa while the Parliament Building was still beflagged for the State Opening by H.M. Queen Elizabeth II which had taken place on the day before. Here I photographed Billie talking to a Royal Canadian Mounted policeman, a mackintosh covering his ceremonial dress from the torrential rain which had just ceased. The population was still in gala mood and the arrival of Alaska-Canada-Minxy came at a happy time. Publicity snowballed.

Above: Our run from Ottawa to Miami took Billie and me through many famous American cities, including Boston and New York, before we came to Philadelphia, which is where the Declaration of Independence was signed and now is America's third largest city. Here we had this photograph taken; our companion is Peter Manning-Smith, the British Vice-Consul. Shortly afterwards we set off again for Baltimore and Washington.

Left: The Rootes' dealer in Baltimore, Mr. Thompson, had every reason to look pleased. Everywhere we went publicity for British cars in general and the Minx in particular was attracting really enormous crowds.

Left: Billie, photographed here on the beach during our short holiday in Miami, hasn't forgiven me for making the palm tree appear to grow out of her. In vain did I plead that I hadn't even noticed the tree...

Below: Still in the deep South we moved to New Orleans where France lives yet in what is now the United States of America and where this Negro family posed for us. The South is a glorious mixture of sweet, slow talk, tobacco, honeysuckle and bourbon; but, even in this most conservative of all regions, things have changed and still are changing.

kindness and discipline. Give them intolerable hours at the wheel, let them feel you sincerely don't care if you do die at their hands, and they blossom.

*   *   *

Mail awaited my return in Vancouver. I was surprised to received a letter from the eccentric little Canadian writer whom I had first met in New York. He congratulated me on the Alaska drive and wrote: "Let me know if you still want dollars, I'll loan you some." He concluded with the following:

> Genius is only the power of making continuous efforts. The line between failure and success is so fine that we scarcely know when we pass it; so fine that we are often on the line and do not know it. How many a man has thrown up his hands at a time when a little more effort, a little more patience would have achieved success. As the tide goes clear out, so it comes clear in. In business and life, sometimes prospects may seem darkest when really they are on the turn. A little more persistence, a little more effort, and what seemed a hopeless failure may turn into a glorious success. There is no failure except in no longer trying. There is no defeat except from within, no really insurmountable barrier save your own inherent weakness of purpose.

I re-read the letter with pardonable bewilderment and chuckled at intervals. Peering from the notepaper I could visualize the writer's face; the ironical twinkle in the piercing eyes behind the pince-nez.

"This letter is from a fellow author," I remarked to Billie, "I'd like to hug and kiss him and say thank you."

"Oh, why?"

"Because once I'd have liked to transform him into a beetle and gladly would have stepped on him."

"What did he do to you?"

I laughed ... "He merely injected me with a strong dose of Westward Ho, in New York. Sometime I'll tell you about it, dear."

*   *   *

A few days later, Ian Garrad took Billie and me to dinner. From the outset there was something pleasantly mysterious

113

about his attitude; an expression of amusement in his eyes. He studied us both so comprehendingly.

"Ah, Billie," he said softly for the second time, "it's wonderful to know you are such a good driver at speed."

"Thank you, Ian," answered my fiancée with obvious pride, if a little perplexed.

"For God's sake," I told the Manager of Rootes Motors, "stop giving Billie a swollen head. The speed limit is fifty over here, but when men praise a woman's driving she is apt to demand a car which will do ninety."

Before parting, Ian suddenly asked, with a smile on his lips: "Wouldn't you two like a glorious holiday in Florida, lovely sub-tropical Miami?"

"Oh, yes," I replied, momentarily taken aback, "who pays?"

Garrad laughed heartily.

"Rootes Motors, of course!"

He described finger spirals in the air by way of emphasizing his remarks.

"Beautiful palm trees, sun, romance, gaiety, swimming, life, laughter."

"You mean, all this, free?" queried Billie, "a reward for the Alaska accomplishment, perhaps?"

A faint negative sigh was the response.

"Oh yeah," was my comment, "a very nice idea. You seem to put an unnecessarily personal significance into the suggestion. What's cookin', Ian?"

Garrad avoided giving any direct reply.

"If it's a gift," I went on quickly, "and we must return to London, I think it would be a brighter inspiration if you suggested a fortnight in Paris. Boy, oh boy, the beautiful honeymoon trip."

"No, no," was the startled answer. "It must be the beautiful Gulf of Mexico, or nothing." He closed his eyes and murmured. "Mexico, the palm beach land, the Everglades, American Society's winter paradise."

"C'mmon dear," I urged Billie, "he's had one over the eight!"

Chapter Eight

First 1958 Car Across Canada

The journey of thousands of miles begins with one pace

IAN GARRAD carefully outlined his plan. It was the outcome of the Alaska record drive, and the far-reaching stir it had aroused. Publicity chiefs in England planned large advertisements for national newspapers; in addition, a documentary film called "Bold Journey" would be made of the Alaska adventure. The record had been enthusiastically acclaimed by dealers throughout Canada and the U.S.A. They hoped that Alaska-Minxy would go on a showroom tour. It was patently obvious to Rootes in Piccadilly, that if the original car could perform further feats on the North American Continent, publicity would be terrific. This is what Ian Garrad suggested to Billie and me. First a race across the width of Canada from coast to coast, then a continuation down the eastern side of the United States of America to Miami, in the Gulf of Mexico. There Billie and I could have a holiday in luxury.

However, neither she nor I looked on the proposition with favour. Carefully I gave reasons for turning down the project. "One," I began, "speeding across certain sections of Canada would be dangerous, especially in October. Two, getting right down to the Gulf of Mexico would be a strenuous, concentrated programme. Three, even if Billie is a splendid driver, it is asking too much for a slight woman of seven stones to stand up to 6,000 miles across the breadth and length of the North American Continent at racing speed."

"Women are wonderful these days," Ian murmured, "Billie would be a good British Ambassadress."

"Maybe" I responded hotly, "but there is no real place for women in feats of hazard. Women cannot respond in crisis like a steel spring under tension. And you know as well as I do Ian, that a drive like this is beyond female strength."

Next I said the wrong thing, I put my foot in it.

"If I'd been unattached and had a co-driver like David Roat, it might have been different."

"Oh!" exclaimed Billie sharply, "you think I couldn't take it, you think women are just hot-house plants for home decoration?"

I turned to her affectionately: "No offence dear, it's just a trip physically beyond women."

"Nonsense," her reply was spirited, "there's far too much exaggerated emphasis on men and what only wonderful men can do." She flushed with indignation. She snatched a breath. "This is a woman's world as well as a man's. I could jolly well endure most of what you and Roat could take, so could half the normal women of the world, if they had to."

"We now have to think of ourselves," I answered in a flat voice.

Billie rose and walked from the office.

"What do you think of that, Ian," I gasped.

We chatted for a few minutes. Then suddenly Garrad exclaimed: "I'll wager my salary that Billie would make a monkey out of you if she co-drove across Canada!" He tittered, "You under-estimate the moral fibre of the fair sex."

I snorted. "Not on your life, it would kill Billie. Moral fibre, my Aunt Fanny."

I didn't know she was standing behind in the doorway.

"Try me and see," I heard her say. "Only your stupid driving would kill me."

My heart bounced and beat faster; I swung around.

"You mean you'd risk this whing-ding of a drive with me, sweetheart?"

"Of course."

"But Honey," I murmured disbelievingly, "you were rigidly opposed to the whole idea."

She took a single step, paused, and said casually; "I want to make you eat your words about women not having stiffening in their back bones. I also think this trip will assist you in settling down." She smiled sweetly, "Besides, I'm a Kiwi, Mr. Yorkshireman!"

Ian Garrad beamed. . . .

*　　　*　　　*

Later, discussing arrangements with Garrad, I scoffed jokingly . . . "Women!" But I felt an undercurrent of excitement at the prospect of my first woman co-driver.

Garrad raised his glass: "Maybe it's a good thing men don't understand women," he laughed. "Women understand women and don't like them."

*　　　*　　　*

Before Red China increased her territorial contact with Russia by seizing Tibet, the boundary line between Canada and the United States of America was the longest between any two countries in the world. This unarmed border, a most imaginary line, extends for four thousand miles, touching seven of the ten Canadian provinces, and thirteen American States. Billie and I would follow a highway from the Pacific to the Atlantic, from Vancouver to Boston, roughly along the Canadian-U.S.A. border, and seldom far from it (the 49th parallel).

When we started it was not possible to cross the whole breadth of Canada on a good motor road. It must be remembered that a tremendous obstacle to an east-west route across Canada has been the physical formation of the land. Nature has defied rather than tempted men to make a single trans-continental road. There were many gaps and detours along the long route which stretched before us; many of the roads we were to use were surfaced with dirt and rough gravel. Today, however, the Canadian Federal Government is behind the creation of a national highway. National pride and the country's ceaseless and colossal development demand it.

From the first coming of the white man transport and communications have been two of Canada's biggest problems. In

this land of vast distances, forest, prairie and mountain provided the principal natural obstacles, but special difficulties were
to come from rivers and some of the land surfaces such as
muskeg and gumbo. With these the climate combined to add to
man's troubles.

For the pioneers roadmaking in the forests was comparatively
straightforward. Once the direction had been determined the
task largely was one of felling trees and clearing a path. On
the prairie the governing factor was water. This heavy and
bulky commodity could not be carried in quantity without
seriously cutting down the already none-too-large pay-load of
the freight wagons. So both for man and his draught animals
there had to be water at the end of each day's drive (some 20 to
30 miles); at the most a wagon train could face but one dry
camp. So trails had to run from water supply to water supply.
But here open country stretched to the horizon; wagons had no
need to follow one behind another and there was no need of
an engineered roadway over the rolling land. In the mountains
the problems were finding passes, engineering suitable gradients,
and re-making the tracks each year after the floods of the
springtime had washed the road away downhill.

With the replacement of the draught animal by the steam
engine and the railway line the conquest of some of these
difficulties was greatly simplified; others assumed a greater
significance. For the engineers of permanent way the muskeg
(large areas covered by damp and rotting vegetation and dead
trees sometimes to a depth of fifty feet) and gumbo (deep belts
of heavy clay) posed special problems. In gumbo it is the winter
of central Canada that brings trouble. In the bitter cold the
ground can be frozen to a depth of three feet. The water within
the clay turns to ice and expands; the surface of the soil is
forced upward, often by several inches. Sleepers are uprooted;
rails distorted. On the roads any asphalted surfaces are cracked;
gravel-covered stretches become rough and hummocky. When
the warmth of spring turns the ice again to water and soil
subsides, the wreckage of the winter must be made good.

At first the roads of Canada were dirt tracks of local importance, principally used for bringing the produce of the farms to the local market centres. To the markets of the world the railways were the routes. So roads were mainly the responsibility of the municipalities, though with some, usually those connecting areas within a province, there was some sharing of responsibility by the provincial governments. There being no national roads there was no provision of Federal Government finance for them. When roads of more than local significance were constructed they usually ran from north to south. They were links between Canada and the markets in the United States of America and later served to link Canada's farmlands in her southern acres with the minerals discovered in her northern territories. The factors which kept the roadways north to south were not economic only. The majority of Canada's rivers and mountain ranges run roughly north to south. Roads from east to west would have to find a way across and through the mightiest of nature's obstacles. For this there was no great demand until after the First World War.

With the development of the internal combustion engine the range of the road user began to grow. No longer had he to think of seeking water every 20 or 30 miles; rather was it his supply of oil and petrol on which he had to keep his eye. With the ability to travel over longer distances there grew a demand for more and better roads. Indeed as early as 1910 the idea of an east to west, coast to coast highway was mooted. But there were many difficulties. Local governments saw no profit or advantage from the vast financial expenditure involved. There were the problems as to where should lie responsibility for roadways through the national parks. But soon after the end of the First World War a start was made on road-building. It was not a major or generally planned start, but a start it certainly was. It's first big boost came from the post-war depression. The Federal Government encouraged, and in large measure financed, road-making as a means of relieving unemployment. By this time the volume of motor traffic had grown to proportions that made the provision of a trans-Canada Highway desirable. But any possible impetus in that direction was killed by the Second World War. It was not until 1948 that the Federal Government tackled the problem of the trans-Canada Highway seriously. There were many difficulties. Such a road would have considerable interest for tourists but the various provincial governments still saw little advantage to themselves in the enormous capital outlay. (In some areas a single mile of road has cost more than £335,000.) So the Federal Government had to undertake a great part of the cost. All the provinces except Quebec eventually co-operated.

It is hoped that soon a car may run on a motor way having no sharp bend or steep gradient from St John's in Newfoundland on the Atlantic coast to the seaport of Victoria on the island of Vancouver in British Columbia on the Pacific coast. There has had to be special provision for the roadway through Canada's national parks; there has had to be collaboration in planning the linking of stretches of road in one province with those in the neighbouring provinces; there have been delays because in years of prosperity there has been a great demand for earth-moving machinery and for labour both skilled and unskilled, and in that demand the claims of the trans-Canada Highway could have no priority; the different stretches had each to wait its turn for men and machines. But the difficulties are being overcome. When we made our trip across Canada there were some gaps in the great Highway, but already the great project was within sight of completion.

Billie and I were to trace a line through wild and beautiful terrain which provided a variety of both scenery and motoring conditions. The highway, many parts of it in bad condition, would wind around mountain sides at high altitude, through gorges, over open country and forest, across vast, flat plains; around the Great Lakes in all their wilderness glory. It was October, too, and good weather was fading out. We had been warned of the savagery of sections of the route, especially preceding the Rockies. Billie could not reproach anyone, she had been warned of the risks she ran. We had been honest with her from the first.

*   *   *

It was minutes after midnight on 12 October in Vancouver when Billie headed Alaska-Minxy inland from the Pacific Ocean where the mountains meet the sea. Well-wishers had gathered to see us off. Billie was attractive in a dark tartan skirt and smart red motoring coat with white buttons. She appeared confident, perhaps a trifle gayer than usual. Prior to "take-off", however, I detected in her laughter, a slightly brittle quality that hinted of inner tension. An official from the Shell Petrol Company remarked: "The girl with an hour-glass figure who has to make every minute count."

We felt mutual relief to be on our way.

"O.K. dear!" I exclaimed, "drive for the first four hours, don't waste a skid. It's 800 miles to Calgary over the Rockies, and we're due there at 4 p.m., today."

"It's so exciting, don't you think?" was the reply.

The lights of civilization dropped away as we twisted higher into the cold, stern, empty, coastal ranges. Silence fell between us: the engine roared reliably. It had again been tuned to perfection. I entered up the diary as Billie tugged around the mountain bends. Scurries of white dust blew across the highway under our shrieking tyres. Within a hundred miles the old spell of Alaska-Minxy enveloped me, I knew too, Billie was breathing more easily, feeling a growing confidence. Her shoulders had relaxed, but her slender fingers rested with firm control on the steering wheel. In the dim light her face was set with a curious intentness as she followed the road ahead in the bright light of the headlight beams.

The thought painfully uppermost in my mind was, could she stick the pace? This was my first serious motoring venture with one of the opposite sex. Each would represent to the other the unknown under trial, an unknown that could both attract and repel. Courtship under normal, happy circumstances was something totally different from being cooped up in a thudding, roaring car across thousands of fast, non-stop miles. It would be a strain being polite and pleasant at all times. With acute tiredness even to blink sleep-hungry eyes would become an effort. Weariness made one not exactly normal. I was resolved to try to reach Toronto on Lake Ontario, 3,025 map miles to the east, in 3½ days. This total time of 84 hours would include Press interviews, a radio interview at Calgary, time for refuelling, meals, detours, cine-photography and any other delays. Average speed would have to be 36 miles an hour; our intention was to race the fast trans-continental train to Toronto. The scheduled time for the crack Canadian express across a track mileage of 2,074 miles was 70 hours. Road distance, however, was considerably more. After Toronto we would catch our second breath, then race for Ottawa and Montreal, before entering the U.S.A. for Boston, and the run down the Atlantic seaboard to Miami.

*   *   *

Hours had wings. Without chatter or complaint, Billie calmly drove the car at a rollicking lick. Most of the road was tortuous, rising at interval to a considerable height. We strained upward and streaked downward, we wound through millions of mountain acres. A tremulous glow, rapidly growing white, heralded the dawn; it dispersed the shades of night in the vast dome of mountain sky. Friendly twinkling lights, seen at intervals across the unbounded emptiness, faded away. I thought about this long, long continental line. Today, for military purposes, Canada and the U.S.A. are one nation; people living either side of the boundary need no instruction on the art of brotherly co-existence.

Along the length of the frontier are 150 customs and immigration entry points, but this imaginary line means more to Canadians, I think, than to Americans. Canadians have an unusually deep spiritual attachment for their boundary, just as they possess an extraordinary love of their country. They have discovered loyalty and beauty in her lonely magnificence, in the wild glory of her autumns; even in the raging blizzards of her Januarys.

*   *   *

We drove towards Grand Forks in a maze of high ranges that vaulted Pacific-ward. All about us was an excessive sprawl of mountain scenery, where distances seemed different. Forests boasted the multi-coloured party dress of autumn; foliage flamed with red and gold. The sun pierced a light mist, glorifying still more the earth, water, vegetation, scent and colouring. I marvelled at the size of Canada.

Around us reared the Monashee Mountains, ahead of us the spectacular Selkirk range; and beyond, the mighty Rockies themselves. After crossing them we would then come to the interminable plains and prairies—and greater speed. Speed, soul satisfying speed! My nostrils twitched at the pure, cool air. The weather was not raw, but it was too chilly to drive without using the heater. The first snow of the season had fallen farther inland. It had thawed soon afterwards, but it had left clear indication of approaching winter. Visibility was exceptional in the most translucent air imaginable.

We encountered no other motor car. A brief halt was called near a canyon. A sheet of white, foaming water roared like a runaway freight train. Hungrily, we dipped for the first time into our food box; I washed the glass of the headlamps and replenished the radiator from a stream. On that wind-beset mountainside Billie powdered her face and applied lipstick. I thought: "Women are crazy about their make-up. Fancy daubing up in this realm of beauty where nature's cosmetics are beyond equal for allure!" But I was careful to say nothing.

*   *   *

The highway surface deteriorated, the number and degree of the curves increased. We came to the start of the fifty-mile dirt and gravel road which snaked through the Cascade Mountains. Spectacular terrain slid past our windows, a dramatic preview of wonders soon to come. Slowly the mountains ahead came closer, finally to hem us in. Patches of snow gleamed above the dark-purple foothills. Here was the typical rolling, wooded slopes and the granite-pocked terrain that covered half of the country. Here, too, was a region of bold ramparts and upswept peaks. Above, enormous cumulus clouds, white and lazy, seemed to form and disperse in a cobalt sky. Warning raindrops splashed the windscreen fifteen minutes later. A veil of descending moisture drifted, softly, slowly, over the mountainous landscape.

The road over the Cascades hugged the cliff face; it was narrow, rough, slippery. To the right were drops of hundreds of feet. After five miles of nerve-chafing driving, and a nasty skid, I braked and laughed.

"I think we'd better go back," I told my partner. "We'll cross into the U.S.A., and miss this section, then re-enter Canada, near the town of Trail."

Billie's brow knitted in thought. "But that will add on another hundred miles," she replied, "let's carry on."

"Famous last words," I snapped, "I'm not making a habit of sticking my neck out with you in the car."

This was our first row.

Said Billie in a rebellious tone: "Keep going, and stop saying 'I' and begin saying 'we'. If you've always taken defeat bitterly and personally, now we'll share it."

"O.K. drive the blasted thing yourself."

Billie took the wheel without a word and drove along the wet, sloping, dangerous road. It was skilful, slithering rib-cracking driving. We got through without mishap. I put my arm about her shoulders, and murmured appreciatively: "Wouldn't have suspected you of knowing driving tricks like that." I laughed self-consciously. "Your hunch was right."

She took my hand from her shoulder.

"Please," she said sharply, "we don't want any fancy goings-on while we're going on."

I'm not likely to forget that fast drive over the wet Cascades. Even if it was a lousy track, it was still an epic feat of engineering for man to make there any road at all.

To cross Kootenay Lake we made a five-mile ferry trip. An elderly gentleman approached us during the crossing.

"I suppose," he said, "you expect to be asked questions with such an interesting looking car, and such magnificent maps painted on the doors."

Mr. Cameron, a reporter, introduced himself. We had an interesting conversation. He advised us for interest's sake to view a large house on the other side of the lake made exclusively of bottles. We paused at this odd dwelling to take pictures. The owner of this most amazing edifice was a retired undertaker. The whole elaborate home was built from thousands of empty embalming-fluid bottles. I imagine they had been collected from every funeral parlour in Canada.

Chapter Nine

From Calgary to Montreal

The English look upon the Canadians as English trying to act American. The Americans look upon Canadians as Americans trying to act English.

W HEN we came to Banff 720 miles had been clocked. This resort in the Canadian Rockies, named after the Scottish town by Lord Strathcona, is one of the holiday wonders of the world. It also represents the headquarters of one of the country's finest national parks. Speeding along the road through glade and forest setting, we saw elk, moose, deer and shaggy mountain goats. At one point, a coyote, like a large, pale rough-haired dog with a bushy tail, sprang from the undergrowth. It was fast, but we were speedier; it was killed outright by our crash bar. Later we halted, and two black bears enlivened the scene by ambling fearlessly to within a dozen feet of the car, squinting inquisitively. These great beasts have become artful in begging for "handouts" from travellers.

When Banff was left behind we continued across the province of Alberta en route for Calgary, referred to formerly as a "cowtown" but now, since recent "strikes" in the vicinity, more properly as an "oil city". We were honoured by a police escort at the city limits. Billie had chosen to re-christen the car Canada-Minxy, which the press and radio reporters who awaited our arrival duly noted. A big fellow in a checked shirt and sombrero type of hat, grinned and said: "Nice to see you again, Dick."

It was an uncommonly nice surprise.

"Hell, Al," I gasped, "it's good to see you after all these years, you certainly look different out of uniform."

I again met Al Priest's pretty English wife, Helen. Al and I had been attached to an R.A.F. squadron on the Isle of Man, in 1945.

Refreshed, we set off at a spanking pace to bisect the province of Saskatchewan. Here more wheat is grown than in the rest of Canada. Following the great Regina plains we would then slash east into the next province of Manitoba, and so to Winnipeg, the metropolis of the prairies. This second leg of 845 miles we hoped to accomplish in seventeen hours. The road would allow for sustained speed through undulating and fertile wheatlands.

Around Regina, we roared through a gently rolling landscape. We drove in relay throughout the night and into the day. It was desolate country, but as the landscapists would say, full of character. Along a vanishing horizon of endless plains, at wide intervals, occasional houses and sparse trees might have been signalling to one another across the lonely miles.

The car was running at its magnificent best, and Billie, now showing signs of fatigue, nevertheless was driving at her best. The air was cool; summer had gone. The golden scythe of harvest had swept over a thousand miles of rich, ripe wheat. Almost to the verge of the Great Lakes we were to travel through these gleaned fields where the wheat that supplies our daily bread had won its race against rust, grasshoppers, hailstorms and other possible disasters. We alternately drove and rested in the swing-back passenger seat that had been fitted, but the car engine never relaxed. Prairie, prairie, prairie, and overall a quiet gloom and a vast cloudy sky.

We neared Winnipeg. In spite of being dead tired, Billie diligently applied her make-up; her eyes had a strained look; her voice was hoarse from the dust which had filtered into the car and settled in her throat; but still make-up was of paramount importance.

"Warpaint for Winnipeg," she laughed.

There was no let-up on arrival. Rootes agents welcomed us.

The Press boys talked to us. Later we met the members of the Winnipeg Sporting Car Club. More time was absorbed in Winnipeg than we had bargained for, but Billie did manage to snatch a little rest. Thereafter we entered on another headlong dash through the night. This time out of the province of Manitoba into the seemingly limitless expanse of Ontario. The prairies were thrown to our rear and we merged with the central coniferous regions. In a short two days we had come into our third time zone. We had begun with Pacific Standard Time, changed to Mountain Standard Time, now to Central Standard Time; at the end of the drive we would be in Eastern Standard Time.

Next morning we arrived on the western shore of Lake Superior, that great inland sea, having ridden 460 miles through the dark hours. We had a meal at the lakehead port of Fort William before tackling the last 1,000 miles to our finishing point. From reports received, this promised to be quite gruelling. There were many detours and incessant rain had played havoc with the unmetalled surfaces.

I accelerated northward to the lonely highlands of Ontario; I was full of driving fever. Our route would take us high around Lake Superior and Lake Huron, then south to Toronto and Lake Ontario. We would penetrate a vast and rugged region. Billions of trees would reach out endlessly like a great green rug, around hundreds of isolated lakes. We were following, in the main, the route of the early explorers. It was a thrilling, unforgettable drive. Ontario's immense northland has been shaped and moulded by nature for more than a thousand million years. It lies on the pre-Cambrian Shield.

This pre-Cambrian Shield is one part of the original hide of the world, the crust that formed as the molten globe cooled. It covers half Canada in a great horse-shoe shape, holding a million lakes imprisoned in its hollows and undreamed of riches locked in its bosom. Rich minerals and precious metals have been discovered. Today, thousands of scientific problems remain to be solved. Canada, rich in promise, offers inexhaustible

"Can't believe you got 90 outa this peanut," said this patrolman of the New York State Police, his handsome face expressionless, when he stopped us for speeding. Billie spoke him fair and earned forgetfulness of our offence. I resented "peanut" as a description of the Minx. Of course, from the picture below, which was taken in London, and shows a Minx standing behind a large American car, you can see what the policeman meant.

Left: At a halt under the frowning mountains on the Mexican border Billie fills the tank. Not only did my fiancée drive, she took a fair share of the many other "chores" inseparable from long-distance driving.

Below: By the Grand Canyon of the Colorado Billie was deeply stirred. So, too, was I. This, the world's mightiest gash, is Nature's story of creation. Far, far away below, like snakey grey twine, roars the Colorado River, a 300-foot wide stream of tremendous power. The rock walls that bound it are a cross-section of the earth's crust. They have been cut out by the wearing of water over thousands of years. To a small boy in a cowboy suit it meant little: "Golly, what a gulley!" was his comment.

challenge to the courage and pioneering impulse of man. The great natural resources which still lie hidden in these areas through which Billie and I passed spell an increase also to the wealth of the world.

Billie's slight figure lay still in the lean-back seat. Her face was paler than usual and registered weariness. With closed eyes she listened to an impressive radio programme covering the opening of the Canadian Parliament in Ottawa by Her Majesty Queen Elizabeth and His Royal Highness the Duke of Edinburgh. The Royal couple were in Canada on a State visit. Across the width of the land we found people for the most part, patriotically stirred. Though in some few parts, feeling was less strong than others, Canadians generally are intensely loyal to the British Commonwealth.

It must not be overlooked, however, that Canada is a rapidly changing nation. Since the year 1900, 6,500,000 people have immigrated to Canada. Between the years 1950-7, alone, 1,300,000 Europeans were transplanted from the Old World to the New. With its present population of 17,000,000 the breakdown ratio among British, French and other ethnic groups is, 4:3:2. The majority of cool-minded, deep-thinking Canadians have a natural aversion to overdone blah about antiquity, ritual and outmoded tradition. These virile people of the North American Continent are as progressively modern as tomorrow. They peer into a future with little time for nursing the unprofitable past. An elderly Canadian engineer said to me: "Every man is his own ancestor, and every man is his own heir. He devises his own future, and he inherits his own past."

Most of Canada's trade dollars flow south of the border, but I believe that this nation, which is rapidly assuming an increasingly important position in world leadership, will stick firmly to Great Britain in the foreseeable future as long as British economic and trade doctrines intermesh constructively and comfortably with Canada's essentially independent policy. John George Diefenbaker, the present Prime Minister, is rapidly becoming a major personality in international affairs. Similarly, Canadian people in an era of their country's rapidly growing structure, seek to lead rather than to be directed. They feel the "vision of Canada's awakening future", nationalism is not lukewarm, they have a faith to espouse, and a trust in themselves which grows. May British and Canadian ties never be impaired, it would be a major tragedy if the New World lost interest in the Old.

*   *   *

Far to the north above Lakes Superior and Huron, we received quite a few stones from fortune's sling. Sections of the highway were a quagmire after the heavy rain, some parts were a squelching mess; in a few places detours had hastily been carved out by bulldozers. In Ontario, too, there are patches of that muskeg which we had encountered during the drive to Fairbanks. "Muskeg" perhaps is worse than the gumbo (heavy clay) encountered in prairie lands.

In northern Ontario, when the world suddenly seemed liquid in the sunset, I handed over the wheel. Within minutes I was asleep. Some time later Billie started jabbing me.

"Richard, look, wake up, it's the Sputnik," she cried.

"Stop," I groaned, "to hell with the ruddy Sputnik." Billie halted the car and I was made to wake up, and sit up. From the heavens hung the ghostly gossamer curtains of the Northern Lights.

"See it, see it, over there, Richard?"

I saw it all right. It might have been a fast moving star on a smooth course.

At the time of our drive, all the world was Sputnik-conscious and many people were afraid of what the future might hold. At one place we'd passed through, an enterprising confectioner had manufactured "Sputnik Candies"! Billie watched the bright, moving object and said:

"It's a scientific horror!"

I laughed cynically.

Suddenly Billie's eyes were streaming with the tears of exhaustion, or Sputnik distress, or both together. "Isn't the world being very silly," she murmured.

130

I took over the driving. The Sputnik had disappeared, but not the eerie spectacle of the Northern Lights. The wan glow made me feel restless. We drove the last few hundred miles in a dream, and when a signpost informed us that we were 25 miles from Toronto, my intellect at first found it ridiculous.

Dick Williams, a splendid Yorkshireman, and the Toronto Sales Manager of Rootes Motors, made us welcome at his office. There were many guests, and a grand reception. Somehow, Billie and I managed to keep bright and cheerful and forget our weariness. Television teams stood by. A huge twenty-foot frame covered with paper had been erected. See picture facing p. 112. Painted on one side were the words:

"TRANS-CANADA RECORD—FIRST 1958 MODEL ACROSS"

We drove Canada-Minxy through this paper wall for the TV cameras. Crowds massed themselves around the car. The general comment was: "What an incredible performance for a four-cylinder car."

The already sensational Alaska-Minxy again received widespread praise. Our clock mileage on arrival and after the detours showed 3,095 miles. Actual driving time for the race across the continent was 55 hours at an average speed of 55 miles an hour. Total time for the 3,100 miles was three and a half days (85 hours). I think Billie and I can safely say that we beat the time of the Canadian Trans-Continental train.

While we were still at the Toronto reception Dick Williams received a message asking him to get us moving towards Ottawa without delay. The day before, the Queen had opened Parliament, and the next day at noon, the Royal couple were leaving the capital city for Washington D.C. The Press boys wanted us in Canada's capital for photographs before Parliament Building. Ottawa was gay with flags and bunting, the population in patriotic and gala mood. If Alaska-Minxy arrived on the scene, affectionate feeling towards British cars would be enormous, publicity great. So Williams put it to me that we ought to start forthwith.

"Don't jest," I told Dick, wearily, and yawned. "We've driven across a Continent, we're worn out."

It was a difficult situation. Dick Williams was one of the grandest fellows I've ever met. It wasn't his idea; but he'd been told to get us there. I felt sorry for him, so I compromised. He drove Billie back to her hotel, myself to my motel. We arranged that Dick would arouse us at 5 a.m., and get us off for Ottawa, 265 miles to the north-east. We were yet bleary-eyed when we did leave Toronto. We were getting "browned-off" with publicity. We liked the driving job, but not the public-relations side of the adventure. We were beginning to feel like goldfish in a glass bowl.

*   *   *

Publicity snowballed. Montreal dealers, too, wanted to see Alaska-Canada-Minxy. We hastened to this bustling city of culture, history and gaiety, where two-thirds of the people speak French by preference. But that doesn't mean that if one asks a question in English there may be language difficulties. The city's population seems to be bilingual I am glad to say. Dining out seems to be the chief occupation; Billie and I tried it and approved whole-heartedly.

*   *   *

Driving near the boundary between Canada and the U.S.A. we had witnessed considerable evidence of a co-operative enterprise unique in international relationships, namely the construction of the St. Lawrence Seaway.

For thirty years, Canada has been striving to begin this work. The long delay resulted from the fact that the area of the projected Seaway was international territory. It was only in 1954 that both nations came to a final agreement, and the Seaway Bill was signed by President Eisenhower.

In 1959 the old boundary where British redcoats once patrolled was to become the busiest and largest inland water highway in the world. Human imagination must be stretched to grasp the results of this stupendous project. It is a vaster feat than either the Suez or Panama Canal. In constructing the

Seaway, more than 20,000 acres of borderland are being flooded, completely eliminating two towns and six villages.

H.M. Queen Elizabeth and President Eisenhower formally inaugurated the St. Lawrence Seaway on 26 June, 1959. Today, liners and freighters from all over the world sail through this 2,350 miles long waterway from the mouth of the St. Lawrence River to the west shore of Lake Superior. Toronto, Buffalo, Detroit, Milwaukee, Chicago and Duluth all have become great inland seaports.

*   *   *

We speeded to Boston, U.S.A. From here would begin our second marathon. A run down America's eastern seaboard to Miami in the Gulf of Mexico. Whatever our personal accomplishment, the really significant fact for me was that we had proved just how tough a British car was. America awaited us. Could the indomitable little record-making vehicle continue to keep it up?

Chapter Ten

Encirclement of the Mighty "48"

America, vast in contrasts and wonders, is the ultimate in motoring friendliness and sightseeing value.

IT IS DIFFICULT, even for an American, to form a clear idea of the vastness of the United States of America. It is equally perplexing to understand the nation's diversities, its geographical and climatic variations, the many facets of its fascinating history—or the intriguing conglomeration of its people. The U.S.A. rightly boasts many of the earth's greatest spectacles, both natural and man-made. In this age of turning wheels, it is small wonder that it is essentially the motorists' domain, more so than any land on earth. Almost everything, directly and indirectly, is planned about, and evolved with the automobile in mind. America has one car to every three of the population. Distances are immense when judged by European standards. To make appreciation of this a little easier, remember that thirty-three islands the size of Great Britain could be accommodated within the borders of the United States.

This land mass is tied together by a network of good highways. Along our route, even in small and remote places, motels and drive-in accommodation existed.

Our small car was still in fine fettle. If the third adventure were to be successful, it would prove that British baby engines possessed the speedy virtues, bull-dog endurance and tough constructional qualities usually associated only with much bigger cars.

Press, TV and radio followed our progress with unusual interest and enthusiasm. Our car had news value. When the

American Press is interested in anything, no trouble is too great to acquaint the nation with relevant information. People all over the States are avid for news about Alaska, their far northern possession. They call it the "Last Frontier". I doubt whether our trip around the "48" would have won any particular attention had not Alaska-Minxy already attracted so much publicity for her exploits in the far north. Crowds looked Alaska-Minxy over critically. One American remarked: "Gee, it must be atomic. Fancy that sewing machine licking Alaska, and now trying to wrap up the 48."

America, today, is small-car conscious to a degree which is causing Detroit to raise its eyebrows.

*   *   *

We found American people refreshing and generously broad-minded. The best that America has to offer in hospitality, sight-seeing and good-natured fellowship is a stranger's for the taking. I wish that vast numbers of British and Continental motorists could drive around the States as we did. Much would be achieved in correcting various wrong impressions, for the most part "movie manufactured", of our American friends. All too often, Europeans overlook the fact that Americans originate from all parts of Europe; they are kin to Europe.

If present international problems followed the American pattern of national unity towards moulding our conflicting world into a single, harmonious, social, industrial and economic brotherhood, little would be amiss. War fevers would vanish.

Billie wrote in her diary what an American expressed in Washington:

> Democracy is a way of life. Democracy is sincerity, friendliness, courage and tolerance. If your life and mine do not exemplify these characteristics, we do not have the right to call ourselves full-fledged citizens of the world's greatest democracy.

*   *   *

Billie was excited as we entered the New England States. On the strength of the new venture we lunched at a smart restaurant where emphasis was solely on sea food. I was intrigued at what was printed on the menu:

135

THE AUTOBIOGRAPHY OF AN OYSTER

I am born without jaws or teeth; but I've got fine muscles, liver and a heart. In each year of my life I produce 1,200,000 eggs; each of my children is 1/120th of an inch in length; so 2,000,000 little ones can be crowded into a space of one cubic inch. I am ready for the table in from one to five years after birth. You will never find me in cold parts of the world. I dislike cold. In Ceylon I sometimes grow to a foot in length. One of me there makes a stew, when I am half a foot broad. I am not of much account in England unless I am imported there from America. It makes me very sad to think of fetching up in the sand—I, who was discussed by Tiberius and Julius. I have been the cause of much bloodshed. Men fight fierce battles for me all along the American, the Italian and the coasts of Kent and Essex. If you eat me raw you are not at all likely to regret it, for I am in a raw state very nutritious and easily digested. As I fry I am likely to be uninteresting and heavy. So few know how to fry me. I am about the only animate thing that can be eaten with impunity in a raw state. Parasites cannot exist in me as they can in chops and steaks and fruits. I am a pretty good friend to man. And to women. Look at the pearls I've given her. Thackeray has compared me in a raw state to a new baby. Yet I never kept him awake at night. I'm not half bad in a stew; but as a roast in the shell all the poetry in me comes out. Then I sizzle with emotion, in butter, red pepper and a little sauce. The clam is like the driver of a hansom cab then—not in it with me. The clam! That commonplace fellow! I avoid him as much as possible. I am not a snob, nor yet a cad, but I really must not be expected to fraternize with the clam, nor can I discuss him. The line must be drawn. He's not in the Four Hundred. Well I am.

Signed:

Blue Pointe

Whilst in America we assessed food and cooking, living standards, and aspects of life compared with Britain, and New Zealand, impartially and objectively. Billie wrote in her diary:

Americans take far greater pride in cooking, and also talk a great deal more about food than we do in New Zealand. Curiosity lures the American cook into culinary experiments, with the result that meals are more varied.

I added:

America makes one realize very abruptly that we British have cultivated a studied indifference to enticing dishes, and the art of good food preparation. Average American housewives would never tolerate the traditional British "cut off the joint and two veg". It must not be forgotten, however, that American cooking has been enriched by national dishes introduced by immigrants from every country in the world.

*   *   *

New England is crammed full of stirring history. Everywhere one finds rich historical backgrounds, homes, public buildings and shrines going back to the beginnings of America. It was easy to re-live the story of the Revolution, to bring alive Paul Revere and Samuel Adams, also the Britishers who fought thereabouts. As I drove, I pictured the village greens of Lexington and Concord, noisy with musket-fire. Billie and I followed in the steps of the Pilgrims. Not many people in Britain are aware that six years after the Puritans coming to Massachusetts in 1630, Harvard College was founded. A famous American historian said of it: "The best thing that ever New Englanders thought upon."

It was thrilling motoring this New England territory. Perhaps 75% of the place names are of British origin. Guildford, Windsor, Avon, Ipswich, Salisbury, and the like. The climate, also, is akin to Britain's; much of the setting is remarkably similar to English scenes. There were pubs, too, but these were nowise comparable to the genuine English versions.

Boston, the first great city we reached, is a leading seaport and internationally famous as a cultural centre. We received an official welcome with civic trimmings, a foretaste of America's acceptance of us, and the car. In half a day we did six broadcasts, a TV show, and managed a stroll to the harbour and the identical spot where the Boston Tea Party created the big rumpus which led to Boston's punishment, thence to the Revolution.

*   *   *

We forged powerfully ahead along a four-lane super-highway

137

leading to New York. We slipped past sleek American cars with a pleasant whoosh! We were hustling because an important reception had been arranged at Rootes Motors, Park Avenue. To reach New York by noon meant fast moving.

Unobserved, a State patrol car lay in wait off the four-lane highway. When it crept up behind, I arrogantly mistook it for one of the elegant models I had whooshed past.

"Someone wanting to take me down a peg," was my erroneous conclusion.

Came a smooth, downhill grade. It enabled me to spurt Alaska-Minxy up to 90 m.p.h. The car was running sweetly under my loving touch. The sun shone, the tyres purred, this was America and I felt like a contented cat. The big Dodge maintained an even distance until the end of the gradient. Then I saw a flash of black and my own precipitous pace seemed slow. The Dodge might have sprung at me. As it zoomed along-side an awful siren let off with an immense clatter. A roof lamp flashed a menacing red. I glimpsed a furious face under a State policeman's hat. A hand signalled us to stop.

Billie glanced at me, I looked at her. Said she: "You just keep quiet, let me handle him, please!"

The traffic officer was a huge, handsome man; his uniform was impressive, too. We were studied with cool, quick eyes. So was the map on the door.

"Can't believe you got 90 outa this peanut," then a disdain-ful sniff as a finger pointed to the map. "What the hell are you selling, Alaska real-estate?"

I gave Billie an apprehensive look.

"Talk mister," invited the speed cop, his face frozen and expressionless.

My hand at my side touched Billie's.

"Why the devil doesn't she start talking," my mind twittered. Then she came to the rescue, resolutely.

"Good heavens officer," she said sweetly, "just what is the trouble?"

The big man responded with a sniff, a scowl and a growl.

"55 miles an hour speed limit, ma'am." The voice became rasping. "I never let likes or dislikes influence me, ma'am."

Billie spoke again. I looked on and felt like a monkey in a cage.

"But surely this wonderful super-highway was built without speed restriction, officer?" She smiled. "We've got to learn, we're new to the States, you know."

"Where do you reckon you've come from?" she was asked.

Billie hurried on. Within five minutes the officer had been acquainted of the history of Alaska-Minxy, Canada-Minxy, and then with a catch in her voice, Billie added: "If you don't dismiss this incident casually, you might be responsible for the end of Yankee-Minxy."

The handsome one spluttered, frowned, then sprawled limply against our bonnet, after slapping the car disbelievingly.

"Ma'am," he said in the same slow voice, "it sounds a corny tale. You wouldn't be trying to pull a fast one, it's a very old dodge?"

Billie seized on this. From her handbag came a dozen Press cuttings.

I became agreeably aware that the traffic officer's lips had pursed pleasantly; his eyes revealed amusement. With mock gravity he inveighed eloquently about faked publicity stunts.

"It's all true," Billie put in calmly, "terribly, terribly true."

Hurriedly she reached into the car and drew out a copy of my book, *Cape Cold to Cape Hot*. It was thrust into the American's hands.

"Do have it with our compliments officer, you must read how my fiancé drove through the Sahara, and the Congo."

"Yeah," was the acknowledgement.

"Oh, and far above the Arctic Circle, too, officer."

The big man pondered his responsibility for a few seconds and looked me up and down. Turning to my fiancée, he exclaimed: "What's he supposed to be, an author or a transient of the world's highways and byways?"

Billie bestowed a ravishing smile: "If we're allowed to finish our American trip I intend to reform him."

I was given a pleasant wink: "O.K. no charge!"

Turning to Billie, he remarked: "I think he's a thorough going bad 'un, and downright odd rushing a nice lil gal like you around on his cuckoo trips."

He laughed good-naturedly and I was offered a firm hand to shake.

"O.K. on your way at 55," I was cautioned.

I thanked him nicely, and even took his photograph (facing p. 128). Came a parting shot . . . "If I were out of uniform I'd like to go on a bender with you two, and hear more."

We nosed towards New York. Billie chuckled delightedly and a light kiss brushed my ear.

"Wasn't he handsome, dear?"

"Nuts," I growled, "I wish you'd allowed me to say something. Fancy him calling this car a peanut!"

*   *   *

John Panks, the important one of Rootes Motors, New York, entertained us at one of the 20,500 eating places in the gourmet belt of the city, roughly between 40th Street and the low 60s. It's an exciting and strange eating town; New Yorkers are as varied, exclusive, sane and eccentric as the thousands of available menus.

This city struck me as having a special affinity with Heaven, an unfettered sense of the infinite. Gazing from the Empire State Building over a medley of man-made casings, two proverbs winged through my mind.

"To follow the will of Heaven is to prosper; to rebel against the will of Heaven is to be destroyed." And, "planning is in the power of man, executing is in the hands of Heaven".

*   *   *

John Panks was a logical man for so big a job. He reflected a suave English side to himself. He'd got good looks, a well-set-up figure and knew how to wear his clothes. He possessed tact and a pleasant manner. I imagined he could pull strings adroitly and organize with ability.

He repeated his question: "Now you quite understand what I want you to do?"

"Quite," I affirmed, "spend approximately a week in Miami before driving Alaska-Minxy back home to you here in New York."

"Exactly!"

John Panks went on: "Alaska-Minxy has been through hell. Remember there are no infallible motor-cars made anywhere as yet."

I laughed reassuringly: "Don't worry, the damned thing is running like a dream."

"A fat lot I care," was the swift retort. "The Minx is a celebrity now, under the spotlight, everybody's looking on."

Billie gave him one of her sweet, good-natured smiles.

"Don't worry, John," she said, "we'll bring Alaska-Minxy back alive."

"Thank you, Billie. Go as fast as you like to Miami, but please nurse the engine all the way back to New York. Every part of that little car has just about had enough. Metal fatigue is metal fatigue, and a breakdown would undo all the excellent publicity to date. Racing it back is a risk without any compensating gain in prospect."

*　　　*　　　*

We left the world's most exciting island. Of the five boroughs that make up New York City, only Bronx is part of the mainland. On these islands and their neighbouring peninsula exist nearly 8,000,000 people. Daily they come to the wonder city by ferries, through tunnels, across bridges. From one island to another they pour into Manhattan's skyscraping buildings, shops, entertainment centres and immense industrial installations of Brooklyn and Queens. The city is always in a state of building flux. As a Mayor once said: "New York will be a beautiful city if ever they get her finished."

*　　　*　　　*

When we reached Philadelphia, third largest city in the U.S.A., and known as "America's birthplace", and "Cradle of Liberty", we visited old, dignified Independence Hall. Here, under the historic Liberty Bell, the Declaration of Independence was signed. It was here that Washington accepted command of the first United States Army, and men like Benjamin Franklin wrote the Constitution and led the new nation in the first steps under it. My movie camera was busy for the documentary film which would result from this trip.

On to Baltimore, where I discovered there's more to American history than I ever thought. Such history had seemed dull before travelling in the original colonies, the Revolutionary and Civil War country. This was territory abounding in association with Washington, Lee, the British, the French and the Indians. But if I want to study the past I must not be committed to fast motoring in the present. We went on at speed to Washington, D.C., the nation's capital. Everything here is of a splendour and dignity worthy of the Republic for which it stands. Washington is a demonstration of what history has achieved at short notice.

Chapter Eleven

The South

No race can prosper till it learns that there is as much dignity in tilling a field as in writing a poem.

W E RACED southward through North Carolina, South Carolina and Georgia, towards our journey's end in Florida. The very word South evoked warm and colourful images. All Americans and foreign visitors are deeply stirred subconsciously by the South. We headed for names delicate upon the tongue, gentle upon the ear, evocative of grace, delight, elegance, leisure. Most Americans appear to dream of the South, as of no other region of their country, a never-never land, an earthly paradise.

Southern living is characterized by a warm humanism, in sharp contrast to the hard business and tough commercialism in other parts of the States. The South still endeavours to maintain its own glorious way of life and traditions. Today Southern hospitality is still spontaneous, as Billie and I so well experienced. One Yankee visitor said to me: "It's all devouring, one can't resist this South. It's anesthesia, a glorious mixture of sweet, slow talk, tobacco, honeysuckle and bourbon."

Billie and I had to press on regardless. We didn't want to. We adored driving through the South, not so much on account of its colonial mansions and beautiful gardens, but because of the kindly people with their fascinating drawl and universal invitation: "Y'all come."

Three of the most popular National Parks of America are in the South. Great Smokey Mountains, in Tennessee and North Carolina; Shenandoah, with its famed Skyline Drive in Virginia; and the Everglades, with its fascinating tropical flora and fauna. But we had not time to see them.

We roared into Florida. Highways were superb, driving a thrill; no mountains or rugged surfaces. Here was a tropical paradise, immense beaches, whispering palms and heavenly warmth. This was the playground of millionaires. Big-game fishing, yachting and sailing, racing, gambling, luxury and leisure all can be experienced. We skirted a deep blue sea, we saw tropical flowers, palatial hotels, vari-coloured villas facing the ocean; the lairs of financiers, sportsmen, boulevardiers and movie stars.

We were officially welcomed at West Palm Beach by the President-elect of the Chamber of Commerce, Mr. Frank Frazier. We were surprised, and honoured, to receive the Freedom of the City. There were newspaper interviews by the *Gulf Stream News*, the *Tropical Leader* and the *Palm Beach Times*. A television appearance was scheduled on station WEAT at 11 p.m. A grand fellow, Mr. Bill Belton-Smith, Rootes Motor representative, was our appointed escort in Florida.

So far, we had fulfilled every call made upon us, carried out every engagement; we were both very tired. Quite a programme had been organized in Miami, the official finishing post. A police escort had been laid on to lead us in with sirens screaming. More TV shows had been lined-up.

Billie sighed longingly.

"What a glorious relaxing thought," she murmured, "soon I'll be able to dress up, walk in high-heeled shoes, talk like a normal woman again, get the infernal engine noise out of my ears, no more hell-for-leather driving. No more reporters, just sanity, I'm so very tired of being an ambassadress for motor cars."

I kissed her. "But I'm madly in love with endurance-driving."

"Well, it's got to finish for evermore, in Miami," she retorted with a trace of vehemence, "or my endurance won't stretch to being madly in love with you!"

A left hand was dangled threateningly under my nose. The

144

thumb and first finger of the right hand started to unscrew our engagement ring.

"No, don't Billie, don't," I pleaded shrilly, "I'm reformed!"

The ring was slipped silently back on her dainty finger.

*   *   *

That night, John Panks phoned from New York and offered his congratulations.

"Wonderful," he said, "now you two can relax and take it easy before you bring our precious Alaska-Minxy carefully back to New York." He stuttered and spluttered. "Richard, my boy, is she going to be a hit! By the way, how do you feel?"

"Rotten!"

"Why?"

"We've spent most of our 700 dollars expenses getting here," I replied, "can you let me have my dollars worth of agreed air passage home, also Billie's air-fare back to Vancouver?"

"Is it urgent?"

"Sure it's urgent. We want to relax and give it a tonk down here. Be a sport and send the money, chum?"

Mr. John Panks, the man with the engaging personality and good-looking face, authorized immediate payment. Secretly I felt a bit of a heel; he hadn't an inkling of the outrageous plan which had drifted into my head, nor had Billie. My bones felt a bit melty when I thought of how I would broach it to her. I visualized with extreme distinctness the diamond ring on the third finger of her left hand. Would she agree? Would she think I was dishonourable? Would I get the ring rubbed in my hair? I prayed she would appreciate the motives behind my plan; my machinations for further glorifying Alaska-Minxy. I never slept a wink the first night in Miami for thinking about it. Billie meant everything in the world to me. If she disagreed, I wouldn't follow through. I wished the idea hadn't come to me, but it had!

*   *   *

As late as 1912, the town of Miami had a population of only

7,500. The sand bar across the bay was inhabited mainly by crabs and mosquitoes. Miami and its famous beaches reached their zenith during the First World War. In those days, land down-town sold for tens of thousands of dollars a front foot. Money paid out for construction in a peak year exceeded a hundred million dollars. Today the population of Miami is 157,000.

More than a hundred varieties of game fish flourish in the azure waters which are warmed by the Gulf Stream. Wealthy visitors come to wager money in sport, big money. At the three nearby race tracks, days when a million dollars change hands in the betting are not unusual. Even greyhounds draw as much as a hundred thousand dollars a night. In Miami money disappears as quickly as a tropical mist.

At the end of the mainlands is the "highway that goes to sea", a giant causeway that takes one to exotic fishing villages, 25, 50 and 100 miles to sea. Here is a contrasting fusion of Old Spain, of Cuba and modern America. At Key West, an old, old Spanish city of legends dating from the days of the pirates, turtle fishing is a mainstay industry. Billie and I were fascinated by the big "crawls". Florida is a seafood mecca. Anywhere on the Panhandle coast, a dollar buys an enormous meal of stuffed crab, oysters, scallops, smoked mullet or pompano. We sampled Conch Chowder, Key Lime Pie and delicious turtle steaks. Elsewhere, one can dine quite inexpensively at excellent Spanish restaurants.

In southern Florida luxuriant jungle with hundreds of tropical plants and exotic flowers of every shape and colour flourishes. Orchids bloom in profusion. We wandered through some of it. We photographed a parrot colony. There seemed to be millions of rainbow-coloured birds, parrots, macaws and cockatoos, flying free.

Next day we explored a monkey jungle and photographed hundreds of Malayan monkeys running wild. Later in this realm of thrilling natural beauty, we came upon a large crystalline pond against a breath-taking background of rich, purple bougainvillea, hibiscus, the passion flower, pandorea, flame vines and palms. Around the water's edge were poised at least a hundred beautiful pink flamingoes. We watched this scene spellbound; as the golden sun filtered through the foliage, the surface of the water glistened red and orange. Below the glittered surface were thousands of goldfish. When one is in these exotic, primeval forests, it is staggering to realize that civilization is only just around the corner.

When we rolled out of Miami we were en route to New York. At least that's what everyone but myself imagined. Rootes' representative in Florida notified Mr. John Panks that we would arrive on the fifth day. Our instructions were to drive leisurely and shoot some movie film for a future documentary. Once in New York, Alaska-Minxy would be handed over for showroom display. We would say good-bye to the stout little car. Billie and I would then fly to Vancouver, our original starting point.

I was pre-occupied with my thoughts as the white ribbon of road unwound below the wheels.

Exclaimed Billie, "I haven't heard your voice for a long time. What's on your mind?"

"Oh, nothing very much," I said lightly. "Guess I'm a little sorry it's all over. It'll be a wrench kissing good-bye to Minxy."

Billie smiled understandingly. "Yes, you two have been through a lot together."

"You know what!" I exclaimed nervously, plucking up courage.

"What, Richard."

"How would you like to finish off this trip by going all around America. Complete encirclement of the Forty-eight States?"

Billie shrugged her shoulders: "Don't be idiotic, Alaska-Minxy must be utterly worn out. Mr. Panks would never hear of it."

I growled: "The car's in first-class fettle. It could polish off the other 5,000 miles around America and never feel it." I laughed scornfully. "Everyone is dithering to get her to New York safe and sound. What timorous minded . . ." I broke off, half afraid to reveal more.

"Stop getting silly ideas in your head, Richard," I was severely told. "New York is the end. That's definite. I've had enough of rushing around uncomfortably."

"Yes, dear." My reply was meek.

*   *   *

We had been requested to call at Fort Pierce, 120 miles to the northward. Dealers sought to meet us, also reporters for a final interview. We drew closer; my dilemma grew more aggravating. Publicity had already translated itself into sales. A dealer in Miami had placed an immediate order for 400 Minx models.

My scheme to abscond with Alaska-Minxy would have to take effect at Jacksonville, on the State border of Florida and Georgia, or not at all. I thought about it nervously.

I knew that Rootes, New York, would not in a thousand years of Sundays grant permission for the car to be flogged for a further gruelling 5,000 miles. Alaska-Minxy had to retire on her laurels. To suggest driving through America's hot, tough desert regions would give the big-wigs cold creeps. On the other hand I was convinced both that encirclement of America would more than ever impress potential American and Canadian buyers and that Billie, I, and Alaska-Minxy could do just that.

Our business over in Fort Pierce we pressed on. I'd feet of clay, and I was further harassed and unhappy when the fan belt snapped. A few miles on the engine began spluttering.

Billie remarked: "Minxy is merely telling you she's nearly dead with fatigue."

"Fatigue my foot," I snapped, "it's a dirty carburettor. It should have been cleaned in Miami."

"How do you know it's the carburettor?"

I nearly ate my cigarette.

"My God," I muttered, "women should swallow a sleeping draught before they start analysing engines."

Two hundred miles north of Miami, and near a small resort

called Titusville, petrol was reaching the engine in fits and starts. A halt was necessary. We found a select hotel.

"O.K. Billie," I said, "I'll fix Minxy; we'll push off in the morning."

My fiancée gaily welcomed an opportunity to get dressed up and to enjoy a nice dinner. Following the porter to her room, she clutched the electric iron. I was not sympathetic towards that crease-killing instrument; I'd called it all names under the sun. It never seemed to have a fixed lodging place in the car. Once I found it on top of my crushed photo-flash bulbs. On another occasion it had sneaked from under my seat at sixty miles an hour and positioned itself between the accelerator and brake pedals. In South Carolina it had been wrapped up in my R.A.F. sports blazer for loving protection, then stored in the dirty boot. My blazer did not benefit. I did feel some contrition, however, at the way I treated it when Billie appeared immaculate in her dresses on social occasions.

How was I to know when the carburettor trouble began, that fate had decided to help my plans?

After dinner we found ourselves in argument with four racing enthusiasts, who had driven competition cars on the world's fastest speedway at Daytona Beach. This speed centre of the world was barely sixty miles distant. On this beautifully hard, smooth beach, the late Sir Malcolm Campbell set up a world speed record of 301 m.p.h. over the measured mile in 1935.

The four drivers all knew about Alaska-Minxy. They had listened to a broadcast I'd made on a sporting programme edited by a national commentator, Bill Stern. In addition, they had given the car outside a close scrutiny. We all had a couple of drinks. We chatted about Daytona Beach, before veering to Alaska.

The big man with the smiling, craggy face, remarked:

"Dammit, it's asking a lot for us to believe you squeezed a thousand a day out'a that lil' hop-a-long you've got outside."

149

Billie thrust out her chin: "It's true, why don't you check the records?"

Tony, a sleek-haired, swarthy man, seemed to be quietly enjoying himself. He asked:

"How many bench-balanced engines were laid on. Guess it was stressed suspension, too?"

I sniffed and replied casually: "Just an ordinary stock model, gents. The same engine is the one right outside."

Billie gave further release to her feelings: "What's more, it came across Canada flat-out in 55 hours, and then it ran down to Miami."

Another strong-faced, sun-tanned driver remarked listlessly: "Okay Bill, I'm inclined to believe you against my better judgment."

"Don't call me Bill," snapped Billie.

I liked the chap with the craggy face, though I knew he was egging me on.

"Heck," he grinned, "steward prunes and daisies! When you pitched up here, your engine sounded more full of phlegm and asthma than my old Grandma."

"A dirty carburettor," reported Billie, knowledgeably.

"Say," chuckled the fourth driver, "what's it do now flat out, 22.6 miles an hour?"

"Dry up," I retaliated as nicely as I could, "stop taking the mickey." I downed my drink. "When I've cleared that carb," I said challengingly, "that lil' hop-a-long will pace any of you chaps at 70 on a good road."

Then I said the wrong thing.

"If I raced it on your blasted, beloved Daytona it would do 80 and snigger!"

There was a concerted chuckle from the four. Craggy face said: "A bet, eh? We'll get you on the measured mile. I suggest a stake of 200 dollars."

I gulped and looked at Billie. She blinked and looked at me. Said she: "I won't allow him to sacrifice that car heartlessly."

"Why not, Billie?"

"Because we are under orders to drive it back to New York."

The men glanced at each other, and I thought to myself: "If you blow Minxy's guts you'll make yourself and the car a laughing stock. These boys will treat it as the joke of the year."

"O.K.," I stammered. "Make it a bet of 250 dollars. Line up Daytona Beach tomorrow. I've only myself to blame if I finish up as sea-shell."

Billie stared . . . "You mustn't do it, Richard, you'll get yourself into trouble."

"I don't care a hang now," I retorted. "The only thing that matters is to get 80 out of Minxy or . . ."

"Or, Richard?"

"Or we'll have to start pawning things!"

*　　　*　　　*

The sand is so hard-packed at Daytona Beach that a car may cruise over 17 of the 23 miles of continuous beach to Ormond. The most perfect strip, of course, is the famous measured mile.

It was 4.30 p.m., the following day, the time when the sand was firmest. Cameras were set up and the boys pulled out their stop watches. I did four preliminary runs to get the feel of the beach. The most I opened up to at any time was 60 m.p.h.

"Here's our 250 bucks," said Tony brightly. "Got yours?"

I gave him the covering sum with a show of uneasiness.

"Let Billie hold on to the 500," I requested in a low voice. "She's neutral."

"Sure. Okay by us!"

After making the wager the previous evening, I had revealed to Billie everything on my mind about taking Minxy right around America, off my own bat. She had flared angrily. Then methodically, she'd weighed facts and figures. Out of my 420 dollars air-fare money, I'd 320 left. From Billie's 270, there remained 200.

"520 dollars," she said with exasperation, "to take us right across America, and up its west side, too. Are you going plain potty, Pape?"

"We've got the ruddy Shell credit card," I put in defensively, "we don't beg gas!"

"Oh no," she answered crossly. "You can't use that on an unauthorized journey. It's criminal! It's unlawful! It's awful, and you'll go to gaol."

"Never," I murmured sulkily, "Shell are too big-minded. They'd understand. I'd risk it!"

I was reminded of the possibility of breakdowns, emergencies.

"Could always sell my cameras," I admitted uneasily. "Have faith, Billie."

At last she agreed.

"All right," she murmured, "win the 250 dollars tomorrow and I'll turn rebel with you, but if you fail to do 80 m.p.h. on Daytona, the deal's off. It's back to New York."

I agreed.

The prerequisites for a 250 dollar Daytona win, were:

1. That I entered the measured mile at not less than 60 from no more than a mile run-up.
2. That I built up to 80 or more from the start of the mile to the end of it.
3. Four stop watches would be used. No percentage of a mile would count. The average of the four stop watches would be binding.

I took Alaska-Minxy rearward a mile. The sand was white and I aimed for the gap between two markers. I let in the clutch and tickled the accelerator. I breathed a long "Ah" and relaxed. The needle rose to 50, 55, 60, 65, 70, 75, 76, 77, 78. . . .

"C'mmon Minxy," I bellowed, "250 bucks or bust!"

79, 80, 81, the whole tableau was one of sand, sea and light. I seemed to be flying. This was no Malcolm Campbell occasion; this was just a pub bet. All the same, on that honoured beach I felt as good as Campbell. I wished I'd been behind the wheel of a car with a hundred times greater horsepower. 86, 87, 88! Minxy roared her guts out. We flashed across the mile marker and eased the car to a stop. Then I turned back to the starting point for the verdict.

"You've won 250 bucks," Craggy face announced. "Over

85 m.p.h. Nice work buddy, we lose. Now let's all go and have a few double doubles."

Billie was still clutching the wad of 500 dollars.

"Climb in dear," I said jubilantly. Turning to the foursome I yelled. "That puts things right. So-long . . . we're heading east to west, then south to north if anybody wants our postal address. B'bye, bless you all for the bucks." I could not resist rubbing it in.

Chapter Twelve

Rebels and be Damned

To get through the hardest journey we need to take only one step at a time, but we must keep on stepping.

WE CAME to Jacksonville, our point of no return on the Florida/Georgia border. Here began our escape westward towards America's badlands, the great desert regions of Texas, New Mexico and Arizona. We were excited at the prospect of taking Alaska-Minxy over these arid regions with their weird, spiky cactus growth, yawning canyons, arroyos and soaring mesas. Daily the sun would be a blazing, living presence, we would be free of schedules and publicity demands. Centres of civilization would be widely strung out. Once in Texas we would head for the Rio Grande on the Mexican frontier. It was my intention to remain as close to the outside edge of America as possible.

The shortest road distance from Miami on the Atlantic coast, to Los Angeles on the Pacific seaboard was 2,800 miles. I had no intention of following the shortest route (providing the Shell credit card procured me uninterrupted supplies of free petrol). In fairness to officials awaiting our return to New York, I promised Billie to send off a telegram to Rootes Motors in New York and to cable to London on the day we were supposed to roll into New York City. If money allowed, more telegrams would go off at intervals to keep Rootes informed of our progress.

"What if we have a hopeless breakdown?" inquired Billie, forebodingly.

"Don't meet trouble half-way, dear. If we do, no cables, of course."

Before we came to the start of the barren desert areas proper, a thousand miles had to be motored.

In relay we drove almost non-stop to New Orleans, among the few places where France lives on in what is now the United States. Once it was the only French metropolis in the New World. Here remnants of a bygone culture persist behind the weathered facades of old houses, in flowered patios and along narrow streets. Here we loitered and saw Negresses carrying bundles on their heads and housewives hauling up groceries in buckets to cast-iron balconies.

New Orleans' water-front streets bear names known the seven seas over for every kind of indulgence. In famous old restaurants, many of them completely unpretentious, Creole cuisine combines the delicacy of the French with the piquancy of the Spanish, but we could spare but little time to sample it.

Alaska-Minxy was running well. The credit card brought us petrol and oil without question. So we opened up across Louisiana, driving by the river roads and bayous. On every hand we saw colonnaded plantation homes of a serene and gracious yesterday. In these beautiful ante-bellum mansions, aristo-cractic landowners of the deep South achieved a social status unequalled in any other period of American history. Those were fabled days of sugar-cane-plantation empires, cotton kingdoms and Negro slaves. Each plantation had its iron bell to summon slaves from the fields at mealtime. It was then a noted custom to cast silver dollars in the molten iron to produce a more pleasing tone.

Billie hummed, "Way Down Upon The Swannee River . . ."

In this Old South, thoughts stir towards Negro spiritual songs with their nostalgia and pathos. But the days of slavery have gone forever. We observed Negroes with happy faces and well dressed. Many own big new cars. Certainly things have changed and still are changing even in the slow-moving ultra-con-servative deep South.

*　　　*　　　*

We skirted the Mexican border and that historic river, the

Rio Grande. This was Texas, then America's largest single state. Alaska-Minxy had begun her penetration into the vast stretching distances of the South-west regions. Here was territory very different from any other part of the U.S.A.; without definite boundaries, where barrenness and aridity are the principal overall characteristics. This was country enormous in scale, offering amazing contrasts of climate, geography and people. America's South-west includes superlatives such as the lowest land, the biggest canyon, the highest mountain, the driest deserts, the hottest valley, the richest mines and the oldest towns in the United States. This was America's real Indian country, too. Three of the main tribes on this purple-rimmed plateau-mesa land are the Hopi, Navajo and Zuni Indians.

After leaving San Antonio, we seemed to have entered a new realm of earth, sky, sunlight and colour. Nature produced the most glorious tone renderings over the strange, rugged mountains, basic red earth and painted plains. In the late afternoon a magic mantle of blue shadows, suffused with pinks and flecked blood-red, gave the wilderness setting a dramatic, and frequently changing enchantment.

We were motoring in what is known as the "Big Bend" area. Our last point of civilization was a place called Marathon, fifty miles to the north. Southward, the view was dominated by the rugged Sierra del Carmen, Fronteriza, and other spectacular mountain ranges in Old Mexico. We had decided to risk going a further eighty miles to the Chisos Mountain Basin at an elevation of 5,400 feet. Here cabins were available and we could get petrol and groceries. Limited dollar funds necessitated careful spending and no luxury.

Billie accelerated over the semi-arid trail hedged by scrub and various cacti. The spectacular Chisos Mountains ahead were now softening and dissolving into graded layers of purple mist. The sun had gone in a plunge of triumph after burnishing the mountains and sand with a reflection of molten fire. Dusk deepened, the glaring desert became a realm of stealthy shadows. On either side of the road, not far away, lonely rock outcrops revealed a greeny luminosity about their ridges.

We were winding through a gorge between high ridges when Billie yelled: "The windscreen, what is it?"

I saw running moisture on the driving side. I stared stupidly, not understanding.

Braking the car, we inhaled the air with startled amazement.

"Petrol!" we cried simultaneously.

Examination revealed that the petrol pipe connecting carburettor and filter had broken above the union. It was a damnable situation, I had no replacement among my spares, and an attempt to burr over the end of the old pipe was not successful. I dare not risk loss of fuel; the tank was not full.

A rising moon silhouetted gaunt rock formations. One in particular looked appropriate for the Rio Grande frontier. It was shaped like a bent old man with a big hat, and draped with a shawl silvered by the moonlight. All was eerie, quiet and at peace. It was obvious that we were stranded until daylight. The prospect of a night in this empty desert was not jarring to me, but to Billie the region was frightening. She thought it a god-forsaken wilderness. At first she was prey to a natural feeling of terror. I explained it was not a life or death mishap. This was not the dreaded, pitiless Sahara, a waterless, heat-racked plain, void of all vegetation and life.

"Don't worry, dear, " I told her, "we'll be on our way again tomorrow."

I pitched my small tent. Billie remained in Alaska-Minxy.

*   *   *

Dawn light was ousting the darkness when I first became conscious of noises not very far away; a series of muted squeals and grunts. I had no knowledge of the ecology of this "Big Bend" locale, it was obvious, however, that species of animal life must exist. In the early light, gripping my swordstick, I sneaked downwind between the cactus growth and rock clusters dotting the desert floor. I stopped in my tracks. Fifty yards away in a small ravine was a small pool.

There were predators in the form of ten wild pigs at this

water hole. They were peccaries, otherwise known as javelinas; they possessed razor-sharp tusks and hoofs capable of inflicting deep wounds. I stopped rigid. Minutes ticked by. I watched these ferocious beasts and listened to the slurp of water as they drank greedily. I dared not move.

Then I spotted something else. At first it was no more than a slight movement behind a screen of cactus.

I gripped my swordstick and unlocked the blade, I wished I had a rifle. Wild pig are dangerous, but I sensed that the movement I had detected had been made by some much larger animal. Presently the creature moved quickly yet stealthily from the clump of cactus to another. The glimpse I got suggested a big and powerful jaguar. The wild pigs now sensed that danger lurked close by. Off they stampeded, screaming in shrill rage, or fear. A flashing, feline body pursued them. With relief I moved back toward the car.

I found Billie combing her hair.

"Where have you been?" she asked, "and what was that funny noise I heard just now?"

I laughed and kissed her good-morning.

"We've just missed some bacon for breakfast," I answered, "the squealing you heard came from nice little pigs."

"Pigs!" she exclaimed in surprise. "There must be a farm around her."

"Perhaps dear, maybe a zoo, too."

*   *   *

It was several hours later that help came to us in the person of a young Federal ranger. His mount was a Chevrolet car, not a horse. At his home near Panther Junction, a few miles away, while repairs were made to our defective petrol line, I asked him about the large cat-like mammal I had seen near the water hole.

"Say fellah," I was told in a Southern drawl, "that critture was a mountain lion."

I learned that black bear also were present in the Chisos ranges. We were told quite a lot by the helpful Texan. The territory we were now in, the Big Bend, contained upwards of 700,000 acres of land in the National Park System for conserving the scenic, scientific and historic heritage of the United States. Early Spanish conquistadores and missionaries had once been active in the Big Bend where today the Rio Grande forms the boundary between America and Mexico. The Spaniards recorded that the Apache Indians were living there when they arrived. The Comanches, famous fighting Indians of the Great Plains, also travelled through the Big Bend on forays as far south as central Mexico.

*   *   *

"Stop humming 'Deep in the Heart of Texas'," scolded Billie, laughingly, "because this is New Mexico".

We were now covering the thousand miles which separated the Big Bend in Texas on the Rio Grande from the Grand Canyon astride the Colorado River in Arizona. We travelled in a vast, arid region; it was uncomfortably hot. Temperatures frequently soared above 110° F. in the summer months. Cactus-covered desert wastelands made it hard to believe we were still on the North American Continent. The outlook in some areas had a lunar quality; dust-devil plains, ancient and weird rock formations, scorched red-canyons, and overall a dazzling whiteness.

We kept Alaska-Minxy moving fast, hour after hour; in this sparsely-inhabited region of natural wonders the old Spanish influence was strong; in fact, three cultures existed side by side: the Indian, the Spanish-American and the Anglo-American. Under a limitless blue sky and blazing sun we traversed what was once part of the Spanish colonial empire. Archæology reveals that preceding the arrival of the conquistadores, mankind inhabited what is now Arizona as early as 20,000 years ago. For countless centuries this land was the hunting grounds of the Indian, particularly the warlike Apaches, of whom there are still about 50,000. We called a halt at a picturesque adobe village and were given to understand it had been continuously occupied by Indians for over 900 years. I was amused to learn that even today among Apache Indians an ancient and inflexible law operates. It is taboo for an Apache male upon marriage ever again to speak or even to look upon his mother-in-law.

"Pretty smart rules," I told Billie, "at least they do try to preserve peace inside their own ranks by counteracting a number-one source of disharmony."

Rather than face another day of desert heat and glare, we agreed to continue driving and take advantage of the cool night air. If Alaska-Minxy was kept rolling, we calculated we should arrive at the Grand Canyon about noon on the morrow.

At a desert service station we filled our tanks and containers. A grizzled attendant looked intently at Billie as though considering something.

"Say! You ain't gonna drive the desert tonight are you ma'am?" he asked at length.

"Yes we are," was the reply, "we're heading north to the Grand Canyon."

The old man studied me. His face creased into what was meant for a slight smile.

"It ain't no good, mister, drivin' wimmin through that desert at nighttime. Guess I've seen plenty of 'em hollerin' and bawlin'."

"What do you mean?" I asked.

"Wimmin just get scarey, then screamy, then full o' hysterics by them big Saguaro cacti." He spat before continuing: "After a few hours of moonlit drivin', them cacti sorta' come alive, real spooky like." He spat, then went on: "They start movin', walkin' and grabbin'."

"Grabbing?" I queried. "How? What?"

"No kiddin' mister," his speech was solemn. "Them big limbs on the Saguaro grow out live, evil arms. You'd sure swear they was tryin' to grab you off the road; real deceivers, they are."

"Well, Billie," I asked hesitatingly, "do you want to go on?"

"Of course!" Her tone was mildly irritated.

"Okay, mister," grunted the gnarled attendant, "lots of wimmin' folk go nutty lookin' at them big cacti in the

Above: From the sun-scorched region of Los Angeles and the "warm" greeting of John Panks, who had imagined us safely in New York with his precious Minx, we came to the fair city of San Francisco and the Golden Gate Bridge. Once across the bridge (4,200 feet long and having the longest single span in the world) we reached the avenue that is lined for more than 100 miles by those oldest of living things, redwood trees. We passed one great California redwood giant even bigger than the Chandelier Tree, pictured on the right, through which we drove the car. Then we raced back again to Vancouver and to our parting from the Minx.

Left: As he gave me a whisky Admiral Dufek said: "Enjoy it; then forget the stuff ever existed until you return. Any kind of alcoholic stimulant is forbidden except by order of a doctor to men of "Deep Freeze" in Antarctica.

Below: Arneb and one of the ice-breakers cleaving through pack ice near Queen Victoria Land.

moonlight, it's a phenomenon, and don't say I didn't warn you."

We motored reasonably fast into a dramatic blood-red sunset. All was quiet; here was room for thoughts and vision. The dusk deepened and the stars hung low like brilliant prisms. The limitless plains were bathed in a majestic sheen of moonlight glory. Long limbed Saguaro (Sah-war-oh) or Giant Cactus (*Cereus giganteus*) reared everywhere in stark, eerie silhouettes. These cacti reached to a height of from 40 to 50 feet. They had lived on that desert from 150 to 200 years.

Billie had been driving for perhaps a couple of hours when she awakened me. The car was stationary.

"What's the trouble, dear?"

She replied in an unsteady voice.

"That old garage man was right. It's becoming unendurable. Those terrible cacti defile everything." With that she hid her face in her hands and cried. "Richard, it's horrible," she added, "they seem to move and threaten."

I attempted to laugh at what I knew was ridiculous, and to reassure my fiancée. The scene outside, however, was utterly unbelievable. It made one feel stunned. Patches of silvered sand looked for all the world like frozen sheets of water. Giant cacti were near and remote, a thousand different grim and threatening shapes. In combination, I had to admit they did give one the creeps.

"O.K. Billie, I'll drive, put your head down and try and sleep."

I pressed on, sceptically, but after a time those damned Saguaro cacti made me restless. Some of the great arms drooped forebodingly. Others were raised rigidly towards heaven, clutching helplessly at emptiness in a pose of primeval pleading. On that arid desert the atmosphere of melancholy was thick and heavy. Later, when the sinister outlines and weird shapes appeared to come to life, waving their arms and swinging alongside, I cut the motor.

"Bloody desert devils and moonlight madness," I told myself. I wasn't risking being mesmerized and perhaps slamming the car into one of them.

Dawn split the heavens like a relieving angel.

"Ah, joy," murmured Billie gratefully, "what a beautiful experience a dawn can be."

*   *   *

We strolled a few yards. Suddenly before us yawned an immeasurable abyss. This was the earth's mightiest gash. Transfixed, we gazed out over a gigantic spectacle, it was afire with tints and glows; a vari-coloured miracle. Above this ultimate of silent grandeur and beauty lay the glaring desert unrelieved by shadow.

The first sight of the Grand Canyon benumbs heart, mind and brain. It bursts upon one's awed imagination like a wonderful truth; it represents a billion new and unimaginable ideas. Spectacular rock sculpture is there and a serene harmony. The mysterious moods of its colours and rays are like soft and delicate thoughts. It takes a little time for the first sight of the Grand Canyon to secure a foothold in reality.

Billie paled and trembled, she was deeply stirred. I felt lightheaded and could only gasp. Something happens to puny mortals when they gaze down for a full mile into the earth over a magnificent vista of painted rocks. It is a view exquisite and breathtaking. The Grand Canyon offers strange spiritual reward to all those who stand on its rims. It stirs piety, ecstasy, wonder and meekness. It is nature's story of creation, it seems also to purvey a glorious spirit which ennobles and chastens thought. It provides a placid mental quiet that ordinarily never emerges from the whirl of our rushing, matter-of-fact existence.

Far, far away below, like snakey grey twine, roars the Colorado River, a 300-foot stream of tremendous power. God and the Colorado created the Grand Canyon. The rock walls that bound this river are a tremendous cross-section of the earth's crust. The longer one peers down, down, down into the colossal abyss and across the sweeping panorama of whole ranges of mountains buried in its depths, the greater grows a deepening sense of the infinite.

A little boy in cowboy suit interrupted our gaze and reverie.

"Golly, what a gulley," he shouted. His mother didn't reply; she, like ourselves, was hushed into reverence.

This titanic gash in the earth's face is 217 miles long, 8 to 10 miles wide and more than a mile deep. It was first discovered by Spaniards in the year 1540. It will always remain one of the world's greatest wonders. The story of its origin is as simple as any that Nature offers. Water has been the principal fashioning agent. Over endless aeons the water has worn away the surface of the land. Identical erosion can be seen in the most ordinary gulley anywhere, but here is on a vaster scale alike in size and time. Even yet the story is by no means finished.

*   *   *

The next big leg of our adventure was towards Los Angeles on the Pacific, via San Diego, a run of 750 miles. Alaska-Minxy had stood up to the prodigious drive better than our most sanguine expectations. She showed no disposition to falter or fail. Billie, too, had held her own in spite of exhausting heat and long sessions at the wheel.

We were in the Yuma Desert near the Californian/Arizona border. Not far from the Gila River we called a halt. While Billie was preparing a meal, I wandered off to fill a water container to top up the radiator. Evaporation in these badlands was considerable. I was moving from the water hole when I spotted a pulsating body in a rock pile. It was the largest, most sickening, pop-eyed toad I've ever seen and I'd certainly observed some outsize horrors of that sort in the Belgian Congo. It was all of nine inches long, an enormous, repulsive amphibian. I examined it. Dropped a stone on it. Prodded it. The preposterous creature bumped off to the pool, plopped into the water and created a miniature tidal wave. At a safe distance, half-submerged, the foul thing glowered at me with protruding, bulbous eyes.

I was in for a far greater shock on return to the car. Unknowingly, we had chosen a very disturbing area in which to eat our lunch. It was a typical desert environment, uninhabited and intensely hot. All around were various communities of cactus, including the "green stick", one of the beautiful trees of desert and foothill regions. When it blooms it is a blaze of shimmering yellow-gold.

Billie was some yards away, moving with dainty steps among the various plant life and certainly oblivious of lethal snake life.

I picked up my camera and moved towards her. A few pictures of my fiancée among the giant dagger cacti and other growths would be interesting for the record. I paused to focus. Unexpectedly, Billie froze in a motionless stance.

"What's wrong?" I asked, puzzled and straightening up.

Her face showed petrified horror. She was erect, silent, unmoving. I moved toward her. I heard a quick, vibrating rattle; I saw a two-and-a-half-foot, diamond-backed rattlesnake. Its dreadful head was raised in striking position eighteen inches from Billie's leg.

The rattle seemed to rise and reverberate.

I moved closer, trembling. Seconds slipped by with agonizing slowness. I swung the heavy Rolleiflex camera by the carrying strap. My aim was true. The venomous reptile carrying its dreaded noise apparatus in its tail received a rattling good clout on the head. That cracked the crisis.

Billie found her voice.

"Dear God," she murmured, "I was so frightened. My limbs were paralysed."

"No more deserts, dear," I promised. "Tomorrow we'll be safe in Hollywood and civilization."

*   *   *

We hastened from the blazing desert to the delightful Santa Monica shoreline. Again, Alaska-Minxy had crossed a great continent from coast to coast. We gazed over the Pacific Ocean in the morning sun. Only 1,500 miles remained to complete our circuit of all the 48 states of the Union. We were in Southern California: in Hollywood, the centre of the world of films. We were sun-scorched and tired and resolved to rest for a few

days. We decided to drop in on Rootes Motors, Los Angeles, and
face the worst, or the best.

*　　　*　　　*

"May I see your manager?"
"What name, please?" asked the receptionist.
"Richard Pape."
Eyebrows elevated.
"Do take a seat," she said, and swiftly departed.
The door opened. Out strode Mr John Panks. I thought I was
seeing a desert mirage. Momentarily I felt powerless. It was a
shock. His appearance seemed theatrical. The great mogul of
Rootes Motors, America, had flown in from New York. I'll
never know whether he came to await our arrival, or to attend
a premiere at Sid Grauman's Chinese Theatre.

For some moments we observed each other curiously,
suspiciously.

"Mr. Pape," his tone was polite, "do you realize this is Los
Angeles on the west coast, not New York in the east. Why
such a mistake in navigation?"

I wasn't going to implore forgiveness from Mr. Panks.

"Fancy now," I retorted with a touch of stiff-necked pride,
"you must pardon me. All my awful life I've had a habit of
swopping east for west and north for south."

Mr. Panks realized that there was little profit in probing past
happenings. Of course many people were thrilled at Alaska-
Minxy's latest performance. Mr. Panks couldn't very well blame
us for adding materially to profitable publicity. So he forgave
us.

*　　　*　　　*

In the sunshine of California we set out for San Francisco,
the city of all nations, the "Paris of the West", an impressive,
shining-white metropolis. It is built on fourteen hills and
washed on three sides by the sea. We sped over the Golden
Gate Bridge to the Redwood Highway, which for more than
a hundred miles is bordered by centuries-old trees. The red-

woods, oldest of all living things, grow to great size, many exceeding 300 feet in height, and 20 feet in diameter. We passed the world's tallest tree, a giant redwood towering 364 feet by 47 feet in circumference. Alaska-Minxy also passed through the "Drive-Through-Tree", reputed to be 3,500 years old.

We flashed out of Northern California into the State of Oregon, next into the State of Washington. This was for us to be the last of the 48. Soon we had 150 miles to go, then 100, 50. As we neared the American/Canadian border, the 10,750-foot-high snow-capped cone of Mount Baker on the U.S.A. side was the last American monument of nature that we saw, a nice and natural farewell.

*　　　*　　　*

It was in the gloaming that we crossed into the Dominion of Canada on the evening of 22 November, 1957. Spanning the frontier zone was a majestic white stone structure, vaster I think than London's Marble Arch. This was the "Peace Arch". It carried an inscription in foot high letters: "Children Of A Common Mother: May These Gates Never Be Closed." It was paid for by the children of both nations; it arose in meaning and beauty for their cents and dimes. It is symbolic of the freedom and friendliness between the two great nations on the great American Continent.

"Oh, that all the world's frontiers were the same as this," whispered Billie reflectively. Slowly she uttered the words of Benjamin Franklin which she had learned by heart during the American drive:

> God grant that not only the love of liberty, but a thorough knowledge of the rights of man, may pervade all the nations of the earth, so that a philosopher may set his foot anywhere on its surface, and say, "This is my country".

*　　　*　　　*

We were welcomed back by Ian Garrad and Dick Williams of Rootes Motors.

"Nice work," laughed Ian.

It was all over! Our tripmeter revealed 11,707 miles

traversed. An hour later indomitable Alaska-Minxy was handed over. She was out of our lives forever. It was a sad parting. How dearly we had grown to love an inanimate little motor car. Billie, affectionate, almost reverently pressed her mouth against the windscreen and left lipstick imprints. There were genuine signs of tears in her eyes when she murmured: "Goodbye Minxy, darling, we're going to miss you dreadfully." I gave the grand little car an affectionate slap, turned and walked into the Vancouver Hotel. The best thing I could think of in the circumstances was to buy a bottle of champagne and toast my fiancée-co-driver and Alaska-Minxy. It had been a great adventure-drive, now I had to turn my thoughts towards settling down.

Rootes Motors issued an official release. It stated:

Complete Circuit of the forty-eight States. Back in Vancouver the full mileage was checked . . . 11,707 miles in a total of 39 days. Actual driving time amounted to 20 days—or 585 miles a day—at an average speed of 35 miles an hour.

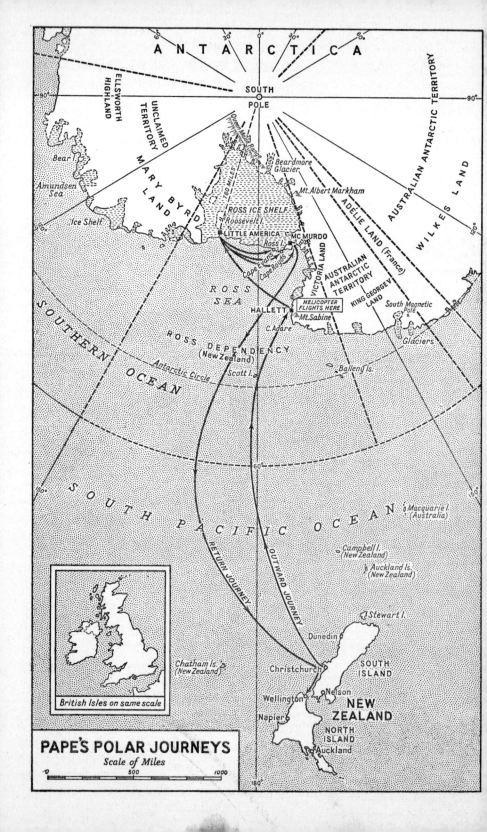

PAPE'S POLAR JOURNEYS

Scale of Miles

Chapter Thirteen

Antarctica

Let us probe the silent places,
  Let us seek what luck betide us;
Let us journey to a lonely land I know.
  There's a whisper on the night wind,
There's a star agleam to guide us,
  And the wind is calling, calling, let us go.

Robert W. Service.

ROM my window, I soberly contemplated swirling snow-flakes. This was Britain, I was back in the provincial calm of Norwich. I thought of Billie and wondered where she might be in the Pacific. It was hard to believe that a bare two weeks had passed since we had driven Alaska-Minxy through sunny California.

With the American drive finished, Billie and I had taken separate routes. Billie had sailed for New Zealand and home on the *Oronsay*; I had flown via the North Pole route to London. I had promised my fiancée to write frequently, and to head as soon as possible for her country, where we would marry. Throughout my motoring adventures on the North American Continent, I had perforce ignored my business affairs in England. Quick return had been imperative.

Immediately I had cleared up my business issues, I sailed for New Zealand, arriving on 12 August, 1958. Our wedding date was fixed for 23 August. I had given a lot of thought to the future, and had resolved to be a worthy stay-at-home husband. I imagined that my consuming passion to wander from trodden paths had burned itself out. In Wellington, however, despite my resolution, the flame began to flicker.

We were at a cocktail party. Fred Butcher, a friend of Billie's family, who was attached to the American Embassy staff in

PA6*

Wellington, remarked: "I'm showing a 'Deep Freeze' film at my place, Thursday. You and Billie must come along."

"Deep Freeze?" I did not know what he meant.

Lois, Fred's charming American wife came to my rescue: "It's about Rear Admiral Dufek landing at the South Pole. It's so exciting and adventurous, you'll be thrilled by it, Richard."

Fred explained that the name "Deep Freeze" was the operational designation applied to America's International Geophysical Year role in Antarctica.

"Who is the Admiral chap?" I asked.

"Rear Admiral Dufek," I was told, "is the first man after Scott in 1912 to set foot on the South Pole. He landed there to survey a site for setting up a scientific station."

"The South Pole station where Fuchs and Hillary joined hands?" I asked

"Exactly."

"We'd love to see this 'Deep Freeze' movie," I accepted, "but honestly, I've never been enthralled by geography's great unknown. Isn't it better left alone? I must admit that Antarctica has a great historical value, I confess it has been the scene of great human exploits, but. . . ."

"Yes," inquired Fred, "but . . .?"

"That was in the great pioneering yesterday of raw, magnificent courage, but today is different: with technical advance exploration has become a cold-blooded and unexciting scientific operation. Ten nations and forty-four IGY stations are in Antarctica. The place is full of starry-eyed scientists who make good Press stories."

A small, keen-eyed American, also from the Embassy, had been listening. Now he joined in: "There is much in the Antarctic to be seen, studied and explained, and explorer-scientists will be going south for a long time to come."

I listened attentively.

"The ice-wilderness," he went on, "the so-called last continent, is rapidly assuming paramount importance where political and strategic ambitions are concerned."

"What does he mean?" I murmured.

Fred grinned. "Well," he concluded, "I would say that our 'Deep Freeze' operation is a combination of strategy, science and adventure, and the Free World should have no complaints."

The "Deep Freeze" colour film was a remarkable presentation.

The film showed drama and dangerous adventure; it was vivid, vital, yet without exaggeration. It was a private film which belonged to Admiral Dufek, secretly I wished it had been shown on every television circuit in the world. Instinctively one flinched from the effects of frostbite on raw flesh; similarly one glowed at the warmth of human comradeship on a freezing plateau, where the thermometer registered 40° F. below zero.

The exploits by ordinary men of Operation "Deep Freeze" in the face of the extraordinary natural forces on the world's most extraordinary continent excited me. We watched men struggling in pitiless temperatures to erect huts at the South Pole itself. "Deep Freeze" was as modern as the hour and backed by the last word in American technological development, a great deal of cash and some very thorough planning. Neither the heroic Scott nor the indomitable Amundsen could in their wildest dreams have imagined the like of what was taking place on their beloved white continent.

In some way the film I saw, dispelled my previous aversion to and misconceptions about Antarctica. The white continent aroused my imagination and stirred my heart.

I thanked Fred Butcher for a magnificent show.

Then I tackled Billie. I wanted to write about "Deep Freeze": would she let me make a trip south?

"Aren't you the limit!" said she. "We are to be married in two days and you want to be 'Poles Apart' almost before the ceremony is over!"

"Poles Apart," I muttered, "what a fine title for a book."

Billie, too, came to like the idea: in the end she agreed to let me go.

* * *

After marriage, while Billie and I searched New Zealand's far north for a spot where we could settle awhile and I could write, I tried to get American approval for my inclusion as a member of Operation "Deep Freeze IV (1958-9)". Our home hunting prospered. We found Russell. It is a small community in the enchanting Bay of Islands. The fates were being propitious, I had no idea then that the beautiful Bay of Islands whispered of past ties with the white continent.

Our home, high on a hill, commanded a superb view of a wide expanse of dark blue ocean. In the distance, rolling hills of light green grazed the sky. This was the Bay of Islands, discovered by Captain Cook and named by him in 1769. Frequently, from my writing room, I tried to envisage Cook's 400-ton Navy ship, the *Endeavour*, anchored there. I was prompted to think across 12,000 miles to a quaint Yorkshire township called Marton, the birthplace of Captain Cook. I, too, had been born nearby, and in my youth had played "Cowboys and Indians" in the fields near Marton.

The Bay of Islands (termed the cradle of New Zealand history) is true Maori country. I formed friendships with many of these good-humoured, self-reliant people : one particularly interesting character was Mateka, an old and picturesque Maori, who held forth with a quaint, half-humorous anger about the wealth of the traditions, the myths and legends, so inseparably a part of his race, and now being disregarded and even ignored.

Casually, one day I mentioned Antarctica. The result surprised me.

"For centuries," said Mateka, "my ancestors have recounted curious stories of a white-faced, cruel-hearted land far to the south. Before your Captain Cook discovered our Bay of Islands my Polynesian forbears found mountain graveyards of ice. Both my father and my grandfather told me many legends of what must surely have been Antarctica."

I began to investigate. I learned that the Maoris did indeed possess many legends of a vast white land with great ribbed peaks far to the south. Yet to me it seemed unbelievable that the original natives of New Zealand, in frail canoes, had penetrated 2,500 miles across freezing, unknown seas.

* * *

Billie appeared before the open window, blotting out the central view of the bay. I was handed a cablegram.

"Intuition tells me," she said, "that here are orders for Antarctica." In the same breath, "Now I must darn those wretchedly heavy socks you refuse to throw away."

I ripped the envelope. Billie's foresight wasn't phoney.

* * *

Permission had been given to me to join the "Deep Freeze" Operation. I was assigned to the USS *Arneb*, an armed attack vessel attached to the Amphibious Force of the United States Atlantic Fleet. The *Arneb* was a ship with character. In the Second World War she had seen a lot of scraps, she'd had a place in the invasion of Okinawa. After the war and metal surgery, and to cool off, she crossed the Arctic and Antarctic Circles. She re-crossed them to make sure she had regained her composure, and the U.S. Navy assigned her to Operation "Deep Freeze" in 1956. On one occasion, polar ice gripped her like a vice and tried to crack her ribs, but *Arneb* had survived. Later, when she was locked in frozen ocean, a big iceberg bore down on her. "Prepare to abandon ship," was the order. But the iceberg nosed past the stern, a few feet away. *Arneb*'s current mission was to carry men and equipment to scientific stations built in Antarctica for the International Geophysical Year. A further function was that of tracking cosmic rays.

* * *

The Bay of Islands was behind me for quite some time to come. Billie would remain with her parents until my return. As the plane flew southward toward Christchurch, headquarters in New Zealand of America's "Deep Freeze" operation, I reflected with certain nervousness on my impending interview with Rear Admiral George Dufek. For years I had been away from military discipline, now I was voluntarily submitting to it again. I felt honoured, but experienced an awkward shyness;

rather akin to being a boy at a new school. Its headmaster, the man I was going to see, was the Commander of the American Naval Support Force, Antarctica.

* * *

Admiral Dufek was born in Rockford, Illinois, in 1903, and graduated from the U.S. Naval Academy in 1925, becoming one of the few officers to qualify for command of air, surface and sub-surface units. He had served in battleships, submarines, cruisers, aircraft-carriers and destroyers. During the war he was Senior Naval Aviator in the Mediterranean, assisting in planning the invasion of Salerno and Southern France. He is credited with sinking the last German submarine of the war. In London, for a spell, his duties involved mission studies and exchange of information of assistance to the Allies. He had commanded Naval air stations in Japan; during the Korean War he had been in command of the aircraft-carrier *Antietam*.

The Admiral had been navigator to the famed polar explorer, Rear Admiral Richard E. Byrd, and had made the first flight over the Thurston Peninsula in the Bellingshausen Sea. He was also the first man since Britain's immortal Captain Scott to place his feet at the South Pole. By direction of President Eisenhower, in 1957, Rear Admiral Dufek was designated U.S.A. Antarctic Projects Officer and Senior U.S.A. adviser on political, scientific, and legislative activities affecting America's prodigious Antarctic programme and its future development.

Here was a person who had won many honours and decorations around the globe, and was acknowledged as one of the world's top-flight cold-weather experts. Dufek was a man whose leadership was active and very real. When in 1946, he had been responsible for the rescue of the crew of a plane that crashed on the Thurston Peninsula it had spurred Admiral Byrd to say: "Captain Dufek's rescue of the six survivors is in many ways unequalled in all the history of polar rescues."

* * *

The interview was at Admiral Dufek's home. From the moment I shook hands, sharp, steady eyes focused on me.

"Sit down, Pape."

"Thank you, sir."

"If you care to smoke, Pape, smoke."

Admiral Dufek was tallish, he had well-formed shoulders and a good head of hair, wavy and white.

I looked into a bronzed face; it was strong and interesting. The tan was intriguing. It suggested seasoned oak and seemed to have been born of the sting of frozen snow, the lash of the winds at sea, and to have grown in air scorched under a blazing sun. I was before a man hardened to life and climates.

"Had your medicals?" I was asked. "You have the certificates, of course?"

"Yes, sir."

"Good! You will report to Commander Merle McBain at Headquarters tomorrow, 9 a.m. You will thereafter report to Captain Schwaner, commanding *Arneb*, berthed at Lyttelton. You will sail for Cape Adare and Hallett Station in Victoria Land."

"Yes, sir."

The Admiral rose and strode to the window of his drawing room. He spoke without turning.

"Like a drink, Pape?"

"I would, sir."

"What?"

"A whisky, sir."

It was poured and I was handed a tumbler. The Admiral said: "Enjoy it; then forget the stuff ever existed until you return. Any kind of alcoholic stimulant is forbidden in Antarctica. A man's mind must always be as crystal clear as the atmosphere. Only the medical officer is entitled to prescribe stimulant. If you fall in the sea, survival time is eight minutes."

"I understand, sir."

"Good!" His eyes searched my face. "You like life, Pape?"

I stared back and felt a trifle uneasy.

"Very much, sir."

"Right! Then remember that taking chances in the Antarctic

is foolhardy." He paused, sipped his own drink, and continued. "For instance, crevasses in shelf and land-ice are notoriously treacherous. They lie under a thin bridge of blown snow, concealed from the most experienced eye but ready to drop men and vehicles hundreds of feet into oblivion."

The Admiral continued: "You have done a lot of flying?"

"Yes I have, sir."

"I am making a long-range helicopter available to you. I want you to visit Scott's base, also Shackleton's hut. You must! These men spot-lighted Antarctica. They give it a soul, purpose and idealism."

The Admiral concluded: "I have invited Captain Schwaner, Commander of the *Arneb*, also his second, Commander Roohan, to lunch. Will you join us?"

"I would be honoured."

Above: The ice-breaker *Northwind*: the rounded forepart of the hull enables her to ride over ice instead of being gripped by it. By pumping water from one to another of a series of port and starboard tanks the vessel can be rocked to help break a passage. Progress, though sure, is slow.

Right: With my cameras before the helicopter in which I flew. Each ice-breaker had two of these machines which were invaluable both for spotting "leads" (stretches of relatively open water amid pack ice) and for rescue operations when accident or weather stranded men in inaccessible places.

Arneb anchored to sea ice. There was no need to drop an anchor to the sea bed; it was much simpler to dig a shallow hole in the ice and to drop in a sleeper with the cable attached. The sleeper froze to the ice instantly, then there was no chance at all that the anchoring would drag.

Our unusual behaviour astonished—and sometimes annoyed—the residents in Antarctica. On the right a crab-eating seal surveys our unloading. To do this expeditiously we loaded our stores into a trailer (*below*) which had been lowered into a landing craft of the kind that made possible the famous landings on the Normandy beaches in the Second World War. We ran this vessel on to the ice. Then a Sno-cat from the camp hitched a cable to the trailer and towed the whole load up to the storehouse.

Right: This cross overlooking Mc-Murdo Sound from Observation Hill is of Australian jarrah wood and nine feet high. It commemorates those great and gallant adventurers, Captain Scott and his companions who died on their return march from the South Pole in March, 1912. Their stirring epitaph from Tennyson's "Ulysses" may yet provide both a reminder and an inspiration for adventurous spirits of generations to come:
"TO STRIVE, TO SEEK, TO FIND, AND NOT TO YIELD".

Below: The American encampment at McMurdo Sound, the gateway to the great Beardmore Glacier.

Chapter Fourteen

To the Southern Continent

The ice was here, the ice was there,
  The ice was all around;
It cracked and growled, and roared and howled,
  Like noises in a swound.

Coleridge.

THE 13,950 tons of dignified grey *Arneb* slid clear of the wharf. It was 8.30 a.m.—a bright and cheerful morning. the sky was blue; the air warm. A crowd of young women in colourful dresses waved to American sailors at the stern rails. The port of Lyttelton has been the point of departure for famous polar expeditions. During the first half of this century, great leaders like Scott, Shackleton, Byrd and Mawson all had affectionate ties with and indebtedness to Lyttelton and New Zealand. Today it is no different, there is a powerful flow of mutual goodwill between Kiwis and Americans.

We were saying goodbye to scenic softness, colour, trees, green growth and easy orthodox civilization. Soon we would come to stark solitudes as we cut into the Antarctic Circle and beyond. *Arneb* swung proudly for the open sea.

The lofty hills in the background quickly lost their sharpness of outline and freshness of colour. This high ground behind the harbour was the last we were to see for a very long time of the sort of land I knew. We were heading for a white wilderness which can test Man's combative and creative prowess to the utmost.

*　　*　　*

We throbbed southward, the latitudes fell rearward. *Arneb* steamed across the roaring forties, through the furious fifties, and plunged resolutely into the shrieking sixties. Thrusting

Pole-ward in these high, cold latitudes towards the frigid seventies stirred a consciousness of having entered what amounted almost to a different universe. The boisterous, pewter-coloured sea and the sombre, lifeless sky possessed an overpowering sense of loneliness.

Here the ship was utterly alone and faced stupendous forces. The southern oceans are the most storm-racked in the world; weather changes with notorious suddenness. It would appear that the vilest demons of wind, sea and ice haunt these empty spaces. Here they can cavort in frenzy and arouse the elements into titanic fury. En route to the pack-ice we were fortunate not to encounter any of their worst outbursts. *Arneb* was a trusted fighter, and the regular creak and groan of her structure, the scrape of metal on metal, quickly lost its strangeness and became rather a soothing assurance that all was going well.

*   *   *

Meteorologists are making intensive study of the ice-capped continent and its environs. It is recognized as being the womb where the world's most monstrous weather and mysterious celestial phenomena are born. The weather is thrown outwards and upwards about the globe as far as the Equator, and it is said beyond. If man is to master the weather to his own profit he must learn the secrets of the refrigerator of the great white south.

I shall not forget the last time I saw the stars of the heavens before crossing the Antarctic Circle into brilliant summer daylight which lasted round the clock. The stars, it seemed, were aware of the short time left, and, in a spate of reckless glory thrust themselves unusually close and bright. Imagination led me to believe that a vast artificial ceiling of vibrant black had been lowered from above. This spectacular low roof might have been punctured at random with millions of differently-sized holes: from behind, lamps of unimaginable brilliance appeared to reflect the flash and fire of rarest diamonds. Never have I observed so low a canopy of stars, or such sparkling animation.

178

I wished to reach out, seize fistfuls and hurl them into the brooding ocean to dispel an escorting glow of eerie phosphorescence.

*   *   *

Four of us were drinking coffee. Suddenly I sneezed.

"Excuse," I said, "my pipe."

The M.O. waved a hand towards me: "If it's a cold in the head," he said, "get rid of it. I'm not transporting germs."

Jimmy laughed: "Bugs haven't got a show down there, anyway. If they do sneak into the seventh continent, they go to the wall, quick."

Captain Schwaner asked: "What are the facts about germs, Morris?"

"Well, sir," said the doctor, "I'm safe in saying that Antarctica is free of bugs, bacteria, mould spores and fermentation. There's no moisture except in frozen form, and metal does not rust; wood does not rot, either."

"What about food?" inquired the Captain.

"Food and materials are preserved indefinitely, sir."

"That's right," said Jimmy, "a bunch of our 'Deep Freeze' boys tested in 1957 some of the food that Captain Scott had brought to Hut Point in 1901, and it was as good as the day it was produced."

"Quite true," confirmed the M.O., "and the men of the British Falkland Islands Dependencies Party found a lot of cached food left by the Swedish explorer, Nordenskjold which provided satisfactory meals after forty-five years."

"One thing everybody is certain about," chuckled Jimmy Roohan, "it's damned cold down there. Do you know Richard, the coldest temperature ever recorded was minus 109.5° F. at the USSR Sovietskaya Base in the interior at 12,139 feet, in April, 1958. Prior to that, the coldest recording was minus 102.1° F. at the U.S. South Pole Station, in September, 1957."

"But that was deep in the heart of Antarctica in winter. What about summer?"

Jimmy was a walking encyclopædia on cold facts about Antarctica.

"During Antarctic summer, that's from December to March, temperatures rarely go above freezing even along the coast. Inland, on the ice-cap, they almost never go that high."

I was suitably impressed.

*　　　*　　　*

Davis, my Negro steward, rapped on the cabin door.

"Boss," he said laconically, "there sure is a big berg bearing down on the starboard quarter."

This, our first iceberg, encountered in latitude 65.38 S, was massive and gleaming. We were entering the iceberg-infested regions, a great wilderness of ocean where these weathered monsters roamed. The one ahead was the van of an unforgettable parade. I was reminded of a stupendous flat-topped wedding cake over a quarter of a mile long. Ice precipices rose sheer to 130 feet above the surface of the sea. A frightening thought was that eight-ninths of this giant tabular berg lay unseen under water.

A high, biting wind whined through *Arneb*'s superstructure. It had ripped the cloud wrack into a weird, shredded formation, making a most imposing background. In a small, blue pool of sky, a shining sun glorified our first berg with ten thousand glints and sparkles. While setting up the camera tripod, my hands were soon numbed; I had yet to learn how to operate my movie equipment while wearing gloves. Captain Schwaner nosed the ship as close to the berg as he dared. The lustrous blue glints from the ice were breathtaking. As this great, glistening mass silently loomed abreast, we seemed for a few moments to have ceased to move. The wind lessened, for we were in the lee of the floating ice mountain, but the coldness of the air increased noticeably. As ship and iceberg crossed paths one could actually feel the awful chill of its dangerous presence. It was dying on its journey northward; the pounding of a ruthless ocean and the influence of warmer temperature would crumble this ice marvel into the water from which it had been created.

An officer on watch, whose face was completely hidden by a black cloth mask in which were only three small apertures, strode to my side. These face coverings were necessary protection from the lash of the wind.

"A nice ice-cube," he yelled. "You'll see so many of them that in the end you won't cross the deck to look at one."

Four hours later, the radar screen showed thirty bergs in an area of fifty square miles.

That evening I said to Jimmy : "The berg I saw today was one of the grandest sights I've ever seen."

He replied genially, "A goodly spectacle for a lil 'un." He then explained that these great square-shaped icebergs, mostly with tops as flat as a kitchen table, were sloughed from ice-shelves surrounding Antarctica.

"In November, 1956," he said, "one of these tabular bergs was sighted by a 'Deep Freeze' icebreaker between New Zealand and Antarctica. Boy, did it rock 'em !"

"Why ?" I asked.

"That berg was 208 miles long by 60 miles wide. If you work it out, that's approximately the size of the State of Connecticut."

Captain Schwaner said thoughtfully : "It's frightening to think of the risks early sailing ships took. No radar or modern aids, and those hard bergs creeping out of mists like crushing ghosts !"

Entering the frigid 70s, I saw the most spectacular berg I am ever likely to see. Someone christened it "Disneyland". It was a weathered veteran, and the elements had sculptured it from base to summit. It was pitted and eroded, yet still a towering mass of strength, twice the size of Trafalgar Square. In the wan glow of a greenish-haloed sun, it shone ghostlike. As we drew closer, I could scarcely believe my eyes, it was a riot of carved shapes. Weather had chiselled cathedral spires, pinnacles, terraces, grottoes, canyon walls and a huge, horse-like head. The range of delicate blue tones was absolutely magnificent, rivalling the most exquisite coloured glass imaginable. Ice walls were seamed with fissures, and along the base, caverns, into which waves rushed and boomed, had been gouged and bored by the beating of the sea.

*   *   *

I was roused from sleep: the ship shuddered; the air pulsed to hideous grinding and hissing, as if some giant were sandpapering the hull. As I left my bunk *Arneb* paused for a moment, shuddered and pressed on. Still in my "long Johns" I made for the next cabin where I found Peter McIntyre working at his easel. McIntyre is an outstanding New Zealand artist, probably the only true Antarctic artist today.

"What the hell is all the noise about?" I asked.

At that instant the ship jerked and trembled again. Without looking up from his canvas, McIntyre answered imperturbably: "We're in the brash, or the slush on the outskirts of the pack."

"What's brash, exactly, Peter?"

"Rotten, sodden, old ice, mushy stuff that's been pulverized by gales. Not very interesting really."

McIntyre was *au-fait* with ice-conditions. He had been in Antarctica the previous year. In 1928 he had tried to join Admiral Byrd's Polar Expedition as a messenger boy, only to be replaced before sailing by a 19-year-old American Eagle Scout. Today that former scout is Dr. Paul Siple, the "Deep Freeze" scientific leader at the South Pole Station. He has been nicknamed by America, "Mr. Antarctica".

From the deck I surveyed a vast conglomerate of small floes, honeycombed with decay, through which the reinforced bows of *Arneb* sliced. Occasionally in the debris we encountered a hard "growler" which caused the ship to shudder slightly as she cleaved it apart.

"Even this porridge can't be treated lightly," a young officer explained, "a quick freeze-up can unite the damned stuff into a solid mass as hard as cement."

*   *   *

Clear of the brash, we encountered an area of loose, drifting floes and a lot of pancake ice, the latter being roughly circular and about ten feet across. Thereafter, unexpectedly, we nosed into a great lake of open water; the ship's speed was reduced to dead slow. In this clear area I could not understand our apparent caution.

Captain Schwaner, muffled in Arctic clothing, paced the bridge which he was not to leave for almost two whole days. We were approaching the Ross Sea, noted for having the most extensive pack ice in Antarctica.

I met Jimmy Roohan. I thought the second-in-command's face showed some concern.

"Why the back-paddling?" I asked.

Roohan shrugged. "The pack is much closer than we expected, a pretty solid surface with few leads according to advance information."

"You mean we can't bash through it, Jimmy?"

The Executive Officer lit one of his beloved Bobby Burns cigars.

"Sure we'll get through; we'll have assistance from a couple of icebreakers."

"Icebreakers," I was surprised, "where?"

"Yep, the *Staten Island* and *Northwind* are coming to help." He puffed, "They'll smash a path for us all right. In the meantime, we await their arrival."

"Heavens, I thought *Arneb* could crash through any ice, any time."

Jimmy didn't agree: "Tackling ten feet of ice with a supply ship like this, could be like trying to sail through cement."

*   *   *

Scientists say that 85% of the world's total ice lies in Antarctica; they give a modest estimate of ten quadrillion tons. (10,000,000,000,000,000). I was soon to stare in mute amazement at the tiniest fraction of it; a white desert of frozen ocean stretching away in all directions as far as the eye could see. Over a hundred miles of floe and pack ice separated us from our destination at Hallett, near Cape Adare in Victoria Land.

*   *   *

Across scores of millions of years secrets of the dead continent have been jealously guarded by powerful natural elements. The first line of defence is represented by the stormiest seas in the world. Ice-fields are the next formidable barrier. During the season of the long winter night, Antarctica is an ice-girt land. A solid, rock-hard frozen sea, from three to ten feet thick, extends outward for about a hundred miles. Only during the summer months are supply ships of "Deep Freeze" able to negotiate this second obstacle. In summer when there is daylight round the clock, the great ice pack which shields Antarctica splits and shatters, fissures, which are lanes of clear water, appear among the floes. Even in summer, however, penetration of pack ice is hazardous because the behaviour of sea ice is unpredictable. A summer freeze-up can occur and rapidly consolidate the pack into one vast ice sheet. Where one expedition has found practically no pack ice, a later one will find the same region thickly covered. The most powerful of ordinary ships can be brought to a quick and hopeless standstill, only tough, modern icebreakers are capable of smashing a passage. This is a slow and toilsome task.

*   *   *

I looked out over a dirty green sea to where it met the sky. What I observed is best described as a long tube of white neon light above the horizon; it gave a bright glare on to the dark cloud face.

"What the deuce is that?" I asked Captain Schwaner.

"Ice-blink," he answered, "a sure indication of the icefields we've got to penetrate. It is caused by the reflection on the cloud screen of light from bright ice."

The First Officer, Lieutenant Walshe, who knew the Antarctic well, said in a slow drawl: "You'll have a profound respect for the white land's accomplishments in the way of optical phenomena. Mirages and looming may be wonderful, but they give you the willies afloat. Whole mountain ranges suddenly loom out in front, though the real things are perhaps hundreds of miles away. Then 'hey presto', and they vanish like smoke!"

The Captain provided further information.

"Y'know," he said, "on Captain Scott's last expedition, men saw the relief ship *Terra Nova* long before it arrived. They saw it sailing upside down on a sky background. And Shackleton reported that he saw fantastic false sunsets and sunrises. The darn sun set and then came up again, then set a further five times."

"I've seen plenty of mirages in the Sahara," I said, "and I wouldn't mind seeing a few down here. What happens, exactly?"

"Small protuberances a few feet high in the pack are magnified a million fold and grow into the sky like long fingers and towers."

*　　　*　　　*

It was thrilling to watch the two Navy icebreakers, U.S.S. *Staten Island* and U.S.C.G.C. *Northwind*. They suggested squat, aggressive bugs. Both were less than 300 feet in length, each was driven by a 10,000 horse-power engine. They had round, barrel-shaped hulls which prevented them being crushed by ice. This construction causes them to pop up like peas in a pod whenever ice pressure becomes dangerously high. Thus they escape sharing the fate of Sir Ernest Shackleton's *Endeavour* which was caught in ice in the Weddell Sea in 1915, crushed, and, when the ice melted, sunk.

Time and time again the icebreakers charged the pack. Great, growling slabs of ice reared up, showing eight feet of amethyst blue or luminous green. Crackling reports rang out as the pack was remorselessly rent and riven.

Twelve hours ticked by; the icebreakers never let up; yard by slowly gained yard, changing course as the thickness of the ice varied, they forced a passage. Frequently when the *Staten Island* made a charge almost a third of the ship rode smoothly up and over the ice surface, then the sheer weight of the vessel cracked the ice. Modern icebreakers have ballast tanks which allow the transfer in minutes of hundreds of tons of water from side to side or from fore to aft. This enables the vessel to heel and roll on thick ice and so gradually to break it.

What a battle it was: as gaping wounds were opened in the ice, the trapped sea gushed out from below like green blood, swirling at its sudden release. *Arneb* followed in the icebreaker's wake, but the passage filled with floes even as the vessel passed. It was up to *Arneb* to cleave through this heavy debris. Many times I thought she would be stopped by some particularly large block—but always she responded to the demands made upon her, heaving, crashing, slogging forward. When we ripped into a floe which checked us, the ship would tremble from stem to stern, but the engines never faltered and slowly we continued to advance. When a floe couldn't be split, we pushed it slowly aside. At two knots, or very little more, we bumped south amid a medley of grating, grinding and hissing noises.

Unmindful of the sub-zero weather, those that could stay on deck did so. Within the steel hull the crunching sounds seemed greatly magnified. On the bridge in heavy clothing and wearing dark glasses to avoid snow blindness, Captain Schwaner studied the fighting floes. Ice navigation leaves no time for leisured cogitation; the ship is a vibrant, oppressed thing, constantly twisting; each move must be planned and executed by the officers on the bridge. Now, as we heaved and smashed through the pack, I felt the spice of this adventure. It was an unforgettable experience. Every mile of progress was a battle.

Each icebreaker carried two helicopters. These "eggbeaters" (American Navy slang) flew in continuous relay to help to pick a course through the white desert. From the air "leads" in the ice, quite invisible even from the ship's masthead, could be easily discerned and their location signalled by radio.

At last in a bobble of blue sea, *Arneb* thrust proudly and expectantly towards Victoria Land. The surface was widely strewn with floes, suggestive of beaten remnants escaping from the "pack-ice battle".

In latitude 72° S. natural Antarctic life appeared. Two

beautiful wandering albatross, the world's largest seabirds, wheeled and soared in apparently effortless flight. Later among the floes we saw flights of exquisite, foamy-white snow petrels. Occasionally there showed on the white of a floe a black, slug-like creature. This was a sleeping seal. Adélie penguins, comical, lovely little creatures were becoming numerous. They waddled haughtily to and fro beating their flappers with enthusiasm. Some, squawking excitedly, fell on their stomachs and toboganed around with an ease delightful and amusing to watch.

A zoologist attached to the Task Force drew my attention to the spouting of whales in the near distance. Using binoculars, I could see their dorsal fins.

"Blue whales," he said, "are beautifully streamlined creatures; they are the largest of known animals, they can grow to 100 feet in length, and one which was carefully weighed in sections totalled 160 tons."

"Take the weight of an average person at 10 stones," the zoologist went on, "and you'll require 2,560 folk, or a small township, to equal the mass of that one blue whale!"

*   *   *

Unexpectedly the sun burst through from a misty and over-cast sky. A vast scene of endless desolation was flooded with intense yellow light, but there was absolutely no restfulness for unprotected eyes.

Snowblindness is a painful, nerve-racking affliction; apart from the personal agony, it renders a man absolutely incapable of any work. The men aboard *Arneb* had been hand-picked and specially trained. A big job had to be done. When the Navy ordered that "every man above deck will wear dark eye-shields", the command was scrupulously obeyed. Bravado or stupidity was not to be allowed to check progress. Every man was part of a carefully blended unit, what faced us was a semi-military plan and precise medical instructions were issued.

Each man carried two pairs of dark glasses, in case one pair got broken. All men were instructed how to prevent snow-

187

blindness and how to treat this affliction if necessary. The symptoms are redness, and considerable watering of the eyes, violent headaches, and badly impaired vision. It is overcome by protecting the eyes from light. The patient should stay in a dark shelter or wear a light-proof bandage. The intense pain can be relieved by using compresses, but no eyedrops or ointments must be employed. With careful treatment most cases recover within twenty-four hours.

About frostbite the medical instructions read:

"Frostbite is the freezing of some part of the body, and is a constant hazard in the Antarctic, especially when the wind is up. The first sensation of frostbite is numbness rather than pain. You can see the effects of frostbite, a greyish or yellow-white spot on the skin, before you feel it. Every man must watch the other men's faces to see if frozen spots show. If the tell-tale evidence appears, the frozen part must be rapidly warmed. Frozen parts should be thawed in warm water until soft, even though painful. "Use body heat," the orders ran, "to aid thawing. Hold bare warm palm against frostbitten ears or face. Grasp frostbitten wrist with warm bare hand. Hold frostbitten hands against the chest, under the armpits, or between the legs at the groin. Hold frostbitten foot against companion's stomach or between his thighs. When frostbite is accompanied by breaks in the skin, apply sterile dressing. Never rub frostbite. You may tear frozen tissues and cause further damage. Never apply snow or ice. This just increases cold injury. Do not try to thaw a frozen part by exercising. This will increase tissue damage and break the skin. Do not stand or walk on frozen feet."

Crews called "Seabees", specially trained for work in very cold conditions, were already active preparing eight landing craft. These steel assault ships, with a front ramp that lowered on to the shore, were improved versions of the vessels that transported troops and materials to the Normandy beach-head during the invasion of Hitler's Europe.

We anchored in Moubray Bay, half a mile from a shoreline of jagged ice and a mile from two large, grounded icebergs. This was Hallett, south of Cape Adare, the joint American and New Zealand scientific base. Through my binoculars I picked out the little red huts of the men we had come to relieve and provision after their long winter of isolation. The camp was clinging precariously to a low sandspit jutting out from the base of towering mountains. These massive, icy ramparts descended steeply into the sea; great glaciers tumbled down their precipitous fronts. Away to the right, stood range after high range as far as the eye could reach.

Almost two-thirds of Antarctica's coastline is bordered by mountains rising as high as fifteen thousand feet, and the Hallett location is considered by explorers to be one of the most beautiful on the southern continent. Though the hour was nearing midnight, the sky was a brilliant blue; the sun paraded the horizon. The whole of the magnificent panorama was a glittering blaze of gold. Half way up the white mountains, a motionless layer of cloud was bathed in a breathtaking crimson; the protruding peaks gleaming like satin. The cold was cutting, but the air was dry and exhilarating; purity and brilliance of colour were heightened by the fantastically clear atmosphere. Here was a scene of bewildering beauty; the great ring of mountains reflected eternal solitude and the stark, elemental forces of nature. I felt like an earthling about to set foot on a new planet.

The sailors had no time for idle contemplation; the ship was as busy as an anthill. A landing was to be made on the coast in a few hours. The landing craft were in the water, and our 60-ton boom, the largest of any ship in the Atlantic Fleet, was raising cargo from the holds. Muffled in Antarctic clothing, heads hidden by fur parkas, faces concealed by anti-glare goggles, these "Seabees" were a model of Naval teamwork in action.

I returned to the wardroom and hot coffee, which was to be found at all times. I read through the daily routine orders:

There shall be no wanton killing, maiming or otherwise harming of any wildfowl. Animals or birds may only be taken as biological specimens by scientists accredited to "Deep Freeze" for special investigations.

****POLES**POLES APART**

Medical Note:

Human flesh will freeze at a much faster rate owing to the cooling factor of the wind. Deck or bridge personnel may be subjected to a wind-chill-factor which can produce almost instantaneous frostbite at low temperatures.

Keep an eye out for killer whales whilst moored on the ice.

THREE SHORT BLASTS (repeated). Blizzard three hours away, commence securing equipment.

FIVE SHORT BLASTS (repeated). All shipboard personnel return immediately to the ship. Make preparations to get under way as soon as possible.

* * *

Jimmy came up to me and said with a twinkle in his eyes: "The Admiral's pleased as punch with our ice breaking, this Naval despatch has just arrived."

I read:

U.S. NAVAL DISPATCH
5ND GEN 1807

FROM:	CTG 43.1		CLASSIFICATION UNCLASS	PRECEDENCE ROUTINE
ACTION:	USS ARNEB USCGC NORTHWIND USS STATEN ISLAND			
INFO:	COMNAVSUPPOR ANTARCTICA			

YESTERDAYS OPERATIONS IN THE SUCCESSFUL ENTRY OF MOUBRAY
HARBOR CAPE HALLETT THROUGH A POTENTIALLY DANGEROUS ICE SITUATION WITHOUT
APPARENT SHIP DAMAGE REFLECTS SOUND ICE NAVIGATION AND GOOD
SEAMANSHIP PRACTICES X STATEN ISLAND ARNEB NORTHWIND WORKED
MOST EFFECTIVELY AS A TEAM EITHER ASSUMING THE LEAD OR BREAKING
OUT THE CARGO SHIP AS NECESSARY X ARNEB POURED ON THE COAL
WITHOUT HESITATION WHEN THE SITUATION SO REQUIRED X ALL SHIPS
WERE REALLY ON THE BALL THIS TIME....BT........

RELEASE	CWO	TOR	TOD	DATE	D/T GR
TG COMMON	1422	2057/CT W1/CT		11 JAN '59	11 20 40Z

NAVY—DPPO 5ND NorVa

"That's fine, Jimmy."

"You'd better get to bed," said Jimmy, "you're doing a photographic flight in the long-range helicopter tomorrow morning."

190

"What!"

"The *Northwind* has just radioed you'll take off from her deck at 9.30 a.m. sharp. I hate to remind you, but a few thousand feet up you should experience a cute little temperature of 30° or more below zero."

*   *   *

The large, red helicopter roared and warmed up before my first Antarctic flight in the vicinity of the Admiralty Range. This machine was specially equipped for rescue operations of downed fliers and marooned surface parties. It was also indispensable for photographic survey of coastlines and to verify landmarks. Captain MacDonald strode over to me on the *Northwind*'s deck.

"Meet a remarkable Englishman who was with Shackleton's 1907-9 Antarctic expedition, also Captain Scott's tragic last expedition of 1910-13."

I shook hands with Sir Raymond Priestley, from Tewkesbury, Gloucestershire, a geologist and a veteran of polar exploration. In his late 70s, he was a smiling man, erect and still physically as hard as nails. Under the auspices of "Deep Freeze", Sir Raymond had returned after nearly half a century to the scenes of many of his previous Antarctic adventures.

Chatting and looking into the keen eyes of this jolly, bald-headed, typically English-squire type, it was hard to believe that death had stared him in the face in an ice-cave where he had lived throughout six agonizing months of a dark, Antarctic winter. His team of six, called the Northern Party, were marooned. No ship could reach them; supplies of food and clothing were low. The men, with unflagging determination not to die, burrowed into a glacier with their ice-axes to gain shelter from the bitter winds; for food they hunted seals and penguins. For sheer spirit, courage, and resource, the soul-stirring story of the ordeal of Sir Raymond Priestley's party is an epic of Antarctic survival. They lived because they had inherited the pluck of a race which didn't know when it was licked. It leaves one amazed that so flimsy a creature as man can endure so much for so long.

As the helicopter soared into the air, I peered down on this grand old explorer. What were his private thoughts about this modern mechanized age? If helicopters had existed in 1913, his party would have been rescued. The hundreds of weary miles over which men had foot-slogged, hauling sledges, the journey taking months, were now covered in a matter of hours by air. With present-day clothing and equipment, men can live in the Antarctic with reasonable comfort. They can live and work on the trail at very low temperatures. The Antarctic, however, remains a dangerous and unpredictable land. Men, if they are going to survive there, must never relax their guard. A moment of carelessness can cost a life.

Chapter Fifteen

Wings and White-outs
Over Antarctica

Thou, that roams the polar heavens wide,
The Lord be ever at your side.

W E SOARED over the basalt cliffs, which revealed black patches of bare rock, yet in all Antarctica only 1% of naked land is revealed. The remaining 99% is hidden under a heavy cloak of ice and snow. The long rotor blades twirled faster, creating a glistening disc in the coldest and purest air on earth. I breathed with a pleasant yet painful invigoration; the helicopter door was open to allow of camera operation. A safety wire connected to my harness was comforting.

At 6,000 feet, *Arneb* and the escorting icebreakers were toy-like. Five miles to the north was a white, uninterrupted surface of ice to the horizon. A signal was flashed to the ships. A few hours later wind and tide had drifted this menacing mass into the bay. Again *Arneb* was beset by a chaotic jumble of floes; however, it all drifted out to sea again next day. That is Antarctica's fickleness.

To the right, frozen mountains of the Admiralty Range stood stiffly, cutting the horizon in a jagged pattern. Explorer James Ross had christened them in honour of the British Lords of the Admiralty; the region over which we now flew had been named Victoria Land in honour of the then reigning Queen. We lifted still higher above a cruel and inhospitable landscape, and I realized the extreme difficulty of charting Antarctica's coastline. Land and sea merge together in a white sameness; enormous icebergs can easily be mistaken for islands. Apart from

193

physical coldness. I also felt numb about the heart as I looked down on the face of the world's highest continent, averaging as it does 6,000 feet above sea level. Asia, the next highest, averages only 3,000 feet.

I turned my gaze towards the utter desolation of the interior, an immensity of trackless wastes offering no relief to the eye. It has been the same for countless years, not a shrub tree or any kind of plant, no life of any kind because nothing exists which can support life. I scanned an immensity of eye-aching white under the sun's harsh glare. Few human eyes had even seen it. Antarctica is still largely an unopened book to the world in spite of today's great advance, the dead land is essentially unexplored and knowledge of it is scant.

From the air I experienced a sharper realization of the loneliness of this mountain-rimmed land. I viewed only the vaguest fraction of Antarctica's $5\frac{1}{2}$ million square miles, but what I saw was typical of the rest. It bewildered my imagination to realize that its secrets were locked below unmeasured yards of glacial ice.

Scientists believe that by the time the great Antarctic glaciation comes to an end the human race will have vanished from the face of the earth. Recently United States scientists at a base camp 5,000 feet above sea level, tried to find out what was below them. Instruments revealed that they were standing on 10,000 feet of ice. What lay below? An arm of the sea?

In spite of anti-freeze servicing, the motor of my movie camera froze up, nothing happened when I pressed the button. I drew away from the helicopter's opening; McIntyre the artist moved in to gain impressions.

As we swept over the coastline an officer of the Air Development Squadron pointed to a soaring peak on the eastern side of the Admiralty Range. What I saw was totally unexpected. On a windswept slope, stark and vivid against the snow, lay the wreckage of a giant C-124 Globemaster plane.

The strong-faced American by my side said over the intercom: "Damned tough luck, our boys got into a "white-out" and slammed into that mountain side four months ago."

"What happened to the crew?"

"Six dead and seven badly injured, quite a job getting them down to Hallett Station."

I had been briefed on "white-outs". They are caused by reflected light which fuses ground and sky together into an opaque nothingness. They are not met with in other parts of the world, but in Antarctica are of frequent occurrence. They spell danger to both plane and trail operations. Fliers aptly describe this eerie phenomenon as "flying in a bowl of milk". The horizons and shadows which normally give perspective vanish. "White-outs" come suddenly. They are ten times worse on nerves than zero-visibility in fog, cloud or blizzard.

"Hell of a place for a forced landing," I muttered involuntarily, "numbing cold and nothing else."

The American grinned. "That's how nature made this ice-box!" he exclaimed, "when you're over it you've just got to keep your mind off coming down, and concentrate on keeping up."

Later, as we zoomed above high ground, a strong and unexpected wind blast buffeted us to port, pitching the helicopter up and then causing it to drop sharply.

I learned that a feature of Antarctic weather is that winds blow almost constantly. Air, which is cooled by the ice-cap, flows from the elevated inland plateau much as water flows downhill. It whips up the snow into raging blizzards, before racing out to sea to create gigantic waves.

"Sure hate statistics," said my American friend, "they're soon out of date, but I guess an Australian expedition is likely to hold a wind speed record for some time."

"What was it?"

"200 miles an hour, and no kidding."

We circled above the *Northwind*, hovered, then gently sank to the deck. I had done a lot of R.A.F. flying in my time, and unemotionally calculated the risks of cold-continent flying. I raised an imaginary hat to the "Deep Freeze" aviators. The

thought of operating over that god-forsaken, ice-bound territory gave me the shivers—and not from cold alone.

*   *   *

We took on board a number of heavily-bearded men who had
served a year in Antarctica. Among them was Dr. Bornmann,
retiring Station Commander and Medical Officer, also Kenneth
Salmon, a genial New Zealander, and the station's previous
scientific leader.

*   *   *

Over the next few weeks I met many men of "Deep Freeze"
who had done outstanding things on that cold continent; all
had the same self-effacing manner as Bornmann and Salmon.
It was evident that explorer-scientists in this new age act in the
same tradition as did the pioneers of earlier Antarctic expeditions. The experience of common hardship in the face of great
elemental forces inspires more than a fortitude born of the
necessity of self preservation. Among men there is a marked
spurning of personal risk and suffering when comrades are
threatened with death or danger. I don't think there is a fraternal
spirit anywhere to equal that of the Antarctic brotherhood.

The first news of the crash of the Globemaster, of which I
had seen the wreckage from the air, had been radioed to Hallett
by another plane which had picked up distress signals. The
weather at the time was very bad with severe "white-out" conditions. Dr. Bornmann and Kenneth Salmon, together with five
others, voluntarily set out with two tractors to cross forty
miles of frozen ocean. To reach the crashed machine they had
to travel over a region not previously attempted. Almost insuperable difficulties lay ahead; the cold was intense and
danger lurked everywhere. One moment's lack of care could
have spelt certain death. The seven black specks, and their two
tractor-weasels loaded with medical and mountaineering equipment crawled painfully forward mile after mile. The line of
march lay over treacherous bay ice broken by tidal cracks.
Progress was agonizingly slow, reconnoitring and detours in

evitable. Later, a maze of *sastrugi* was encountered; an area where the ice surface was roughly corrugated and spotted with high hummocks around which they had to thread their way. This switchback surface was hell both for men and machines. Often, one of the weasels threw off a track; this could be re-seated only after hours of hard labour. Frost was ever ready to bite deep into ungauntleted fingers. . . .

Appalling cliffs and glacier faces rose 100 feet high sheer from the frozen ocean, all were quite impossible to climb. But a way up this initial barrier had to be found before they came to the even more gruelling mountaineering on the last stretches to the actual wreckage. On the second day, for a brief spell, the weather cleared; red distress flares were seen coming from the plane's survivors, then approximately seven miles away.

Mile after mile of the glacier walls were searched for a likely climbing place. As the rescue party zig-zagged below the ice mountains, uncanny hissing noises set nerves on edge. These sounds were created by air being drawn in through ice holes as sea water receded, then squeezed out again as the sea returned. Once, when the team found itself among rotten ice and snow, there was an ominous crack beneath the leading weasel. The vehicle tilted on the bobbing ice and began to sink; before it was half-submerged the occupants had jumped for their lives. Miraculously its plunge was arrested by jagged ice on the farther side of the crack, and the medical gear was rescued.

Using a stretcher as an improvised sledge, the men plodded on on foot. Roped together, they frequently had to leap when patches of ice crumbled. Undismayed by hardship and mishap they tackled the mighty, rough-hewn glacier walls. Toehold after toehold was cut.

In the hour of their worst dilemma, the weather relented and cleared, the helicopters were able to fly in and complete the rescue. Seven lives were saved. After three days of racking toil, exhausted and shaking with cold, the men got back to Hallett Station and routine duties.

*　　　*　　　*

Boom! The air trembled as the noise of the explosion rumbled across the sea and echoed around the amphitheatre of cliffs. For three days U.S. Navy men had used high explosive to blast hard rock for the foundations of a modern radio station with air navigation aids, the equipment for which *Arneb* had carried to Victoria Land. Beyond the spit on which stood the red huts that housed the men manning the station, lay a runway on the sea ice. This was capable of receiving long-range planes direct from New Zealand.

Although the International Geophysical Year is a thing of the past, America looks to the future, and continues to pour men, money and machines into Antarctica on an unprecedented scale. The use of aircraft is a major feature of operations where the difficulties of creating and supporting settlements are great. In this age which has seen the development of jet aircraft, atomic power, and earth satellites, many things are becoming possible that were undreamed of in the past. No one with certainty can foretell Antarctica's future, but if it is to yield to man's growing technical skill, powerful aircraft will be a foremost weapon in the conquest of the cold continent.

The big aeroplanes required to carry supplies to the South Pole presented a new problem to Antarctica. They weighed far too much to use skis and had to land on wheels. During the opening phase of "Deep Freeze", snow was cleared from sea ice and a 6,000-foot runway laid out at McMurdo Sound. This was before the Hallett strip had even been considered. The runway worked successfully, until, as the weather grew warmer, the ice surface softened and developed holes that filled with water. For a time it looked as if the South Pole Station would have to operate without some of its men and supplies. In this emergency, the American Army rushed in Dr. Andrew Assur, a civilian expert in the study of ice and its behaviour, direct from the States. At his suggestion tractors crushed thousands of tons of ice into slivers to fill in the holes with a mixture of ice chips, snow and slush that froze solid. This "ice-concrete" solved the problem. Many of the melt holes had been started by a patch of oil or a piece of paper which had absorbed heat from the sun. Admiral Dufek was jubilant over the repaired ice airfield. He said: "If a man so much as walks on that new strip with dirty shoes, or throws away litter, I'll have him court-martialled!"

The United States and Russia use planes to keep stations far inland on the plateau supplied with food, fuel and other necessities. Within a few years, no doubt, all the remaining unknown parts of the continent will have been seen from the air.

In addition to ten first-class Navy ships assigned to "Deep Freeze", two American Air Force Squadrons also form part of the combined operation. The 52nd Troop Carrier Squadron has ten 90-ton Globemasters based in New Zealand for airlifting personnel and priority cargo, particularly for dropping missions over the South Pole. The Air Development Squadron has twenty-four planes both wheeled and ski-equipped which airlift personnel and light cargo to various Antarctic stations. They carry supplies to Navy tractor trains and scientific traverse parties and also fly photographic missions and are responsible for search and rescue operations. To gain some idea of this gigantic and stirring Antarctic enterprise, during the re-supply mission to which I was attached in 1958-9, let it be realized that 2,150,000 gallons of aviation petrol and diesel fuel were transported from New Zealand. Navy ships also carried 9,000 measurement tons of cargo (40 cubic feet per measurement ton) and Air Force planes flew in a further 300 short tons (2,000 lb. to the short ton).

Operation "Deep Freeze" is the greatest-ever Government-backed programme for Antarctic advancement and understanding, and undoubtedly its greatest asset for assisting science to open up the bottom of the world is the aeroplane.

It was Captain Scott who first looked down on the white continent when in 1901, he made the first and only captive-balloon flight to a height of 800 ft. to observe what lay beyond the Ross Sea ice barrier. Who then would have imagined that man's key to the Antarctic lay in the air?

Chapter Sixteen

We Learn from the Penguins —and the Ice

Science is the greatest instrument of social change, all the greater because its object is not change but knowledge.

JIMMY ROOHAN, together with a biologist friend from the station, accompanied me to the Hallett penguin colony. As we approached, Jimmy said: "Scientific calculation claims that there are 200,000 Adélie penguins here!" He screwed up his face and sniffed, "from this considerable smell, I'd say that number has been underestimated."

Brian, the biologist, grinned broadly. "One soon gets used to it, after all, it's quite a friendly reminder that our Adélie companions have been propagating their species in this locality for the last ten thousand years or more."

"How do you know that?" I asked.

"By expert analysis of the guano," he replied.

The penguin rookery was on a finger of land approximately a mile in length by little more than a quarter of a mile wide. It reached back from a shoreline of grotto-like ice formations over black volcanic sand and rocks to the steep sides of sheltering cliffs. Every square yard was peppered by little black and white figures, thousands of them; it was a staggering spectacle which was as full of sound as of motion. At closer range I noticed that most of the rocky floor lay under a thick covering of guano.

The rookery was all bustling activity. Hoarse-squawking comedians waddled to and fro, others were being noisily pursued by strings of hungry chicks, small balls of fluffy, smoke-grey down. Lines of parents trooped seaward, continuously being passed by returning penguins each with paunches swollen by sea food for immediate transfer to the clamouring fledglings. The chicks put their heads into their parents' mouths, their food is brought into the gullet by regurgitation and so fed to the offspring.

I was amazed at the great speed penguins achieve in water. It was thrilling to watch them darting to and fro in unbelievable contrast to their slow, ambling gait on land. They shoot through the sea in a series of leaps, skimming the surface with all the grace and dexterity of porpoises.

"They've got to be fast," said Brian, "in the sea they run continuous risk from leopard seals and murderous killer whales."

When camp construction began, some of the Adélie penguins had had to be evicted from a few acres. There was considerable fuss, fury and protest. The birds were indignant that their barren rookery, penguin property for countless centuries, had been invaded. Beyond a netting fence the penguins long continued loudly to protest their wrath; they squawked, flapped their flippers, and with necks craned heavenward, apparently implored the Antarctic gods to wreak vengeance. As if in sympathy with the outraged feelings of the Adélie penguins, a fierce blizzard broke and *Arneb* was battered and seriously holed by crashing ice floes. The escorting icebreaker, *Northwind*, snapped a propeller blade. After the storm, much to everyone's astonishment, the netting around the camp site was down and thousands of penguins had re-occupied the beach.

Jimmy laughed as he recalled the scene: "Boy, was it darned funny. All the counter-attacking birds were straining on tiptoe and literally were in hysterics of raucous, squawking mirth. Can you imagine how silly our scientists and Seabees felt when they had to repeat the laborious job of eviction before the huts could go up?"

*　　　*　　　*

Adélie penguins are always comical and well deserve the title "clowns of the Antarctic". These adorable little polar creatures stand about two feet high, and are half the size of their bigger cousins, the aristocratic Emperors. Always immaculate in raven-black "coats" and glossy-white "waistcoats", these birds are indigenous to the white continent and have never been transplanted. Scientists have often tried to remove penguins from the germ-free atmosphere of their ice-surroundings, but all have quickly died. Antarctic species have absolutely no resistance to the virus-tainted atmosphere of civilization. I was told the same would apply to a child born and reared in Antarctica, where the atmosphere is practically aseptic.

Penguins seen in zoological gardens originate from more temperate latitudes and over scores of thousands of years have adapted themselves to survival outside the white continent. Zoo penguins, however, do not possess the wit, intelligence, quaintness or lovable natures of the real citizens of Antarctica. The Adélies reveal no fear of man or dog on land or ice. Possibly this is because they have never experienced enemies, other than pirate skua gulls, which steal their eggs and sometimes unguarded chicks, outside the sea.

These quaint creatures are endowed with an insatiable curiosity, and frequently get in the way of people trying to do things around bases. They stand about in a semi-human manner, observing whatever is going on with solemn astonishment from white-rimmed, gollywog-like eyes. Adélie drollery is thoroughly captivating; it has a touch of the pathetic, too.

"They make no objection to our presence," said Brian, "so long as we don't get too close to their nests. If you interfere with their pebbles, every one of which is hard earned, they'll hop up and nip at your leg. Those small flippers, too, really can bruise you."

I was told that Adélie penguins lay their eggs (two at the most) and raise their young during the Antarctic summer. They build their nests of pebbles on bare places where the ice has melted, and, because pebbles have to be carried long distances quite a lot of thieving takes place. The demand is greater than the supply. As winter approaches the penguins leave the land

and follow the Antarctic pack ice out to sea so as to be near the open waters where they find food. To the isolated men of "Deep Freeze" one of the happiest signs of returning spring, after the monotony of the long winter darkness, is the reappearance of bustling, cheerful Adélies back to nest and breed.

Moving among circular groupings of stones in the penguin community, with voracious skua gulls wheeling overhead ready to swoop on any unguarded chick, I could hardly believe that about 200 million years ago, Antarctica possessed a temperate or semi-tropical climate, with swamps and rich primeval vegetation. Fossils of tropical ferns and plant life have been found embedded in rock. In the sandstone of the Beardmore Glacier, less than 350 miles from the South Pole, known coal deposits are evidence of once-great forests.

The squawking penguins at my feet had originated from one of the earliest forms of bird life, when lizards began developing wings. Penguins once flew, just as the cumbersome, lazy seals once owned legs for roaming in Antarctic forests. Then the bottom of the world began to grow cold and freeze over. Vegetation died as the ice mantle enveloped the land. In the course of time, nature adapted the wings of the penguins into flippers for rapid propulsion through water instead of air.

"Don't move," said Brian, "let's see what Alfred does."

Alfred happened to be a formal-looking penguin with a satin-white breast. For some minutes he had studied us keenly with his boot-button eyes. We kept motionless. Alfred gave a squawk. another shuffle, and came within a foot of Jimmy's leg. He screeched ecstatically and waved his flappers in the friendliest manner imaginable. Brian expertly imitated the "Quaawk, Quaawk" . . . Alfred was in raptures at this "bird-talk" answer, and immediately waddled over to a nearby nest of pebbles. It was absolutely ludicrous the way he waited his opportunity at the rear of the stones with a "butter wouldn't melt in my mouth" look.

"Guileless innocence," said the biologist, "watch him, it's a clear indication of forthcoming petty larceny."

Alfred, with a lightning move, snatched a pebble with his beak and made toward us at a running waddle. He was quite oblivious of the indignant noises coming from the stone's rightful owner.

The offering was laid gallantly at Jimmy's feet. Mr. Alfred Adélie drew himself up to his full height, extended his neck and proceeded to make a guttural humming sound.

Jimmy yelled, "Hop it, peculiar, this is the first time I've been mistaken for a female."

Alfred expressed utter dismay and incredulity, then fled.

"What's he done wrong?" I asked.

Brian explained that penguins have difficulty ascertaining each other's sex. This difficulty is overcome during the mating season by the simple expedient of the male offering a small pebble to his intended. If it is accepted with grace and coyness, it's a sure bet that the recipient is a female.

*   *   *

About a dozen varieties of penguins exist. Of the best known are the Emperor and Adélie. The Adélie is the commoner; the Emperor the aristocrat of the ice continent. This beautiful bird stands between three and four feet high; it is a creature of great dignity and polished manners. The Emperors possess superb plumage, snowy white breasts and shiny black backs. The long curved beak has a violet edge, whilst around the neck region is a delicately blended collar of yellow. An adult weighs between 70 and 80 lb., and a blow from its flippers may be strong enough to break a man's arm. Only half a dozen isolated rookeries are known to scientists.

The most unusual thing about this extraordinary aristocrat is that, unlike the Adélies which lay their eggs in summer, the Emperor lays its single egg in the depth of winter. For eight weeks the father bird incubates the egg on the ice and disregards food. The adults do this by first holding the egg, then the chick, on their webbed feet, protecting with a downy fold of abdominal fat the precious possession. Emperors possess a tremendous nursing instinct, and chickless grown-ups crave to adopt any baby unattended for a single moment. Consequently youngsters are almost killed by kindness in scrambles by would-be adopters.

It is exceedingly dangerous for scientists to visit the few known rookeries to study breeding habits and domestic life of Emperors. Unfortunately this takes place during the time of greatest darkness, when blizzards and temperatures are at their worst, when conditions are paralysing. During Captain Scott's second expedition to the Antarctic, an heroic journey was undertaken by Dr. Wilson, Lieut. Bowers and Mr. Cherry-Garrard. This trio visited Cape Crozier to study these eccentric penguins and their embryology. They returned to the camp after five weeks almost dead men.

Captain Scott wrote of them:

> Wilson is disappointed at seeing so little of the penguins, but to me and everyone who has remained here the result of this effort is the appeal it makes to our imagination as one of the most gallant stories in polar history. That men should wander forth in the depth of the polar night to face the most dismal cold and the fiercest gales in darkness is something new; that they should have persisted in this effort in spite of every adversity for full five weeks is heroic. It makes a tale for our generation which I hope may not be lost in the telling.

Today, men are still possessed of the same spirit to take frightful risks in quest of knowledge. I had completed this manscript, but have returned to add a little to this chapter. I have just learned of the lucky escape of my biologist friend, Brian Reid, who took me over the Adélie rookery at Hallett.

THREE MEN ESCAPE WHEN WEASEL GOES THROUGH ICE
Press Assn ... Wellington.

The first field trip of the 1959/60 Antarctic season ended in near disaster, states a report from the Antarctic. In attempting to reach Coulman Island, the site of one of the few known Emperor penguin rookeries, one of the two United States Navy weasels without warning broke through the sea-ice. The three occupants managed to escape from the sinking vehicle. The accident occurred on the second day, about 38 miles from Hallett Station. The five-man team, which left Hallett Station on 19 August, was led by a New Zealand biologist, Mr. Brian Reid of Wellington, and included the station leader, Mr. Charles Roberts, an American.

New Zealand Herald, 26 August, 1959

I saw only one Emperor in Antarctica, that was when we were anchored in sea-ice off McMurdo. It was a magnificent four-footer, and was first seen waddling towards *Arneb* from afar. Slowly it came closer. Once close to the ship it remained motion-less for five minutes looking over the vessel with a gracious formality. When the sailors called to it there was a stiff bow, a soft guttural noise. After another bow it moved on. Captain Schwaner caught up with it some distance from the ship. The bird paused sedately, studied the Captain and his camera with haughty curiosity, waited until shots had been taken, drew himself to full height and set off once more. We watched it wander from sight across a limitless expanse of ice. Where it was heading for on a seemingly aimless journey, no one will ever know. But penguins are known for their roaming inclina-tions, and exploring tendencies, and quite happily wander for miles.

*　　　　*　　　　*

Were they low-lying clouds? We sailed closer. The white ruler on the horizon became an endless ice-wall. This was the Ross Ice Shelf, an impassable barrier 500 by 350 miles in extent, covering an area approximately the size of France.

Our Hallet mission having been accomplished, we had been ordered to proceed to the Little America scientific station, on the northern edge of the Ross Ice Shelf. This camp was being abandoned. To reach its situation in latitude 78° S. meant the deepest penetration of the Antarctic Continent that it is possible to make in a ship. We would be just 699 miles from the South Pole. Once more we smashed and lurched through stubborn pack ice to reach safe ocean; then, after steaming for 400 miles, we turned into the pack to hack and thud our way to the great ice barrier again. In two places the reinforced plates of the ship were badly strained during this tough ice-chiselling; those in the know were a little concerned until the leaking seams had been welded.

The height of Antarctica is caused by ice and snow that have piled up during hundreds of thousands, perhaps millions of years. All the centre of the continent is covered by a high plateau or ice-cap. In places, this ice-cap is more than two miles thick. The great weight of ice causes its outer fringes to move toward the edges of the continent. When this ice reaches the ocean, it moves out across the sea in the form of ice shelves. These shelves are attached to the land at one end and float on the water at the other; they surround much of the continent. From the sea they look like great white cliffs, towering up to a height of about 150 feet. From time to time, pieces of the ice-shelf break off and float away. These are the flat-topped (tabular) icebergs which are found only in the Antarctic. The greatest embayment of ice in the world is the Ross Shelf. As we skirted its edge, the glittering cliffs showed a shimmering blue at their base.

"Over there is the Bay of Whales," said Captain Schwaner, "where Roald Amundsen of Norway had his winter quarters, seventy miles nearer the Pole than was Scott at Cape Evans. From that camp, 'Framheim', he made his sledge dash to the one spot on earth where everything points north."

I was glad when we went below deck. The Ross Ice Shelf is an awesome sight. Those glass-smooth walls appeared to encompass millions of years of silence. The ice appeared to grow out of the sea like a terrible white spectre suggesting the end of the world.

We didn't stay long at Little America, but all that time was an anxiety for Captain Schwaner. We lay-to in the most treacherous ice-filled sea of Antarctica. Here nothing can ever be taken for granted. One day Lady Antarctica is sweet and friendly, the next, full of spite.

On a previous visit the place where we now waited had been thick with bay ice. On that occasion three "Deep Freeze" vessels had been preparing to off-load direct on to the ice. Suddenly, owing to a change in the wind, the ice broke up. The three ships were then faced with the task of discharging cargo over an ice-shelf fifty feet high. A violent swell carried one of the ships against a projection, seriously holing the hull.

We were luckier. Bay ice had drifted from the barrier just before our arrival. When it would return to ice-lock the sea none could foresee. The landing craft moved into a steep and narrow gap in the cliffs, a beach-head; the only entrance to the camp. It seemed a miracle that such a slip existed in an otherwise unscaleable barrier hundreds of miles long, but considerable labour had been employed to improve it.

The members of the Little America party with their personal gear and their precious ice-core samples were taken on board, but little else was moved. Then the camp in its entirety was abandoned. A considerable scientific programme had been carried out there during the International Geophysical Year which had ended a few weeks before. Now we left behind a lot of equipment—perhaps £50,000 worth. This was a wise move. The amount was small compared with what might have been lost had *Arneb*, in staying to load, remained long enough to be trapped by the returning ice. Had that happened, *Arneb* herself might have been crushed and sunk.

Ice is never static. Throughout the Antarctic it is always shifting and splitting; always in ponderous and unending movement. Frequently whole islands, some as big as the county of Yorkshire calve away from the Ross Sea Ice Shelf. I learned that already behind the camp at Little America a giant crack existed. One day it is probable that the whole of the Little America Station may float northward atop a giant iceberg: when the ice melts, the sea will be the station's grave.

The minute the landing craft had been raised from the sea, we sailed.

The little cluster of huts and radio masts stood out against the slate-blue sky hauntingly alone. This was their farewell. In a few brief hours the station had been stripped of life. Now

When camp construction began at Hallett some of the members of the Adélie penguin colony (*above*) had to be ejected from a few of the acres which had been theirs for centuries. When a blizzard broke the netting fence which kept them out they invaded in force, squawking and flapping their wings, evidently overjoyed to have the elements even temporarily on their side. These adorable little polar creatures have never been successfully domiciled away from the germ-free air of Antarctica.

Left: A parent Adélie feeding a chick by regurgitation.

Above, left: Dr. Bornmann, who had served as Station Commander and Medical Officer at Hallett for a year.

Above, right: With the biologist Brian Reid: the fibre-glass sledge might be a life-saver if one fell in a crevasse because it could bridge the gap.

Right: With Captain MacDonald, the Commander of the *Northwind*, and Sir Raymond Priestley. Sir Raymond had been in Antarctica before with Shackleton and Captain R. F. Scott.

Left: The padre, Captain Hammond from Virginia, at the church in McMurdo which ministers to all religious denominations.

Right: The New Zealand artist Peter McIntyre at his easel in Antarctica.

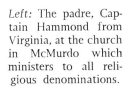

Left: With Captain Schwaner, Commander of *Arneb*; we had induced the Medical Officer to prescribe stimulant and each enjoyed one can of beer.

Above: On shelf ice such as this and three feet thick, Captain Scott's photographer, Herbert Ponting, was attacked by eight "killer whales" which actually broke up the ice and nearly caught him.

Left: This photograph, from a film I took from the deck of *Arneb*, shows a "killer whale" spouting. The animal is about thirty feet in length and extremely savage.

it was alone on a windswept plateau. Around it would swirl the world's most changeable and treacherous weather. The cold and the dark would hem it in until the ice on which it stood broke free and sailed on its voyage of return to the waters of the ocean.

As the camp merged into a veil of mist one of the bearded former inhabitants saluted and wistfully turned away. One man of Operation "Deep Freeze" was not returning. A construction driver, Max R. Kiel, had been killed when his tractor plunged into a deep crevasse. His body lay below a pall of snow on that ice-locked continent.

*   *   *

Scientists at Little America had drilled holes down through the ice to a record depth of 10,000 feet. They had taken samples, temperatures, and estimated the age of various layers of snow and ice composition. A deep-thinking Harvard man, Henry Francis, who had been executive deputy chief scientist at Little America, now shared my cabin. He remarked like a true scientist: "Those ice-cores alone offer sufficient scientific reward to offset ten-times over the cost of forsaking the camp."

"Why?" I asked.

"Because," he answered, "glaciologists will solve much about the physical make-up of Antarctica through those ice cores."

I was astonished when I learned that some ice compositions in the ship's refrigerator, went back to the eleventh century— the time of King Richard the first of England.

"Volcanic specks of dust," explained Francis, "embedded in centuries-old ice, can help more than you'd imagine to lift the Antarctic veil."

*   *   *

We zigged and zagged with circumspection on our return across the perfidious Ross Sea. Our destination was McMurdo Sound, America's most important base, 750 miles north of the geographical Pole. McMurdo, a small bay protected by land, has long been a place of interest in polar exploration. Captain

Robert Falcon Scott built his first camp here in the 1901, *Discovery* expedition, naming his base "Hut Point". In 1908, Sir Ernest Shackleton ventured from McMurdo in an attempt to conquer the heart of Antarctica. He travelled to within 100 miles of the South Pole. In 1912, Captain Scott returned to McMurdo Sound. It was from here that he set out poleward, only to perish with four companions on the return trail.

Forty-five years later, Sir Edmund Hillary, the man who will always be remembered for climbing Mount Everest, with a ground-support party reached the Pole from McMurdo. This was part of the British Trans-Antarctic Expedition under the leadership of Dr. Vivian Fuchs, who successfully concluded one of the most perilous journeys in polar exploration. In 1958 Dr. Fuchs crossed the entire continent, a distance of 2,150 miles. This was the venture formerly planned by Sir Ernest Shackleton, but ending in failure when his ship, in 1915, became beset and crushed in the Weddell Sea Ice Pack. From his take-off site, Shackleton Base, on the Weddell Sea, Dr. Fuchs travelled to the Pole, then onward to journey's end at McMurdo Sound.

The name McMurdo, Antarctica, was thrilling and inspiring. A name on a map, a departure and arrival point on the Ross Sea, but one historically associated with sterling qualities of human courage and fortitude.

The most important part of *Arneb*'s mission was at McMurdo. Here supplies, a large portion of them for airlift straight into the South Pole Station, would be discharged. Runways had been built two miles from the main huts on sea ice rising to a height of 27 feet above the water. On these runways, an area of ice 6,000 feet by 300 feet had been shaved and planed to make a landing surface for the big planes coming in direct from New Zealand, after crossing 2,300 miles of the worst seas in the world, in weather that was rarely friendly.

Icy winds penetrated one's clothing; winter was rapidly getting into its stride. It was mid-January and, owing to adverse conditions, we were already behind schedule. Seasons are reversed south of the Equator. Antarctic summer is from

October, when the first aircraft of the season arrive from New Zealand, until January, when the last aircraft and ships of "Deep Freeze" depart for home. After that, the only contact which personnel in Antarctica have with the outside world is by radio. They are cut off until the winter night is over. They must live with the frequent blizzards and temperatures as low as 100° of frost.

In the area of McMurdo Sound *Arneb* closed with Mount Erebus, Antarctica's only live volcano. This giant-girthed pyramid rising 13,350 feet, stiff and cold, looked almost ethereal. From sea to summit it was cloaked by immense snowfields. A thin steam-cloud issued like a weather vane from the cone. It stretched, like a broad, white ribbon across a bright blue sky. The volcano itself soared into the air like a sentinel guarding the Ross Ice Shelf. It had been discovered and named in 1841 by Sir James Clark Ross. In 1908 six men of Shackleton's expedition climbed to its smoking crown. The active crater, they reported, was approximately half a mile in diameter by almost 1,000 feet deep; three times the depth of that of Mount Vesuvius.

Once we were beyond Erebus, Antarctica decided to become awkward. McMurdo Station was barricaded by thick ice, we could get no nearer to our destination than ten miles. Before us stretched a solid white plain.

Progress was out of the question, *Arneb* just couldn't push through a solid sheet of ice nine feet in height.

A signal came from the icebreaker, *Northwind*:

"It's tough stuff! With luck we may chop out two miles of passage a day."

But the indomitable icebreaker was being optimistic. It took longer!

With non-stop persistency the *Northwind* hacked at the strong barricade, crunching, banging and grinding. For two days we watched the icebreaker lunge and thrust her bows over the stubborn, white-blue ice. With a metallic scream she would come to a shuddering halt, then, her weight pressing downward, she paused as if for breath. Reluctantly the white sheet groaned, then rapidly divided. Yard by fighting yard a channel was opened up. But for a week or more we would not be able to reach McMurdo Station to off-load heavy equipment. Turning about, we sailed for Cape Royds. Here, not far from Mount Erebus, Shackleton had built his quarters during the 1907 expedition. Here a small party of scientific personnel was put ashore by one of the landing craft to inspect the original hut and historic surroundings.

En route to Cape Royds a number of geologists had been landed at Inaccessible Island, which grew from the sea like a huge cake over which icing sugar had been randomly poured.

I learned that some work has been done in Antarctica to determine what may be under the ice. So far, about 175 minerals have been identified, including coal, gold, silver, and copper, yet less than one per cent of the continent has been studied for minerals. At present the thick ice-cap makes it impossible to mine these minerals except where rocks crop out above the ice and snow.

*　　　*　　　*

There are powerful reasons why Operation "Deep Freeze" has been followed with close attention. In view of its great strategic importance in a military sense, Antarctica cannot be neglected. Though the Second World War did not touch the White Continent, it came close to doing so. Hitler had sought to establish German sovereignty there in 1938. He described an area south of the Weddell Sea as "New Schwabia". Topographical features were named after prominent Nazi officials, and a team of experts under Dr. Ritscher were sent out there in a vessel named the *Schwabenland*. Had Germany then possessed long-range rockets and atomic war heads, South Africa, New Zealand and Australia could have been bombarded from Antarctica. As it was, German commerce raiders sheltered off some of the sub-Antarctic islands and were even successful in capturing the Norwegian whaling fleet. This so alarmed Whitehall that Britain in 1943 sent a military force to the Palmer Peninsula under the command of Lieut.-Cmdr. J. W. Marr, who had begun his experiences in the Antarctic as a Boy Scout on Shackleton's last expedition. Marr established two bases: one near the west coast of the Palmer Peninsula and the other in the near-by South Shetland Islands. After the war, these bases continued to be used and Britain has opened others, ten in all, for scientific research. They are listed under the Falkland Islands Dependencies Survey.

Today, there are five well-established Soviet stations on the southern continent; U.S.S.R. teams fan out on daring and ambitious journeys both exploratory and for scientific study. Russians, like the Americans, are in Antarctica to stay. It remains to be seen whether the various stations will be used for the fruitful development of scientific research, or the eventual creation of military bases.

No cut and dried territorial rights in Antarctica have ever been internationally settled. A host of nations assert claims to slices of the continent. Antarctica still represents more or less a hunting ground for all, in spite of certain dog-in-the-manger attitudes. Claims to sovereignty appear to have been inspired largely from historical and economic motives. The latter, on the part of individual powers for protecting prosperous whaling fleets. Antarctica, says the United States, belongs to nobody. Secretary Charles Evan Hughes proclaimed in 1924:

> It is the opinion of the U.S.A. that the discovery of lands unknown to civilization, even when coupled with formal taking of possession, does not support a valid claim of sovereignty unless discovery is followed by actual settlement of the discovered country.

Possibly the outcome of an atomic war will decide the ownership of the polar continent. I only hope that the lofty ideals which inspired the letters IGY, do not over future years evolve into AICBMR (Antarctic Inter-Continental Ballistic Missile Race).

Today, widely-spaced rocket bases are as important as the missiles themselves. It would be fatal to entertain the idea that Antarctica would remain neutralized in any future war. In an age which has seen the arrival of jet aircraft, atomic energy and earth satellites, the polar continent must be evaluated in strategic terms. With the push-button war of the future fast becoming reality, Antarctica might well be viewed as a major launching zone. The Democracies have good reason to study this possibility with disquiet. New Zealand lies 2,700 miles from the Pole, Australia 3,000, South Africa 3,400, South America 2,200. London and New York are approximately 7,500 miles distant. These mileages, great as they may seem, should be studied in the light of what the Air Force Missile Chief of America, Major General Bernard Schriever, said recently:

> It is possible that both countries (referring to America and Russia) will achieve initial operational capability of Inter-Continental Ballistic Missiles at about the same time.

The world has now reached a major milestone in the long history of armed conflict. Every continent has its potential defence and attack value. Antarctica, last great unexplored continent, could well become a hot spot in any cold war.

Since this chapter was written, to be precise, on 1 December, 1959, in Washington, a treaty of which the main provisions are to "freeze" territorial claims for at least 34 years, to promote international scientific co-operation and to provide for complete non-militarization of the area, including prohibition of the testing of nuclear or any other weapons, was signed at the Antarctic Treaty Conference. The treaty expressly permits the use of atomic energy for peaceful purposes. Though it has still to be ratified by the respective governments (Argentina, Australia, Belgium, Chile, France, Great Britain, Japan, New Zealand, Norway, South Africa, the Union of Soviet Socialist Republics and the United States of America) it is nevertheless a most welcome sign of intended international co-operation.

Cape Royds: Shackleton's 1907 Base

Self-preservation is the first law of nature, but self-sacrifice is the highest rule of grace.

FLYING spray cascaded over the open sides of the landing craft. Repeatedly we slammed down hard into a trough of water as we thrashed through a rough sea to Cape Royds. I was excited: here we would find Shackleton's base of the British Antarctic Expedition, 1907.

We crashed on to a beach on low ice; within a dozen paces I looked down on a half-buried sledge. It might have died naturally in the track when the last of Shackleton's men departed half a century before. The hut was not far away, it lay in a small valley protected by a low, sheltering hill. The site was clear of snow and scores of irregularly-shaped boulders lay around; in fact, the hut was built on volcanic rock. Directly behind, Erebus soared majestically upward, its streamer of smoke sweeping across the sky like a giant brush mark.

I experienced a stirring of the heart, and a profound sadness. The very squawks of welcoming penguins on a near-by ridge seemed muted. A few groups of the birds came closer to stand, erect and motionless, apparently in solemn contemplation. They might have been paying silent tribute to the brave explorers who had lived here. In these surroundings the solitude seemed almost a thing of tangible reality. I felt that the spirits of the men of that earlier expedition were not far absent from their former camp site. I came closer to the hut, which was wonderfully preserved and intact, forever free of rot or decay. Among a pile of debris, old hawsers, scrap metal and tins, a skua gull chick, no more than a fluffy ball close against the egg shell from which it had emerged, blinked calmly. This tiny Antarctic creature seemed to be expressing satisfaction at being born amidst such relics and on such historic ground.

Packing cases stood tight against the walls of the dwelling. After departure, Shackleton had said: "Wind velocities were so great as to move cases weighing 50 to 80lb." In such position they acted as wind breakers. Shackleton also said:

> I left at the winter quarters on Cape Royds a supply of stores to last fifteen men for one year. The hut was locked up and the key hung up outside where it would be easily found, and we readjusted the lashings of the hut so that it might be able to withstand the attacks of blizzards during the years to come. If any party has to make use of our hut in the future, it will find there everything required to sustain life.

I stood before the wooden structure and dreamed and wondered. It was a tiny monument to man against one of the mightiest backgrounds of nature I have ever seen. There was something frightening yet inspiring about the scene. Beyond that front door fifteen men once had huddled together, laughing, planning and existing. Here they had battled against sub-zero temperatures and unimaginable blizzards. They had been cut off from civilization, without even radio contact or the advantages which modern polar equipment gives. From this little pivot, dwarfed by mighty Erebus, hemmed in by glaciers, epoch-making journeys had begun.

I visualized Shackleton, a man of great daring and imagination, striding from the door, followed by men of his sledging party for the South Pole. In 1908 Shackleton attained the most southerly latitude which had then been reached by man after ascending the mighty Beardmore Glacier to the Polar Plateau. After 72 days out from Cape Royds, and near the end of human endurance, the party turned back, only 97 miles from the Pole. The Union Jack had been planted in latitude 88° 23" S. This was three years before Amundsen reached the Pole. It was a valiant feat of leadership and indomitable courage. During the 800 mile return journey, starvation stared the sledge-hauling team in the face. At one stage each man had had to survive on one biscuit a meal. Yet those four tiny specks of hope in the great, white wilderness won through.

In imagination also I pictured other parties emerging from the hut. One group had climbed Erebus to the rim of its belching crater, a mountaineering accomplishment of the highest order. Yet another party had reached the South Magnetic Pole for the first time, and another small team had thrown new light on Antarctica's geology by discovering vast mountain ranges hitherto unknown.

I passed into the dim interior of the hut. It was ridiculously small to have been the whole inhabited world of fifteen men. It was 33 ft. × 19 ft. × 8 ft. Within those four sombre walls everything symbolized peace, quiet and repose. Sealskin sleeping bags were lying jumbled on beds built from empty boxes. Cooking pots on the 4 ft. × 3 ft. coal-burning stove contained evidence of the last meal. I thought back to the winter of 1908 when this stove had burned day and night for nine months, in its oven bread had been baked daily. Old jackets hung from nails, one had the name tag of a Piccadilly outfitter; in the pocket was a well-bitten pipe.

Primitive shelves and lockers made from boxes nailed to the walls, still contained possessions. In one there was a packet of barley sugar, scissors, books, two gramophone records and a belt. In another, three pairs of roughly-darned socks, and below, a photograph of an elderly, white-haired woman. It was signed, "To Bertram from Mother". Everywhere I turned, the contents of the hut evoked poignant emotion; The atmosphere was gripping. Here men had lived and performed their routine duties in the light of acetylene lamps. Here they had struggled through the dark months to keep "polar ennui" at bay until the reappearance of daylight. It was hard to conceive how that wintering over party had maintained good spirits, sanity and sociability.

Space had been skilfully arranged and, as Shackleton recorded in his diary, two men were allowed bunk space in an area of 6 ft. 6 in. × 7 ft. In all, the hut had eight such divisions. The occupants had done their utmost to make the tiny compartments habitable and personal. One compartment had been nicknamed, "No.1 Park Lane", another "The Gables", there was a "Rogues Retreat", and also "The Pawn Shop".

Near the door was a tiny dark room, still with photographic plates in the rack. Opposite was a similar den, the laboratory, with a miscellany of bottles and rock specimens. I opened a tin of sardines and ate biscuits; marmalade and canned Irish stew also were sampled. The contents were as fresh and edible as on the day they had been packed. I sat down on various bunks in the hut. The past seemed to have slid away in this land of eternal snow. My feelings were hard to interpret. I kept pausing involuntarily; as a wind gasped about the eaves outside, I expected to hear the shouts of men returning, or perhaps the bray of a pony from the stalls at the back.

I turned toward a large, framed picture on the wall. Before me were photographs of the late Queen Alexandra and King Edward VII. This was 1959 and thus was I made conscious of the evanescence of time. All human life is part of the eternal process of dying. Antarctica has no human life of its own, it is a dead continent, but it preserves intact not the relics alone of what life has come to it, but something also of the spirit that inspired that life.

I paused awhile longer before turning to the door; the portraits of the King and his Queen remained in my mind's eye : of them Shackleton had written :

> Last night as we were sitting at dinner, the evening sun entered through the ventilator and a circle of light shone on the picture of the Queen. Slowly it moved across and lit up the photograph of His Majesty, the King. This seemed an omen of good luck, for only on that day and at that particular time could this have happened, and today we started to strive to plant the Queen's flag on the last spot of the world.

* * *

From the cabin I ventured farther afield to what had been known as "Back Door Bay". A dozen or more crab-eating seals, each a dozen feet long, lay drowsing on the bay ice, contemptuous of my presence. This was my nearest approach to seals. Fully-grown specimens weigh nearly half a ton, they are inoffensive enough and exist on a diet of fish foods. Their great quivering hulks reminded me of jelly tied up in big, floppy bags.

I descended to where land met sea-ice to take photographs, then retreated hastily. I remembered warnings about the danger of lurking leopard seals. "Watch for them," Jimmy Roohan had warned, "take no chances, because if you run your fastest on the ice, the leopard seal will overtake you. It's damned fast."

The leopard seal, ocean carnivore, is as dangerous as a tiger; it is the mortal enemy of peace-loving seals, penguins, and even whales. An adult is quite fifteen feet long and equipped with huge curved fangs and a triple row of blade-like cheek teeth. One snap would take off a man's limb, and the animal will attack human beings without provocation. It is one of the most fearsome beasts of prey known.

If I didn't get chased by a leopard seal I certainly experienced a nasty scare when a number of skua gulls attacked me in rapid succession. At the time I was crossing the rocky peninsula on my way back to the landing-craft, and unknown to me the skuas were nesting thereabouts. In a shrieking hullaballoo they rose around me, spiralled to about a hundred feet, paused, aimed and then dived at great speed. These birds were fully grown and measured over a yard from tip to tip. It wasn't funny having them tearing straight towards my face screaming with anger. It was unnerving. I dropped my gear and used my extended camera tripod to ward off the attackers. Peter McIntyre, the artist who also passed over the same ground, actually was brushed across the face by a wing. During Scott's last expedition, his photographer, Herbert Ponting, was lucky not to lose the sight of an eye. A huge skua dived on him with piercing shrieks and a wing joint struck his face. He lay on the ground for an hour in pain, but fortunately the wide brim of a floppy hat took most of the blow and saved his sight. I learned that these savage birds dive on intruders without the slightest real provocation, but never attack with their beaks or claws, only with their extended wings. It is their habit to fly straight towards a man's face, then at the final moment, lift and pass within inches of his head. I hated these scavenger skuas. They are cannibal; steal the eggs of their own species and create havoc among young penguin chicks in the rookeries.

Our landing craft chugged seaward. Against a distant background of the western mountains, *Arneb* enlarged; slowly it grew real and solid, then at last it towered above us. As I climbed on board my pilgrimage to a little cabin at the foot of Erebus became a precious memory.

Cape Evans: Captain Scott's Base

"Death cannot be and is not the end of life. Man transcends death in many altogether naturalistic fashions. He may be immortal biologically, through his children; in thought through the survival of his memory; in influence, by virtue of the continuance of his personality as a force among those who come after him; and ideally, through his identification with the timeless things of the spirit."

WE FOLLOWED a coastline of crenellated ice walls and volcanic cliffs toward Cape Evans. The scenery was of austere and desolate grandeur, dominated by Erebus with its remarkable beauty and similarity to Fujiyama (Fujiyama is 12,395 ft.; Erebus 1,000 ft. higher). It was zero degrees but the summer temperature was invigorating. Visibility was magical; the jagged and tumultuous white peaks of the Royal Society Range, in Victoria Land (one hundred miles away) were sharply etched against a lilac sky. In the light of the midnight sun they glistened with a far-off loneliness which was wholly indescribable.

We were fifteen miles north of McMurdo, our eventual destination, when the volcanic islet of Cape Evans came into view. Cape Evans had been the wintering-over station of Captain Scott's last expedition. From the hut we were about to locate, gallant Englishmen had set out for the Pole. Tragically, Scott and his four companions perished in a silent wilderness of snow on the return journey in March 1912. Their deeds are proudly imprinted in the annals of polar exploration.

*   *   *

While waiting to go ashore conversation turned again to that most dangerous of Antarctic animals the killer whale. I could not see why anyone on ice could be in danger from a creature which inhabited the waters. So I asked:

"But how the devil do they get on to the ice?"

Captain Schwaner reached for a book and read aloud:

In the Antarctic, one type of porpoise is so large that men have mistakenly named it the killer whale. They are about thirty feet long and are the most savage of all beasts. They hunt in packs and will attack the great blue whale. When they see a man, seal or penguin on the ice, they will dive and rush to the surface, breaking ice three feet thick to dump their prey into the water. Several men have had narrow escapes and have fled for their lives across breaking ice.

Jimmy pointed across the open sea to Cape Evans.

"Over there!" he exclaimed, "Scott's photographer, Herbert Ponting, missed being torn to shreds by eight killer whales because he foolishly went to the ice edge."

"You know what Ponting wrote?" asked the Captain.

"No, sir."

Another volume was selected and the Captain produced frightening facts to support his warning. He passed the book over and I read:

I had got to within six feet of the edge of the ice, which was about a yard thick, when to my consternation, it suddenly heaved up under my feet and split into fragments around me, whilst the eight whales, lined up side by side and almost touching each other, burst from under the ice and spouted. The head of one was within two yards of me. I saw its nostrils open, and at such close quarters the release of its pent-up breath was like a blast from an air-compressor.

Captain Scott also wrote in his journal about the photographer's escape:

One after the other their huge, hideous heads shot vertically into the air through the cracks they had made. As they reared them to a height of 6 or 8 ft. it was possible to see their tawny head markings, their small glistening eyes and their terrible array of teeth, by far the largest and most terrifying in the world.

Later I, myself, shot a cine film of killer whales not a dozen

222

yards from *Arneb*. At the time we were tied-up off McMurdo. The starboard side of the vessel lay flush against the edge of sea-ice for unloading. On the port side, however, there was a patch of open water roughly 200 yards square, in an otherwise endless white expanse. The visible sea formed the end of the channel chopped out by the icebreaker. It was four in the morning and I had just returned to my cabin. Sleeplessness was an affliction and I had spent many hours in conversation in the wardroom. The weather had cleared and visibility was crystal clear. The white peaks of the far off western mountains were bathed in glorious rainbow hues of crimson and gold. Two miles across the sea-ice the camp of McMurdo and surrounding hills were tinted in a delicate bluish-green.

When the knock came at my door I was making diary notes about this silent and soul-stirring scene of Antarctic magic. My thoughts, to say the least, were far away from devilish and bloodthirsty killer whales. At the door was Davis, my coloured steward.

"Boss," he exclaimed a little breathlessly, "Goddam killer whales, right alongside! Captain Schwaner wants you to come on deck with your camera."

I threw on my thick outer clothes with the speed of a fireman and grabbed my movie camera.

I joined the Captain on the lower deck and looked down on four huge dolphin-like creatures, all of thirty feet in length. The bodies rose and sank, spouting and hissing. They blew so loudly that one could almost sense the tremor as pent up force was released. It was a sinister sight. Triangular shaped dorsal fins, all of five feet high, flashed out of the water as the thick black bodies arched and dived. Then suddenly, on the far side of the large square of water, a seal, at least seven feet in length, raised its head and splashed at the ice edge distractedly. Close behind a killer whale spouted, then a huge head shot vertically out of the water and small evil eyes momentarily looked about. The seal had submerged. Half a minute later it appeared on the opposite side rushing and splashing towards the ice edge. With a magnificent effort it projected itself out of the water, struggling valiantly with its flippers to lever to safety a body which must have weighed 600 lb. The Captain and I breathed with relief when the seal flopped on the ice furiously panting.

"Nice work seal," someone yelled from the deck above, "you've sure beaten those baskets."

Some men attached to a cargo tractor transport on the other side of the ship came into view around the bows. One man in a bright green parka stupidly advanced towards the seal with a camera. He paused within a dozen paces. The creature stared at him in blank amazement from large liquid eyes. The killer whales were still diving and blowing in the square of water.

"The fool," exploded the Captain, "the utter idiot. They crash ice. Danger is always present when these carnivorous killers are about."

We gesticulated wildly and shouted to the man to get away from the ice edge. A deck hand tossed an orange crate over the side. Almost immediately there was a spout of water nearby, followed by a flashing head and a glistening black body. It was a full half hour before those four dorsal fins disappeared.

*   *   *

Captain Scott's last polar home had been erected close to the sea. It nestled atop a rising beach of black volcanic sand and appeared reasonably sheltered from winds. The locality possessed morainic rocks, volcanic agglomerates, and large boulders of olivinine kenyte. There was absolutely no soil anywhere, and the sun's heat absorbed by black lava patches resulted in a rise in temperature.

This site was not as picturesque as Cape Royds, but the hut which had once housed twenty-five men was, like Shackleton's last abode, in perfect condition. Here again I felt the sensation that time had been nullified. Entry was not easy. Unfortunately, a window had been shattered by blizzards and snow had driven inside. At least a third of the hut's interior (50 ft. × 25 ft. × 9 ft.) was a solid mass of hard ice. Access to the free part of the habitation necessitated wriggling across a narrow space between ice and roof.

In and about the station provisions of every description were plentiful; I was surprised by the large amount of stacked pickles. A pile of *Illustrated London News* and *Sphere* magazines were as fresh as the day they were printed. Reverently, I examined articles which Scott had brought with him on return to the Antarctic to complete and extend his previous discoveries. I picked up a glass inkwell on which "R. F. Scott" had been painted, also a bottle of Indian ink marked "Wilson". They are among treasured souvenirs.

There was a heart-wrenching pathos about the hut and its environs. From this spot, Captain Scott, Doctor Wilson, Captain Oates, Lieutenant Bowers and Petty Officer Evans had sledged poleward, never to return. The simple wooden building had been the mecca of all their hopes and dreams. I looked to the south. In the great outback their bodies remain without change deep below the snow, their deeds a soul-stirring legacy to men of all races.

Near the hut, I stopped in my tracks and surveyed a grim sight. It was a dead sledge dog, still wearing its collar and chained to a packing case. It had lain there stiff and stark just short of fifty years. It seemed a tragic attestation of Scott's mistrust of dogs for long polar journeys.

I spoke to many authorities about dogs, the oldest form of polar travel. Sled dogs primarily are workers and not pets. Scott's last journey still remains a burning subject of controversy. It is generally believed that if Scott's imagination had allowed itself to be less opposed to dog teams as against his faith in Siberian ponies, he and the others might well have survived. Norway's Amundsen moved fast to the Pole with tough, reliable dog teams, and swiftly returned to safety. Scott's men on the other hand, were compelled to foot-slog and man-haul heavy sledges after the last of the ponies had been shot at the entrance to the Beardmore Glacier. From this point the distance to the Pole and back, was roughly three-quarters of the total

In all, 1,200 geographical miles had to be conquered by five men laboriously trudging over snowfields and dragging heavy loads. Their task was made the heavier by atrocious weather.

It was in 1908, during his first attempt to reach the South Pole, that Sir Ernest Shackleton discovered and traversed the Beardmore Glacier. This river of glistening blue ice is the longest in Antarctica. Born through the gigantic pressure of millions of tons from the two miles high icecap that covers the central polar plateau, it cuts its way for 1,200 miles to reach the sea at the Ross Ice Shelf.

Though it may move only inches in a week, this ice river has planed and sculptured its way through mountains which tower to more than 14,000 feet. As it inches forward over the rough rocks the ice does not maintain constant speed throughout its length. So cracks and crevices, known as crevasses, occur. These cracks may go down deeply into the heart of the glacier and yet retain a thin covering of snow across their tops so that neither man nor machine may discover their existence before the thin snow cover breaks and lets all on its surface into the icy depths. Nor is this the Beardmore's only danger. The glacier varies in width from 5 to 25 miles; always it presses outwards, slowly grinding and cutting. Where its path lies through a pass in the mountains the ice river gradually undercuts the surrounding slopes until they collapse and millions of tons of rock thunder down upon the surface of the glacier, thence to be carried remorselessly to the Antarctic Ocean. To the relatively slow-moving man upon the glacier's surface such an avalanche of rock gives scant chance of escape. Yet for those on foot the Beardmore was the path to the Pole. No man ever is safe on that terrible stretch of ice and even those who fly above it regard the Beardmore Glacier as the devil's own pathway.

I stumbled on a dump of scrap metal and disused motor parts, a vivid reminder of the first two petrol engines used in Antarctica. Scott was the pioneer of caterpillar traction, but troubles and disappointments in those early 1910 engines were heartbreaking. The two crude tractors which set out on the long journey broke down and were abandoned after a combined distance of only 150 miles. Scott's faith, however, was strong in the future development of motor tractors, and he believed the day would dawn when engines would supplant animals in the far south. How accurate was his far-sightedness can be gauged when we recall Sir Edmund Hillary's first overland trip to the Pole and the great achievement of Dr. Fuchs in crossing the great southern continent.

Today, "Deep-Freeze" operation relies on Sno-cat vehicles; in addition speedy, versatile weasels and giant 35-ton caterpillar D-8 tractors with 54-inch treads have been adapted to polar operations. The wide tracks reduce the tractor's ground pressure to the equivalent of a man weighing $11\frac{1}{2}$ stones.

In 1957, "Deep Freeze" transported the material for Byrd Scientific (IGY) Station across 600 miles of frozen desert in uncharted Marie Byrd Land, a tremendous undertaking. The most dramatic way in which these vehicles are used is in tractor trains. A tractor pulls behind it one or more sledges on which supplies and equipment are loaded. The tractor trains that carried the building supplies, food and equipment to the Byrd IGY Station used 35-ton tractors and sleds that, when loaded, weighed twenty tons. When the men ate or slept, they used wannigans. A wannigan is really a hut built on a sled that can be pulled along behind a tractor. It contains bunks, stoves, radio equipment, and other facilities to make men comfortable. To Captain Scott and his men, it would have seemed a fantastic luxury.

Even with steel juggernauts rumbling over uncharted polar wastes, Antarctic travel must forever remain treacherous and dangerous. Great blizzards, which blow up in a few minutes, can last days. They bring the mightiest tractor to a halt. Then there is always the constant fear that a tractor may disappear into a crevasse.

Arneb sailed for ten miles through a 100-yard-wide channel hacked from solid sea-ice. This water lane ended opposite McMurdo Base, but over a mile of white still separated land and ship. We moored to sleepers frozen in to ice holes—a most rigid and stable form of anchorage. Off-loading began immediately. The heavy tractor trains operating on the sea-ice were compelled to make a sweeping detour of eleven miles to reach the station. The shortest route was treacherous, no tractor driver dare stray from the marked trail. I travelled to the base on a 35-ton tractor hauling 20 tons of supplies; it was not a pleasant trip. The most frightening of dangers when operating on sea-ice is a sudden sharp cracking sound and an almost simultaneous downward plunge. During my long, grinding ride, I was prepared to jump for it at a second's notice. My mind kept on recalling vividly the fate of a tractor which had suddenly disappeared in the same vicinity with five men. Four had managed to struggle to the surface, the fifth, Ollie B. Bartley of Kentucky was drowned.

Prior to this accident, on the same McMurdo Bay ice, driver Richard T. Williams had taken a downward plunge in his tractor and died. I was happier when the American padre at McMurdo, Captain Hammond from Virginia, drove me on a journey across sea-ice in a lighter, faster vehicle. The splendid, bearded Chaplain proudly showed me over his tiny church, built from curved corrugated iron. It serves the spiritual needs of 132 officers and men of the U.S. Navy, and civilian scientists.

"Life on the ice stresses human values," he said. "Down here men quickly understand the true meaning of self-sacrifice and discipline. We have no time for prejudices and petty actions. Living in such confinement would be unbearable, if it were otherwise."

He paused outside his little church . . . "In Antarctica, men's hearts," he continued, "seem naturally to expand to the beauty and power of spirit, and the good things of human nature that are unchangeable. Acts of goodness are in themselves inner happiness and contentment. I can say with full-hearted pride there is good in everyone down here."

Padre Hammond pointed to a small cross on the roof of his church.

"Follow an imaginary line from it," he said, "right away to the summit of the high hill behind the church."

I did so, and my eyes rested on the pinnacle of Observation Hill which had figured so largely in Scott's first expedition.

"What do you see?"

"I see a tiny cross up there."

"That cross," said the Padre in his slow southern drawl, "is directly in line with the one down here on my church. It perpetuates the memory of Captain Scott and his companions. It was carried up there by the relief party which found their bodies."

"Amazing how the searchers stumbled on a tiny, snow tent," I ventured to reply, "so many months after the men had died in their tracks."

The bearded Virginian gazed thoughtfully into the far south, then murmured . . .

"How can we close our eyes to the fact that it was not a special act of providence which guided those who found the partially snowed-up tent and the three frozen bodies?"

I answered, "Yes, I have seen some of that white polar nothingness from the air. It was rather a miracle."

The Padre Hammond broke his gaze with infinity.

"Everything is planned," he exclaimed softly, "by a mighty hand for good. Those brave men did not die alone out there for no purpose!"

I drove in a weasel over to Hut Point, to visit Scott's very first cabin which he built in Antarctica, during his 1901 *Discovery* expedition. It lay ten minutes run from America's large compact station of red pre-fabricated buildings, hangers, workshops and permanent helicopter pads. The pathetic little hut seemed strangely out of place. It contrasted sharply with modern Antarctic life and technological development. Not far from the front door of the historical building, two large steel oil tankers had been frozen into the sea ice. Pipe lines as thick as a man's thigh wound around the rear of the hut to large storage tanks. I photographed dozens of seal skeletons alongside one of the wooden walls. Fifty-seven years before, the flesh of these creatures had fed the British expedition.

A helicopter hovered overhead; from the camp came the roar of tractor engines. I returned to the mess at McMurdo for lunch. It was a superb four-course meal, in warm, comfortable quarters. I kept thinking back to those piled-up skeletons, however, and seal meat. In the days of the great explorers it was a major item of food. Captain Scott wrote: "Tonight we had galantine seal—it was excellent." And, "We had some seal rissoles so extraordinarily well cooked that it was impossible to distinguish them from the best beef rissoles. I told two of the party they were beef, and they made no comment till I enlightened them after they had eaten two each. It is the first time I have tasted seal without being aware of its particular flavour. But even its own flavour is acceptable in our cook's hands—he really is excellent."

On the mess wall a notice announced that the film, "Around the World in Eighty Days" would be showing that evening. a movie show goes on three times a week in McMurdo base camp for the personnel.

I thought to myself, "In their wildest dreams the first men who waged warfare on this great white south, could never have imagined such comforts." I countered this reflection quickly, and added, "But life down here is still a lonely, rigorous and dangerous ordeal."

With a companion I decided to climb to the pinnacle of Observation Hill and visit the cross erected to the memory of Captain Scott and his four valiant comrades. It was an exhausting ascent and as we got higher my breath came in rapid gasps; the vapour blew back in my face like smoke. We did not regret making the climb. From a high vantage point we looked out over the Great Ice Barrier, and to our left was a panoramic view of modern McMurdo shoulder to shoulder with Scott's old *Discovery* winter quarters. It was strangely stirring. Seawards was an infinite solitude of ice; *Arneb* appeared as a toy vessel marooned on a vast plain of white. I directed my gaze inwards to the luring land of mystery which has always challenged men to follow their adventures upon this last great frontier racked by the world's cruellest weather. Over the last century, courageous men of many nations have sought to unlock the secrets of the great white continent. It is certain there will always be other brave men who will follow in their footsteps at the bottom of the world. The great unveiling of the once invincible Antarctica is only just beginning. The vast unknown and uninhabited wastes offer room enough for men of all countries to explore and adventure, pooling scientific understanding for the good of all on earth. I trust that the twelve-nation Antarctic conference, which began in Washington in October 1959, will agree to respect the non-military development of the white continent. The future must shortly reveal the sincerity of international goodwill, and the intention for peaceful purposes and fruitful development of scientific research and co-operation.

I reverently touched the cross on the windswept summit. It was nine feet high and made from Australian jarrah wood. In perfect condition as it always will be, the carving on it was fresh and clean as the day it was chiselled. When the ship *Terra Nova* returned to Antarctica for the last time to pick-up survivors of the ill-fated expedition, the cross had been carried to the top of Observation Hill and positioned. This symbol of the Christian faith was the final gesture of goodbye and respect from the living to the memory of the dead. The carved words come from Tennyson's Ulysses and read:

In
Memoriam
Captain R. F. Scott, R.N.
Dr. E. A. Wilson, Capt. L. E. G. Oates, Ins. Drgs.,
Lt. H. R. Bowers, R.I., R.I.M., Petty Officer E. Evans, R.N.
who died on their
return from the
Pole. March 1912.
TO STRIVE, TO SEEK, TO FIND, AND NOT TO YIELD.

On that high hill, I gazed towards the stark white hills,

beyond which was an enormous portion of God's earth never trodden by man or beast. I turned my eyes downwards towards the tiny hut which had been Scott's Ross Sea Base, then I traced a thin imaginary line towards the Beardmore Glacier—the portals of the Pole. I was stirred when I recalled that Scott and his companions had perished less than 140 miles from where I now looked out. These gallant Englishmen had died in their tracks in latitude 79° 50' south. At this position they had lost their great fight, and tragically, within a short, single march of a supply depot. There they would have found fuel and food which might well have saved their lives. But a great and abnormal blizzard had descended and pinned them down in a tiny tent. Elemental fury lasted too long.

The spot where the frozen bodies had been discovered was reached on 12 March, 1912. Scott's final entry was recorded in his diary on 29 March. It was 18 January, 1912, when Captain Scott and his men planted the Union Jack at the South Pole, after incredible foot-slogging and sledge-hauling over a distance of 900 miles. It must have been heart-rending for the five men to find the Norwegian flag already there. The intrepid Roald Amundsen and four other Norwegians had reached the Pole a month before them. Such is the price of exploration and attainment in wresting from nature her jealous secrets. Written in the leader's diary later found on his frozen body were the words: "Great God! this is an awful place and terrible enough for us to have laboured to it without the reward of priority . . ." Then began the desperate homeward journey, anxiety and agonizing hardships and suffering from frostbite and starvation. Scott wrote in his record: "Well, we have turned our back now on the goal of our ambition and must face our 900 miles of solid dragging—and good-bye to most of the day dreams."

I looked to the south once again before I began my descent. Not a great geographical distance away, five bodies lay deep beneath eternal ice, free from all decay. What impact their lives had made upon history, what legacy they had left to posterity. As I picked my way down the steep slope to

McMurdo base I pondered a great deal on the American padre's words. "Yes, Scott may have failed to achieve for his country priority at the Pole, but he left behind a noble tradition. A record of fortitude and unselfishness to fire inspiration, adventure and patriotism in men for generations to come. The good deeds of the dead possess more reality for men than the living."

I paused and looked back a number of times at the simple wooden cross bearing five names. It was growing smaller and smaller. What the padre had meant was growing larger and larger in my mind. That cross represented a glorious proof that the spirit of man is supreme and imperishable, transcending all that is temporal and temporary.

Chapter Nineteen

Life at the South Pole

"If we are to become the masters of science, not its slaves, we must learn to use its immense powers to good purpose. The machine itself has neither mind nor soul, nor moral sense. Only man has been endowed with these Godlike attributes. Every age has its destined duty—ours is to nurture an awareness of those divine attributes and a sense of responsibility—in giving them expression."

EACH year since 1957 a handful of men has lived and worked actually at the South Pole. Theirs is no idle existence; nor is it purposeless. By comparison with the sojourns of Captain Scott and Shackleton their life is luxurious; but it is not without danger. Those early explorers of the barren, white wilderness lived in wooden huts that were, by comparison with the dwellings now in use, cold, draughty, cramped and cheerless.

From the doorway of my own quarters in Antarctica I could see Hut Point and the crude wooden structure which sheltered Scott: such heat as he and his companions had came in part from a not very efficient wood- and coal-burning stove and in part from their own close-packed bodies. Through crevices in the wood the bitter winds came in; those winds, driving powdered snow, howled and screamed for weeks on end. Certainly it was warmer inside the hut than out in the elements; but it could never have been hot.

I studied my comfortable, scientifically-designed quarters. Instead of narrow wood-lengths and tarpaper, Deep Freeze builders had used panels for the sides and roofs of the building. These panels consisted of a layer of plywood, which faced outside, and a layer of aluminium which faced inside. Between the two layers was an insulating material which helped to keep the cold out. These panels arrive in standard sizes and fit tightly in line. They can be slotted and bolted together quickly to make buildings of many different sorts and sizes. When completed, such constructions are air-tight and easy to heat. Oil heating is easy and cleaner to use than coal and the transport of fuel is simpler, too.

There is no dirt in Antarctica save that which man brings in. Scott's photographer, Herbert Ponting, on his return to Europe could show a skin as white as a child's. Scott, however, had only two tractors—and they soon broke down. His transport was by pack pony, dog-drawn sled and man-hauled sledge. Today the petrol-driven tractor and the aeroplane dominate the movement of everything, both men and supplies, and with the increase in motor traffic the amount of dirt is increasing also. A bath in Scott's crude hut was an heroic venture; adequate water supply, when every drop had to be produced by melting ice on a not-very-efficient coal-fired stove, alone was a problem. So if "knights of the grey underwear" then took pride in going for weeks or longer without baths, who really could blame them? Today a welcome relief from the external temperatures in the minus 80s is a session in a steam bath or under a sun lamp!

As I write this chapter in New Zealand, I have just learned that America will beat the winter blizzards at the South Pole and other bases by flying three pre-fabricated atomic-power stations to Antarctica in the near future. The first atomic-power station is to be installed at McMurdo. Soon, the building in which I discussed so many aspects of Antarctica, lying between Scott's old camp and the cross on the hill, will be lighted and heated by atomic reactors. These will be similar to those used to power American nuclear submarines. Such reactors are capable of supplying heat and light to a town of 20,000. This equipment is small and uses concentrated fuel which will last for months without recharging. Surpassing strange things are happening down there! Developments which Scott and his men could not remotely have imagined in their most sanguine dreams.

Now that occupation of the Antarctic has become an accepted thing, and with the first atomic reactors being prepared for the Great White South, undreamed of things are possible. Antarctica, the unconquerable, is slowly bowing to man's growing technical skill. Within a short span, I foresee enormous ice runways at the South Pole, enabling giant planes to wheel-land just as they now do on the sea-ice at McMurdo. Atomic heat will enable snow to be melted for re-freezing into permanent, glass-smooth, rock-hard surfaces.

Deep Freeze Sixty got under way in September, 1959. There had been previously four American enterprises called respectively Deep Freeze I, II, III and IV. The change of title implies no change of policy; it is designed to signify that the planning and financing of the operation have been brought into line with the fiscal year—and since these operations in Antarctica are costing the Americans perhaps a million dollars a man surely that is not inappropriate!

There are four American stations operating on an all-the-year-round basis in Antarctica. Naval Air Facility, McMurdo Sound, is the principal cargo staging base as well as being the scene of some limited scientific investigations. This station is situated on the west coast of the Ross Sea. The other stations are Byrd, which is in the heart of Marie Byrd Land and is named after the famous American admiral and aeronaut who pioneered so much flying at the earth's extremities; Hallett Station, which is on Cape Hallett, also in the Ross Sea, is supported jointly by New Zealand and America; and the Amundsen-Scott South Pole Station, which, as its name implies, is situated actually at the South Pole.

Before I say a word about the reasons why these stations are maintained—and scientifically those reasons are compelling— I shall write of the contrast in man's way of life in Antarctica that only half a century has brought about. Of the enormous improvement in housing I have said something already; food and transport also have been revolutionized. There has been an influx to the Great White South of equipment the very existence of which Scott and Amundsen could not have known.

Let us look first at food, because to all of us that always will be important. Against the wooden walls of Scott's hut there yet lie dozens of skeletons of seals. When I saw them fifty-seven years had passed since the meat of those creatures was a major item in the daily diet that preserved life in the men and animals of the British expedition. Seal meat has a distinctive flavour, hard to disguise and not palatable to everyone; it was a foremost part of the diet of every day. Even seal meat could seem palatable by comparison with pemmican. Weight and bulk of rations mattered greatly when long distances had to be covered on foot with all supplies for men and animals having to be dragged on sledges. So seal meat gave place to pemmican, a greasy mixture of beef, fat, horsemeat, cereal and powdered fruits. That was the staple diet of the old explorers when they were on the trail and even so, such was the meagre ration against the mileage to be covered, that most of the time on travel found the traveller obsessed with thoughts of food ... even of seal-meat.

Operation Deep Freeze planners have given a lot of careful thought to food requirements in the Antarctic. In this aspect, the Navy received valuable assistance from industry and the Food and Container Institute, Chicago. Varying degrees of strenuous activity and exposure to freezing temperatures result in quantitative variations in food intake. Varying increases from normal subsistence requirements have to be allowed for items for which greater than normal intake could be expected, either because of the operating conditions, environment, or the characteristics of the rations. Based on these considerations, the ration was planned to meet maximum food needs under extreme cold and increased physical activity. The load list contained approximately 200 items. Meat comprised about 20% by weight of the food provided, or just over a pound of meat per man per day. As a point of interest objects weigh more at the Pole than they do at the Equator. If 5,000 tons of cargo were loaded on a ship at the Equator it would at the Pole weigh 50,000 lb. more.

The cooks prepare an incredible variety of dishes. In spite of Antarctica being a natural icebox, in the kitchens at McMurdo I looked into huge refrigerators stocked with food. A twelve months' emergency supply is carried. Hams, joints, chickens, turkeys, fish and special meats in tins and skins. There was every variety of frozen vegetables, fruits, and juices that one buys from the deep freeze boxes in stores at home. The cooks prepare fresh bread, cakes, pies, buns, cookies of different varieties and a strong favourite, cinnamon rolls. It is a fact that all personnel on Antarctic stations, odd to relate, have a yearning for dessert ice cream. Twenty gallon ice-cream freezers are always operating to produce sundaes, hot chocolate sauces and whipped creams. It has also been found that men aboard ships in the Antarctic and at land bases consume a tremendous quantity of sweets and chocolate. This has been attributed to the absence of liquor; sweetmeats give quick energy and body heat. The average daily food consumption per man was between six and eight pounds, and a favourite beverage, despite the low temperature, was iced tea!

On any expedition, of course, the most critical, and often the most thankless task is that of the cook. Let him be bad and failure is almost inevitable: let him be good and contentment is in a fair way to be achieved; men have time to think of other things than their unsatisfied stomachs and a way to success stands a fair chance of being found. The Deep Freeze cooks have been selected with great care. Some have had their own problems. There have been odd requests for special dishes—some men actually developed a desire for ginger-flavoured steaks at *breakfast*! There have been odd culinary problems—as when cakes wouldn't bake whatever proven recipe was followed: because the cook was working at 9,200 feet above sea-level every mixture failed to rise. So the cook sent to a great flour combine in America a request for guidance. The answer from Pillsbury in Minneapolis was sent by an amateur-operated radio: "add more flour!" It worked.

This particular cook, Chet Segers, had to plan carefully: most of his three-ton stock of food, which had been delivered by parachute drop, was in tunnels in the ice at a temperature of minus 60° F.; it had to be allowed to thaw gently for about a week before use.

Mention of that food store in an ice tunnel reminds me of one of the greatest dangers facing the dwellers in Antarctica: fire. Should fire break out it would be almost impossible to check because though all around is ice it cannot be converted quickly enough to water for use against a fire. Though every man is constantly conscious of the fire danger, so that vigilance and precautions are second nature, the risk remains. Men without food in Antarctica would live longer than men without shelter. So wherever there is an encampment there is at a distance a spare, emergency hut. It is stocked with fuel and food enough to last twenty men for half a year: to sustain life in fact until the return of the sun and the coming of the supply planes.

Planes play a big part in Antarctic life. Small ones fitted with skis are used to ferry men and supplies between the various stations. Giant planes flying directly from New Zealand, land on special runways on the sea-ice in McMurdo Sound. They bring in and take out personnel and some supplies and scientific specimens. Helicopters have a hundred uses; their principal tasks are reconnaissance (especially for leads in pack ice to help shipping to move) and for rescue work when men come to grief in remote places or in particularly difficult terrain.

In 1956, on 31 October, Admiral Dufek stepped from a ski-equipped plane on to the ice at the South Pole; his object was reconnaissance. He was the first man since Scott to set foot at the bottom of the world. Though it was summer time the temperature stood at 58 degrees below zero. There was a wind blowing at fifteen miles an hour. Almost always in Antarctica there is wind. Wind intensifies the effect of cold on man. So Admiral Dufek stayed no longer than was necessary to test the snow, place markers and set up a flag. After only three-quarters of an hour the Admiral and his companions climbed back into their plane. They had frostbite on their faces: that also is of almost daily occurrence in Antarctica. Their plane was frozen to the ice. That had been foreseen. The machine had special jets under its wings to assist take-off. . . .

From the South Pole Station to the base at McMurdo takes four hours by plane. For Amundsen to travel from the Bay of Whales to the Pole, a distance of 770 miles, took 39 days. That distance is shorter by between 60 and 80 miles than the journey which Scott made from Hut Point to the Pole.

For Amundsen and Scott travel and transport meant men on foot with their loads either on man-hauled sledges or with dog teams or pack ponies. Scott did try tractors, but in 1910 the mechanics of motoring were not equal to the trails of the road-less far-south. Yet some of Scott's experience has helped those who run the tractor-drawn supply trains which today move stores from the ships to McMurdo Base. By his emphasis on scientific studies Scott did as much as any man to ensure that exploration of the Antarctic will continue.

There are sledges and dog teams with the present dwellers in Antarctica. Admiral Byrd always referred to sled dogs as his "Antarctica life insurance". When Admiral Dufek planned Operation Deep Freeze he had similar thoughts. The dogs are kept at "Dogheim Manor" at McMurdo. They are trained and ready for emergencies. Should men strike trouble in mountainous areas those dogs can be parachuted to their aid. Until such an emergency occurs they are everyone's pets, adding a touch of friendliness, almost a nostalgic feeling of romance, to the general picture of Antarctic life. And not only the Americans have found dogs a worth while "life insurance". Sixty were taken out in 1958 by the New Zealanders who formed a part of the British trans-Antarctic Expedition. I visited them. Of course, if one husky howls or barks thirty others join in. When the peace of the camp was thus disturbed I almost could imagine that the calendar had spun backwards and that I was myself in Scott's hut, for I was hearing hideous sounds with which those forerunners of Antarctic exploration must have been all too familiar.

The smooth surface of snow hides danger. On the right can be seen the thin snow covering ("bridge") over a crevasse. If the weight of man or vehicle is too great for such a "bridge" it will collapse; the gap beneath may be as much as 200 feet deep ... So safe paths across snow-fields must be carefully reconnoitred and flagged (below). Because the first crossing can be as dangerous as a journey through a minefield, the vehicles making it are manoeuvred by ropes attached to their controls and operated by men walking behind.

Above, left: Commander Francis J. Roohan, First Officer of *Arneb*, from whom I learned much about Antarctica.

Above, right: Captain H. C. Schwaner, Commander of *Arneb*, under whose authority I was placed during my time with Operation "Deep Freeze".

Below: Tracked vehicles, including Sno-Cats, on a traverse. As was foreseen by Captain Scott, who was the first to use it in Antarctica, caterpillar traction has revolutionized the movement of men and supplies on the ice continent.

Above: Shackleton's hut at Cape Royds, a tiny monument to man against one of the mightiest backgrounds of nature I have ever seen. Here fifteen men had huddled together, laughing, planning and existing. They were utterly isolated, without even radio contact with the world outside, while winter lasted.

Below: The stove in Shackleton's hut: in 1908 this burned day and night for nine months and in its oven bread was baked each day. The sealskin sleeping bag on the bed was left by the Shackleton expedition.

Rising stiff and cold to 13,500 feet and looking almost ethereal, Mount Erebus, Antarctica's only live volcano, dominates the area around McMurdo Sound. From the top of its cone a thin steam-cloud stretched like a broad, white ribbon across the blue sky. The summit was first reached in the autumn of 1908 by four members of Sir Ernest Shackleton's expedition. Some have noted in this mountain a strong similarity to Fujiyama in Japan.

The sound which in fact more commonly assaulted my own ears was the mechanical growling of the 35-ton tractor trains. *Arneb* could not get through all the ice between McMurdo and the open sea. So her stores had to be fetched across a wide expanse of sea-ice. No direct route could be taken because the ice on which those trains moved had to be thick enough to bear them. So the crawling yellow caterpillars bobbed in a shuttle-cock service across a sweeping arc that meant a journey of many miles. The service ran continuously until the stores had all been off-loaded.

That *Arneb* got no nearer was no fault of her escorting ice-breakers. A deal of thought has been given to icebreakers. Without these tireless little sledge-hammer slaves for pulverizing millions of tons of ice, the current Deep Freeze shipping assaults on the cold-continent, even in summer, would be well-nigh impossible. The icebreaker is a comparative newcomer to the navies of the world. Of indispensable value today in attacking ice, it cannot be overlooked that one day it may play a supreme role in ice-defence. Future warfare would inevitably embrace the cold-continent. America's largest and most up-to-date ice-breaker is the U.S.S. *Glacier* which displaces 8,625 tons. Her ten diesel engines, with 20,000 horsepower can drive the toughened hull into the solid pack fifteen feet in thickness and smash it apart. Phenomenal as the power of the *Glacier* is, creditable as its record has been in the icefields, I think icebreakers, like the aeroplane, will undergo considerable development in short time. At present there is a limit to the capabilities of ice-mauling ships. When winter blackness envelops the white-continent, and ice masses seal it off with an impenetrable barrier, ice-breakers, perforce, are halted. There is no getting into Antarctica, and no getting out once you are there until the icefields break up with warmer weather.

In July of 1959, the Vice-President of the United States, Mr. Nixon, and Admiral Rickover, "father" of the American atomic submarine, inspected the Russian atomic icebreaker, *Lenin*, of 16,000 tons, at Leningrad. America has still to produce her first atomic icebreaker. May it be soon. If America is to pioneer and probe farther and deeper into unknown Antarctic areas, economy of fuel with power is necessary. Perhaps even the ice-shield of Antarctica's winter may yet be pierced? For other cogent reasons, America cannot afford to lag behind in the atomic icebreaker race.

* * *

In the days of Scott and Shackleton, when men slept, lived and ate in a tiny hut where privacy was impossible and entertainment was what one's companions could provide, there were, as might be expected, some psychological problems. Now sleeping quarters for one man occupy almost as much space as *housed* eight in 1929. Now there are film shows three times a week; there is radio—but as yet no television—and with the help of "ham" radio men in America, members of the wintering over parties can even speak by telephone to their loved ones in the States!

Of course things sometimes misfire. One call was made from the Pole by a seismologist named Willie Hough. Somehow the ham-radio man co-operating on the American Continent called the wrong telephone number. Thousands of miles away in the realm of civilization a phone bell rang. An irate American picked up his receiver in the small hours of the morning, his sleep sadly interrupted.

"Hello," said Willie Hough, "I'm speaking from the South Pole, is my wife there, please?"

Angry at what he thought was a crazy, practical joke, the man roared . . . "Nuts!" and hung up.

Don't judge communications with Antarctica by that one incident: it isn't typical. Despite the exceptional difficulties—of which more shortly—the standard of communications is high. I had a most interesting conversation with the Radio Officer. He it was who told me that of the 75-foot radio tower built in 1929 at Little America by Admiral Byrd's men only eight feet now project above the snow. He took me to the isolated outpost at McMurdo that is the radio station and introduced me to Robert Allan of California, one of the trio of lonely operators who serve that station.

The impossible is being accomplished daily by Allan and his two companions at the radio shack which is a mile from this base area. These three men keep up a daily routine maintenance and check the transmitter antennae in weather usually featuring winds of gale force and temperature of at least minus 50°. In case of emergency this self-contained group can exist for a month, but normally during weather breaks one of the men drives a weasel from the radio shack to the McMurdo stores to replenish their larder and exchange reading material.

Powerful radio installations at McMurdo keep in frequent touch with other Deep Freeze bases, particularly the South Pole with its seventeen Navy men and scientists. During the long winter night of constant darkness, numbing cold and howling winds, when the ice continent is completely isolated, radio is the only contact with the outside world.

"Transmission with the Pole should be clear tonight," said the Radio Officer, "but in winter, even short-wave radio provides fickle communication during magnetic storms."

Magnetic storms have been traced to explosions on the sun, which look, when seen through telescopes, like spots. The storms caused by sunspots produce one of the most beautiful displays in all nature, the Aurora. Curtains of light in many changing colours dance across the sky. At the top of the world we know them as the Northern Lights, in Antarctica, the Southern Lights. These words express in simple form a complicated truth. The rays that bombard the earth are attracted towards the magnetic poles. The Aurora then occurs at the northern and southern ends of the earth. Atoms and electrons streaming from the sun converge towards the earth's magnetic poles, penetrating the atmosphere and exciting the gases in the air. This excitation, in which atoms become more energetic, occurs about sixty miles high. When the atoms return to normal, they give out the distinctive lights and colours of the Aurora. The entire action is similar to that which causes a neon tube to glow. Although the Aurora is sometimes seen far away from the poles, it is most often seen in a wide belt encircling the earth about 23 degrees from each geomagnetic pole. For this reason, the polar regions are the best locations for observing the Aurora. At the South Pole, observers study the timing, the rapid changes, and the geographical location of the Aurora. They break the light into component colours, using spectroscopes and other equipment. A specially-built wide-angle camera takes photographs of the sky almost from horizon to horizon at regular intervals. The Antarctic is a good place for scientists to study the effects of these phenomena on radios and our atmosphere.

Polar research includes geomagnetism, the study of the magnetic field of the earth and its variations. While its best-known practical uses are in surveying, navigation, and exploration for minerals and petroleum, geomagnetism plays a very important role in the study of the ionosphere. Variations in the earth's magnetism can be traced to two different causes. Those occurring slowly over periods of years or decades, result from slow changes in the earth's molten interior or in its crust. Those happening rapidly come from electricity flowing far above the earth's surface. The Deep Freeze geomagnetic programme calls for systematic measurement of magnetic variations at all stations in Antarctica.

Cosmic rays bombard the earth from all directions. Actually, they are fragments of atoms coming from outer space and travelling at terrifyingly high speeds. They are observed with special "telescopes", which often employ a Geiger counter in the "eyepiece". Most cosmic rays are stopped high in our atmosphere, but they create additional fragments which reach much nearer to the surface of the earth. Their energies are often much larger than any that can be produced by the best man-made atom-smashers.

Some, but not all, of these rays come from the sun. Others have their beginning in outer space, perhaps in the stars. Few of these particles ever reach the earth because they are trapped in a band of light air and gases between fifty and two hundred miles above us. This band, where the rays are trapped, plays an important part in making our radio sets work. When the radio waves strike this band, they bounce back again to earth. This action makes possible long-range radio. If the radio waves did not bounce off this layer they would go straight out into outer space. Therefore anything which disturbs this band affects radio communications.

All these things are important. The lonely Antarctic scientists are helping to enlarge our knowledge of the earth on which we live. Many things have been learned at the South Pole about how to live where it is very cold. How motors and other things work under difficult conditions. The vast, freezing Antarctic is a laboratory to test things as well as a place to increase our knowledge of natural forces.

This knowledge is extremely varied in character; for instance it is not generally known that there is a wavering at the earth's spinning axis. It is a slight wobble called the "Spin Pole"; this wander forms an approximate circular track at the South Pole, ranging from 10 to 100 feet in diameter. The balance of the spinning earth is affected by atmospheric upheavals, atomic explosions, earthquakes and floods. The delicately fine balance of our whirling earth on its north and south poles can be disturbed, scientists have discovered, even by the mass movement of traffic on various continents. Deep Freeze science-mathematicians feel that one day instruments will permit them to record the actual wobble-pattern of the earth, even to marking out the erratic circular movements of the spin pole on the South Pole snow itself.

The South Pole scientific station is unique in the annals of polar accomplishment. Here scientists have located the Pole within a possible error of a hundred feet in any direction. A man can walk round the world down there and cross the date line in a few minutes. That won't make or mar history I know; but many of the more serious accomplishments and discoveries of the scientists in Antarctica are adding greatly to the known facts of a region in which much of the world's weather is born. On this score alone the considerable cost is worth while. And that is only one field in which most valuable knowledge is being obtained and is regarded as cheap at the price.

The huts stand on a 9,200-foot-high plateau of ice and snow. Winds sweep endlessly over the featureless plateau. Seismic echo soundings have revealed that the men live on ice which is 8,300 feet deep. Below this is a layer of rock which itself is 900 feet above sea-level. Over the ages, therefore, snow has built up and compacted to a depth of a mile and a half. At this South Pole station volunteer scientists and Navy technicians are allowed to exist for a year. For half that time they live in a world of continuous, blinding white, followed by constant darkness and the earth's coldest temperatures. These men go there in the knowledge that during the long months of darkness they are absolutely cut-off. There is no escape until the sun rises again and planes can fly in.

Living at more than 9,000 feet above sea level and in extremely low temperatures men spit blood when the capillaries of their bronchial tubes break down. Here experience gained in the Second World War has provided an answer. Anti-cold masks were designed to enable troops to move where an enemy would not expect them. They comprise layers of steel wool that traps some of the heat and moisture from exhaled breath and when the wearer inhales use them to warm and humidify the dry and frigid air.

The first scientific leader for the Deep Freeze operation at the Pole was Dr. Paul Siple. He came first to Antarctica when an Eagle Scout at the age of nineteen with the expedition commanded by Admiral Byrd. In all he has spent 64 months, more than any other man alive, in ice-continent service. Dr. Siple found that all winter long at the Pole the wind blew, averaging between 15 and 20 m.p.h. Although wind adds materially to the effect of cold Siple and his companions could work outside in temperatures below minus 80° F. A possible explanation is that at 9,000 feet above sea level the air, being much thinner, had less conductivity and so less "cooling power". One man even stayed outside for four hours without ill effects when the temperature was very close to minus 100 degrees F. It was common for men to work two- to three-hour stretches in the snow mine, where the temperature deep below the surface remained around minus 60°.

Dr. Siple found that if the polar atmosphere was less chilling, it also contained less total oxygen than air at sea level. Newcomers, especially, found themselves quickly out of breath when they engaged in heavy labour. When personnel arrived on the heels of the departing construction crew that had built the shell of the camp, there was still a great deal of heavy work to be done. There were several noticeable effects. Nearly everyone lost weight. Some who could well afford it lost as much as 30 lb. to 40 lb., but even the lean workers grew leaner. A few felt a gradual attrition of strength, especially noticeable in loss of ability to lift and grip. This affliction ended soon after winter hibernation started, and the men's weights then began to return to normal. Another trouble noticed by some was an arthritis— like aching and stiffness of joints, especially knuckles, elbows, and shoulders. This may have been due to some mild form of anoxia, or oxygen lack, from altitude and to a reduced rate of blood circulation from the cold. For some, heavy exercise or long exposure to the cold tended to cause headaches. But gradually they became acclimatized, and when visitors and replacements arrived at the winter's end, the yearlings had acquired a reasonable amount of stamina.

Of course, serious surgical operations or accidents could cause the doctor at the Pole considerable anxiety, possibly the need to seek specialist advice by radio. Deep Freeze teams, however, at all bases have kept remarkably fit other than for the occasional appendicitis operation. Teeth in Antarctica are the most troublesome part of the body, owing to breathing very cold air through the mouth. Dental fillings have revealed a nasty habit of playing up. Nasal functioning is greatly affected by minus temperatures. Disease germs and epidemics are no worry, however, in this sterile atmosphere. At least, not until the arrival of newcomers from the germ-laden outside world. Once replacements have been purged of bugs by the aseptic climate, all is safe again. On one occasion at the Pole, a man brought in common-cold germs which struck at the veterans.

Paul Siple wrote:

"The colds we caught were worse by far than any I have ever seen before in my years in Antarctica."

He also wrote:

"Probably for me more than for any of my companions this base at the Pole seemed to be spacious and luxurious living. The effort to conserve heat has always tended to force men to live closer together under polar conditions than they would in milder climates. The first winter night I spent in the Antarctic, back in 1929, I was one of eight housed in barracks 10 x 10 square feet. At the Pole our space per man in the sleeping quarters alone was nearly this large. In fact, the total floor space of the Pole camp —6,000 square feet—was about four times larger than at Little America 1929 base, which housed 42 men as compared to our 18. This in itself was a great step towards solving the psychological problems of polar environment. The loosening up in living space gave a measure of privacy to our men. Also, the extra room required more servicing and left less spare time. Busy men are generally happy men, and time speeds by unnoticed."

For the men on Operation Deep Freeze the U.S. Navy has attempted to supply facilities comparable with its bases elsewhere around the world. There are hot and cold shower baths, a washing machine, electric clothes drier, vacuum cleaner, a light over each man's bunk, and linoleum on the floors. An intensive and systematic snow-mining programme provides more than 200 gallons of water per day, or about 11 gallons per man. The men stay clean and comfortable, with the camp tidy and morale high.

There are many communal chores that have to be shared by all hands; mining snow, bringing in fuel, keeping buildings and passages clean (or as locally expressed, acting as "house mouse").

Each man fulfils an essential job, and each is responsible, in his own way, for the success of the operations.

Men volunteering for a year in Antarctica are meticulously screened both physically and emotionally. Nothing is left to chance. Those passing the selection committees are reliable, energetic types, keenly enthusiastic about their individual jobs, and having moreover a deep interest in the closely-knit weave of the complete operation itself. For a tough existence in a barren wilderness of weird settings, high qualities of understanding, goodwill, tolerance and brotherhood are vital.

Experienced eyes are alert all the time for misfits. However, in almost all cases, good personalities become even better under conditions of isolation and hardship. The screening boys at home really know how to pick 'em. The volunteers are good, serious-minded men, and believe you me, slackers get no joy down in the far south.

I asked: "What was the most noticeable effect of Antarctic conditions on human reactions?"

One of the scientists answered: "Well, being cooped up during the long months of darkness and severe cold made individuals crave to be alone. Solitude and the privacy of one's thought were a luxury. As an ex-P.O.W. you should know that there are times when men's hearts long to ask and answer silent questions, when the memory longs to tune-in to loved ones far away."

I nodded.

"Naturally," the soft-spoken voice continued, "men at the Pole and all bases for that matter, brooded about the day when the sun would appear. The thought of the first plane to come in with mail as the months went by grew into an exciting anticipation.

"When the mail did arrive, the mysterious sense of living beyond the rim of the known world vanished. The camp was never quite the same again. *Esprit de corps* was magnificently strong, and, although men didn't talk about it, the realization of the impending early return to civilization became a magnetic prospect and growing obsession." He laughed. "And boy, when the replacements did arrive by plane, did we resent 'em as the corniest bunch of foreigners we'd ever clapped our eyes on! Sort of felt the South Pole belonged to us and nobody else. This land affects a lot of us the same way. Once Antarctica gets under your skin you have great desire to go back to solve its mysteries."

Epilogue

I quote the optimistic words of the late John Foster Dulles:

> You cannot preserve independence nowadays without inter-dependence. Now, who are the people who should set the first example in interdependence? Shouldn't it be our peoples who derive from the same religion, common-law principles and so forth? And, indeed, I doubt whether history shows ever that two countries have been co-operating as closely as we are co-operating at the present time. . . .

*   *   *

*A*RNEB re-crossed the Antarctic Circle. The darkness of the night came almost as a welcome novelty as we headed northward to civilization. An Antarctic adventure was almost over, and I felt nothing but admiration towards America's Operation Deep Freeze. It is the classic, the boldest, of all ice-continent conquests. The U.S. Navy and Air Force had revealed splendidly trained manpower, high morale, and the latest in technological efficiency. Living with Americans on this hazardous undertaking had further increased my appreciation of the people of the New World, capable of meeting any challenge.

Reviewing the entire course of my "Poles Apart" adventures, beginning in the far north of the North American Continent, encircling the mighty "48", then voyaging to the far south, I appreciated that I had been afforded an unusual opportunity for understanding one of the newest of great nations. I had discovered throughout something good, strong and reliable in the overall American character. Years of travelling have taught me to assess human qualities realistically and dispassionately, also not to overlook the fact, that, psychologically, parts may not be true of the whole. What cheers me particularly, is to have discovered by intimate association, a genuine American affection towards Britain.

I found Americans to be dynamic and generous people. There is little which is crabbed or stilted in their refreshingly sane, modern, and broad-minded outlook.

Americans have a vigorous enthusiasm for solving problems of the present and probing the future. They have little time for idling over vain regrets, or losing themselves in the mould of an uneconomical past. America represents the world's greatest experiment in the intermixture of races and cultures. Today, after only four short centuries, it represents the greatest and most successful admixture of peoples since the world began. I found the people of the New World strongly of one culture and vitally one nation. The hopes and aspirations of free humanity are fastened to the U.S.A., for world leadership and support, adequate proof of a country's maturity. Among the broad cross-section of Americans I encountered, I found a sincere peace-consciousness. Americans, according to my findings, are certainly not war-mongers because they oppose weakness.

Isn't the world one, now, and indivisible? Isn't peace, too, one and indivisible? Admittedly, Americans are alert to the fact that a democracy which is not prepared to defend itself and the basic moral principles it represents, is, to say the least, hardly a true democracy. I am pro-English first, but for me America comes next. Any carefully-thinking person will realize that it is the good fortune of the free world to have a strong, unselfish United States, willing to pour its wealth and manpower into the critical regions of the world in the name of peace and defence.

I find it not comforting, however, to hear all too often, recriminating irrelevancies which can and do stab at Anglo-American goodwill. I would not discuss this aspect had I not come heart-to-heart, and man to man with so many fine Americans during my *Poles Apart* journeyings. It is the men, ordinary creatures who count most. They mould and make a country, also win wars. Arm-chair generals voice opinions which are not truly representative. I regret that it seems the ordinary thing for many outside the States to take it for granted that America must inevitably bear the brunt of future struggles, yet at the same time to condemn her youthfulness, vigilant methods and resolute policies. Nations have developed fast since the last two wars, for better and for worse. America, however, has not failed to fulfil her destiny, despite the enormous responsibility which has been thrust upon her broad, young shoulders.

Following my adventures with Americans, the realization has deepened that only U.S.-British close co-operation can checkmate Communist subversion with its fantastic desire for the disintegration of our democratic civilization. This, the greatest partnership of all time, is surely the only answer for the security and happiness of a free humanity. Nothing can be stronger than the greatness of such a partnership for weakening, halting and dispersing a wrong way of life.

*   *   *

The sun shone in strength, flecking a calm sea with a golden glitter. The mainland emerged from a haze of mauve, the sunlight flooding the scene in welcome. New Zealand came up clean and sharp; rolling contours, colour, and softness. This calm and lovely country was again a thrilling reality, all the more beautiful and telling after the treeless, white wilderness we had left behind. The spectacle of multi-coloured green was stirring, heralding soil-life and beauty.

Billie was on the quay to welcome my return. It was a happy reunion; I appreciated a tolerant wife who had not opposed the latest venture. Her philosophy recognized reality in allowing my nomadic spirit freedom for collecting new impressions, and for our own happiness, by co-operation of head with heart. That evening we met Captain Schwaner and Commander Jimmy Roohan for a small farewell party. *Arneb* was leaving next day for the U.S.A., via Australia, where the Commonwealth Government was to honour Admiral Dufek for his leadership of the "Deep Freeze" Operation.

Billie remarked to Jimmy Roohan: "Richard has told me

something about the scenery down there. I would have loved to have seen it, you men are lucky creatures."

"Never mind," Jimmy's reply was intended to be consoling, "I have read that some travel bureaux have promised Antarctica vacations in the future. Think of it, atomic-powered liner-cum-icebreaker pleasure cruises to the southern continent, ski runs on the slopes of Erebus!"

"Yeah," put in Captain Schwaner, "I can visualize the advertisements. Centrally-heated observation decks; dinner-dances among the icebergs with all the amenities that you'd get on a cruise to the Bahamas."

"Which," said I, "prompts me to ask, have any women ever been down there?"

Captain Schwaner leaned back, smiled broadly, and reached for his file on "cold facts about the Antarctic".

"They have," he affirmed, and read:

On 20 February, 1935, a Mrs. Klarius Mikkelsen accompanied her husband ashore in a small boat. She was with him on a whaling expedition, and as far as we know was the first woman to set foot on Antarctica.

"How interesting," murmured Billie, "but as Richard isn't a whaling skipper, I'll have to wait for the pleasure cruises to start."

Captain Schwaner motioned for silence, and went on:

And two American women, Mrs. Edith Ronne and Mrs. Jennie Darlington of Washington, D.C., participating in the Finn-Ronne expedition of 1947/8, were the first women ever to spend a winter on the Antarctic Continent. With the original intention of returning to the United States from a South American port, both then decided to accompany their husbands aboard the expedition ship, *The Port of Beaumont* on the voyage south to the Antarctic.

"But no woman has ever yet been to the Pole," said Jimmy breezily. "Now there is a first for an intrepid gal, if you like." He leaned over to Billie, his eyes twinkling. "What about the 'Papes at the Pole'?"

Billie laughed, demurely smoothing her dress. "You mean 'Up the Pole', don't you Jimmy?"

"There's always got to be a first time," Captain Schwaner admitted. "I suppose one of our planes could carry a woman to the Pole, the same as we fly men in today."

"Good Lord!" I thrilled to a sudden idea, "I'll have to think about that one, Billie."

She shook her head. "Oh, heavens," she said, "his restless nature is speaking again. Only this afternoon he half promised to get a job, and cultivate a nice green garden in his spare time after all the ice he's seen. He rhapsodized about greenery."

I looked searchingly into my wife's happy face.

"Seriously dear," I asked, "would you risk it if somehow I got permission for a South Pole flight?"

At that moment the steward arrived with a tray of drinks.

"You're not serious?" asked Jimmy with eyes that were smiling mischievously.

"How much ice in your drink?" The Captain asked my wife.

"Put plenty in," I interrupted, "I want Billie to get used to it."

"Deep Freeze" Emblem designed by Walt Disney

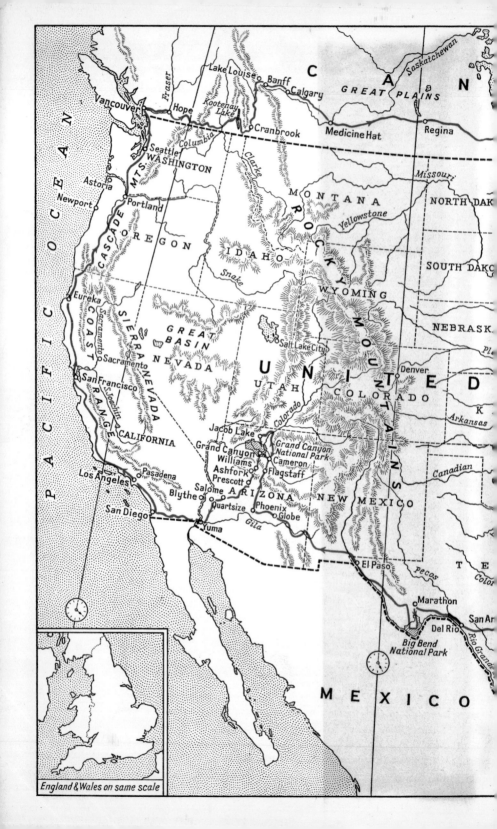

England & Wales on same scale